Society American Anti-Slavery

Proceedings of the American Anti-Slavery Society

Society American Anti-Slavery

Proceedings of the American Anti-Slavery Society

ISBN/EAN: 9783744732666

Printed in Europe, USA, Canada, Australia, Japan

Cover: Foto ©ninafisch / pixelio.de

More available books at **www.hansebooks.com**

PROCEEDINGS

OF THE

American Anti-Slavery Society,

AT ITS

THIRD DECADE,

HELD IN THE CITY OF PHILADELPHIA, DEC. 3d and 4th, 1864.

PHONOGRAPHIC REPORT BY HENRY M. PARKHURST.

NEW YORK:
AMERICAN ANTI-SLAVERY SOCIETY,
No. 48 BEEKMAN STREET.
1864.

THE THIRD DECADE

OF THE

AMERICAN ANTI-SLAVERY SOCIETY.

In accordance with the previous action of the Society, at the occurrence of its First and Second Decades, and in compliance with the generally expressed wishes of its members and friends, the Executive Committee caused the following Circular Letter of Invitation to be issued, in November last:—

BOSTON, November 12, 1863.

The AMERICAN ANTI-SLAVERY SOCIETY will commemorate the Thirtieth Anniversary of its formation, on THURSDAY and FRIDAY, Dec. 3 and 4, 1863, at CONCERT HALL, in the city of PHILADELPHIA, commencing at 10 o'clock, A. M., of each day. Its object, as originally announced, and uncompromisingly adhered to for the last thirty years, was and is the immediate and entire abolition of Slavery in the United States, by all those instrumentalities sanctioned by law, humanity and religion; and thus "to deliver our land from its deadliest curse, and to wipe out the foulest stain which rests upon our national escutcheon." Its measures were proclaimed to be, and ever have been, "such only as the opposition of moral purity to moral corruption, the destruction of error by the potency of truth, the overthrow of prejudice by the power of love, and THE ABOLITION OF SLAVERY BY THE SPIRIT OF REPENTANCE."

At its approaching celebration, the Society will have the sublime privilege to announce, as the result, primarily, of its disinterested, patriotic, and Christian labors, the emancipation of THREE MILLIONS THREE HUNDRED THOUSAND SLAVES, by the fiat of the American Government, on the 1st of January last.

It is not only to revive the remembrance of the long thirty years' warfare with the terrible forces of Slavery, and to acknowledge the hand of a wonder-working Providence in guiding the way of the little Anti-Slavery army through great moral darkness and many perils, that we now invite this meeting, but also to renew, in the name of humanity, of conscience, and of pure and undefiled religion, the demand for the entire and speedy extinction of Slavery in every part of our country.

Your attendance at this Commemorative Meeting, in Philadelphia, on the 3d and 4th of December next, is respectfully solicited and cordially desired.

In behalf of the Executive Committee,

WILLIAM LLOYD GARRISON, *President.*

CHARLES C. BURLEIGH, } *Secretaries.*
WENDELL PHILLIPS,

In pursuance of the preceding Call, the AMERICAN ANTI-SLAVERY SOCIETY celebrated the completion of its Third Decade at Concert Hall, in Philadelphia, December 3d and 4th, 1863, commencing at 10 o'clock, A. M.

The Hall was decorated with the beautiful banners of the Philadelphia Female Anti-Slavery Society, on which were inscribed appropriate mottoes from the writings of WHITTIER, W. H. BURLEIGH, and others. In the rear of the platform, the American flag, now at length the symbol of Liberty, hung in beautiful festoons, extending each way from an Eagle and National Shield in the centre, and surmounted by a white banner or band, on which were inscribed, in conspicuous black letters, the words, "UNION AND LIBERTY." At different points, large white cards were displayed, on which were inscribed appropriate sentences from WASHINGTON, JEFFERSON, MADISON, MONROE, RANDOLPH, CLAY, and other eminent men of the past.

The Hall was filled at an early hour, and some time was spent in mutual greetings and congratulations on the part of friends of the cause from different parts of the country, who all appeared to share one common feeling of thanksgiving and hopefulness.

The meeting was called to order by WILLIAM LLOYD GARRISON, the President; and on motion of J. MILLER MCKIM, to complete the organization, AARON M. POWELL, of Ghent, N. Y., and WENDELL PHILLIPS GARRISON, of Boston, were appointed Secretaries *pro tem.*

Mr. MCKIM also moved the appointment of a Business Committee of twelve, to prepare work for the meeting, and to receive resolutions and other papers, and report them at their discretion.

The motion was agreed to, and the following were appointed as such Committee:—JAMES MILLER MCKIM, MARY GREW, AARON M. POWELL, LUCRETIA MOTT, ROBERT PURVIS, OLIVER JOHNSON, JOHN T. SARGENT, SARAH PUGH, THEODORE TILTON, ABRAHAM BROOKE, ALFRED H. LOVE.

Rev. SAMUEL J. MAY offered a very appropriate and impressive prayer.

INTRODUCTORY REMARKS BY THE PRESIDENT.

BELOVED FRIENDS AND COADJUTORS:—

This is the Third Decade since the formation of the American Anti-Slavery Society in this city. It will, in all probability, be the last one that we shall hold; for who now believes that slavery is to continue ten years longer in our land, rendering necessary ten years longer of anti-slavery effort for its overthrow? We trust that we are very near the jubilee. We know that we are a great deal nearer to it than when we first believed. What was sown in weakness is raised in power; what was sown in dishonor is raised in glory. All the signs of the times, in regard to our glorious cause, are cheering in the highest degree. It is no longer a question confined to a few humble individuals, as against a mighty nation; but it is a nation rocking as by an earthquake, in travail with this tremendous issue. And now, instead of words, the question is debated upon the battle-field, at the cannon's mouth; and, undoubtedly, through this war of judgment, God means to vouchsafe deliverance to all in bondage.

Welcome and benediction, upon this thrilling and joyous occasion, to those who entered earliest into the field of labor; who have gone through with all its toils, its sufferings, its sacrifices, its perils; and who have been graciously permitted to live to see this gladsome day! Welcome and benediction to those who came in at a later period, and to the still newer converts to our cause! Welcome and benediction to all! We may now confidently hope that our labors are drawing near to an end, so far as the abolition of slavery is concerned; but our labors in the field of a common humanity, and in the cause of reform, are never to terminate here, except with our mortal lives. With the liberation of the millions in bondage, we are to have a new field of philanthropy opened to us on a colossal scale, that will tax our means, our generosity, our sympathy, our efforts, to the utmost extent, to meet the solemn demands upon us, on the part of those houseless, homeless, penniless millions, who are coming forth from the house of bondage. This is a work of mercy and benevolence, in the doing of which we believe the great mass of the people of all denominations, and parties, and sects will flow together, and be glad to make a common atonement, though at so late a day, for the wrongs and outrages that have been heaped upon those held in brute servitude for so many generations.

One of the Secretaries will now read some of the numerous letters which have been received from those whose circumstances or engagements prevent their being here. Of course, if all who would like to be here could be gratified, it would be the largest meeting ever convened in the city of Philadelphia. Thousands and tens of thousands are regretting that they cannot be with us on this occasion.

The first letter I hold in my hand is from one who deserves to be held in honorable and lasting remembrance for his early, devoted, and long-continued services in our cause; I mean the first President of the American Anti-Slavery Society, once the distinguished merchant philanthropist of the city of New York, ARTHUR TAPPAN; the benefactor to whom I owe my liberation from the Baltimore prison in 1830; and but for whose interposition at that time, in all probability, I never should have left that prison, except to be carried out to be buried.* I think it is some twenty years since I had the pleasure of looking him in the face; but I could do no less than to send him a letter of invitation to be present at this commemorative meeting, renewing my expression of gratitude for all his kindness to me personally, and my admiration for all he had done in the cause of the oppressed; and I was glad to receive this letter in reply.

[The letter was read, as follows, by WENDELL PHILLIPS GARRISON, one of the Secretaries:]

NEW HAVEN, Nov. 17, 1863.

WM. LLOYD GARRISON:

DEAR SIR,—Few events could give me so much pleasure as the receipt of your note of the 12th inst. During the years that have intervened since we last met, I have often recalled the time when we were united in working for the slave, and regretted that any occurrence should have estranged us from each other.

I shall be glad to attend the meeting at Philadelphia, but my advanced age (78th year) and growing infirmities may prevent.

I am, truly, your friend,

ARTHUR TAPPAN.

THE PRESIDENT. The next letter is from one of the signers of the Declaration of Sentiments; a name known and honored throughout the civilized world; *the* poet of America, JOHN G. WHITTIER, (applause,) who has done so much by his writings as a poet in aid of our glorious movement, that I have no words to express my sense of the value of his services. There are few living who have done so much to operate upon the mind and conscience and heart of our country for the abolition of slavery as JOHN GREENLEAF WHITTIER:

AMESBURY, 24th 11th mo., 1863.

MY DEAR FRIEND:

I have received thy kind letter, with the accompanying circular, inviting me to attend the commemoration of the Thirtieth Anniversary of the formation of the American Anti-Slavery Society, at Phil-

---

* See Appendix A.

adelphia. It is with the deepest regret that I am compelled, by the feeble state of my health, to give up all hope of meeting thee and my other old and dear friends on an occasion of so much interest. How much it costs me to acquiesce in the hard necessity, thy own feelings will tell thee better than any words of mine.

I look back over thirty years, and call to mind all the circumstances of my journey to Philadelphia, in company with thyself and the excellent Dr. THURSTON, of Maine, even then, as we thought, an old man, but still living, and true as ever to the good cause. I recall the early grey morning when, with SAMUEL J. MAY, our colleague on the Committee to prepare a Declaration of Sentiments for the Convention, I climbed to the small "upper chamber" of a colored friend to hear thee read the first draft of a paper which will live as long as our national history. I see the members of the Convention, solemnized by the responsibility, rise one by one, and solemnly affix their names to that stern pledge of fidelity to freedom. Of the signers, many have passed away from earth, a few have faltered and turned back, but I believe the majority still live to rejoice over the great triumph of truth and justice, and to devote what remains of time and strength to the cause to which they consecrated their youth and manhood thirty years ago.

For, while we may well thank God and congratulate one another on the prospect of the speedy emancipation of the slaves of the United States, we must not for a moment forget that, from this hour, new and mighty responsibilities devolve upon us to aid, direct and educate these millions, left free, indeed, but bewildered, ignorant, naked and foodless in the wild chaos of civil war. We have to undo the accumulated wrongs of two centuries; to remake the manhood that slavery has well-nigh unmade; to see to it that the long-oppressed colored man has a fair field for development and improvement; and to tread under our feet the last vestige of that hateful prejudice which has been the strongest external support of Southern slavery. We must lift ourselves at once to the true Christian altitude where all distinctions of black and white are overlooked in the heartfelt recognition of the brotherhood of man.

I must not close this letter without confessing that I cannot be sufficiently thankful to the Divine Providence which, in a great measure through thy instrumentality, turned me so early away from what ROGER WILLIAMS calls "the world's great trinity, pleasure, profit and honor," to take side with the poor and oppressed. I am not insensible to literary reputation. I love, perhaps too well, the praise and good will of my fellow-men; but I set a higher value on my name as appended to the Anti-Slavery Declaration of 1833, than on the title-page of any book. Looking over a life marked by many errors and shortcomings, I rejoice that I have been able to maintain the pledge of that signature; and that, in the long intervening years,

"My voice, though not the loudest, has been heard
Wherever Freedom raised her cry of pain."

Let me, through thee, extend a warm greeting to the friends, whether of our own or the new generation, who may assemble on the occasion of commemoration. There is work yet to be done which will task the best efforts of us all. For thyself, I need not say that the love and esteem of early boyhood have lost nothing by the test of time; and

I am, very cordially, thy friend,
JOHN G. WHITTIER.

WM. LLOYD GARRISON, President A. A. S. Society.

The reading of the above letter was interrupted by the arrival of a delegation of colored soldiers from Camp William Penn, who, as they advanced to the platform, were greeted by a general outburst of applause. These soldiers, having taken the seats assigned to them on the platform, immediately behind the officers of the Society, remained as evidently interested and intelligent auditors during the whole of the protracted morning session.

THE PRESIDENT. The next letter is from a very near, and dear, and revered friend, Hon. SAMUEL FESSENDEN, of Portland, Maine, father of Hon. WILLIAM PITT FESSENDEN, who is one of the leading Senators of the United States. He is now, of course, advanced in years; and, having nearly lost his eyesight, is compelled to use an amanuensis in order to have his sentiments recorded. Among a host of friends and coadjutors, I hardly know of one whom I esteem and reverence more than I do SAMUEL FESSENDEN, of Maine. The circumstances in which I became acquainted with him are to me peculiarly touching, as they are certainly enduring in my recollection. I trust he will be spared to witness, before his removal, the utter extermination of slavery from our country, and to join in the song of jubilee.

PORTLAND, Nov. 23, 1863.

MY EVER DEAR FRIEND:

It was with very great pleasure that I received your kind notice of me of the 12th of November. You do me but justice in believing that I entertain the same views as I ever did in regard to that dreadful curse, the system of Southern slavery as it has existed and been practised in the great Southern section of our country, and which we are combatting in the present war. That system, in my judgment, most entirely embodies the cruelty of Moloch, the brutality of Belial, and the avarice of Mammon; and while, with you and others, I entertain the same views as to its enormity, I cherish the hope, and I believe I may now say the expectation, that God is about to bring this dreadful enormity,— a sin which, next to the crucifixion of the Savior, I esteem the most heinous ever committed by any of the human race,— to a speedy and final end.

I might almost say, that I regret that the infirmity of eighty years' pilgrimage on earth has made me unable to attend the coming meeting of the Anti-Slavery Society; but I am almost totally blind, and it might well be supposed that, trembling upon the extreme verge of four score years, I perceive myself that the powers and faculties of my mind, such as they were, have so far failed as to render me incapable of doing any more for the benefit of the cause which you have so ably advocated—that of the total abolition of slavery in our country.

I shall not probably live to see the total destruction of this accursed system, but feel assured that it must soon take place, and that I now see those glimpses of its approaching end which enable me with confidence to say, "Lord, now lettest thou thy servant depart in peace, for mine eyes have seen of thy salvation," the glory of the people of God, and the returning happiness of our suffering country, in the firm establishment and perpetuity of our free institutions.

With sentiments of the most cordial esteem, I am, in the sacred cause of liberty and humanity, truly and faithfully your friend,

SAMUEL FESSENDEN.

To WILLIAM LLOYD GARRISON.

THE PRESIDENT. The next letter is from one who was not with us in the early part of our struggle, but who has done a noble service since he joined us some years ago, in the common effort for the emancipation of those in bondage—JAMES FREEMAN CLARKE, of Boston.

JAMAICA PLAIN, Nov. 26, 1863.

DEAR SIR:

* * * It would give me great pleasure to accept your invitation, which I feel honored in receiving. Unhappily, I can hardly hope to be able to visit Philadelphia at that time. But whether there or elsewhere, I shall in spirit be with you, and shall sympathize with your satisfaction and pride in feeling that the result for which you have labored so long and so earnestly is almost attained. That slavery in America is virtually at an end, I cannot doubt. The great act of emancipation by the President, under his power as Commander-in-Chief—a power given him by the Constitution—is an act proceeding directly from the Constitution itself, and is therefore a part of the highest law known in the land. The Border States, exempted from the operation of that great edict, will themselves, following Missouri and Maryland, decree emancipation as a measure of public policy. Thus slavery is like a tree taken up by the roots— the life not wholly out of it, the leaves perhaps yet green—but its roots are out of the ground, and it must die.

The Society over which you preside has not only reason to congratulate itself that its labors have contributed largely to this great end; but that it has also given a historical proof that no evil, however mighty, no abuse, however deeply rooted, can resist the power of truth and righteousness, clearly uttered and perseveringly witnessed to. Every advocate of justice henceforth, however humble he may seem to be, will be encouraged by your success to believe that God by him will fulfil the prophecy which declares that "He shall smite the earth by the rod of His mouth, and by the breath of His lips shall He slay the wicked." So that by your fidelity, you have not only helped to put out of the land this gigantic evil and sin, but have also contributed to destroy every other evil and sin which in all time to come shall be brought to an end by the power of truth and justice.

Very truly and faithfully yours,

JAMES FREEMAN CLARKE.

THE PRESIDENT. We hoped to have had the pleasure of seeing with us, upon this occasion, three of the most devoted friends of our cause which the struggle has brought forth; I mean, THEODORE D. WELD, ANGELINA GRIMKE WELD, and SARAH GRIMKE. The letter which they have jointly sent to us expresses their feelings in regard to this celebration. I need not pass any eulogium upon these devoted friends; for you all know, who know any thing of the Anti-Slavery movement, what they have done for it.

WEST NEWTON, Dec. 1, 1863.

BELOVED FRIENDS:

The letter of your Committee invites us to be present, either in person or by letter, to celebrate with you our Third Decade. In place of ourselves, we send a few words of earnest greeting, as our proxy.

The fittest celebration of the past is to gird ourselves anew for the present and the future. The crisis that is upon us speaks its own word. To us, that word is this:—

This Conspiracy is Slavery. The fiend that planned it, that ripened the plot, and now reeks with its perfidies, perjuries and myriad murders, is *Slavery*—Slavery in arms—the whole of it, and nothing else; its body, soul, and spirit; the focus of its life and the furnace of its rage; its mad brain and heart, with all their greeds, plots and hates, ablaze with the fires of their own hell—every muscle and nerve-fibre on the rack—thought and will strained into spasms, and raving in frenzy. By its own act, by God's decree, Slavery's last hour has come, *if the Nation will have it so.* Up from the whole land, from all the earth's ends, the great question comes, million-voiced: "Does the Nation know, will the Nation do the thing that belongs to its peace, and to all human weal?" He that hath ears begins to hear the Nation's solemn voices saying, "We do, and we *will!*" Terrible things in righteousness, just retribution for our partnership in the infinite crime and curse, press up these words to-day upon the Nation's lips. We hear in them the voice of God. We see, in the blow about to fall, the bolt of God, striking dead, and burning up its corpse; leaving not a hair of the accursed thing to taint the air, or stain the ground, or bow down one free grass blade, or tether the tiniest rootlet in the soil.

Hitherto, Slavery's intense vitality has pervaded its whole body; all these life-forces the rebellion has absorbed into itself. From all the extremities, they have rushed to their centre. True blows struck there deal death to slavery, and to all its dragon-brood — aristocracy, caste, monopoly, class legislation, exclusive privilege and prerogative, all legalized oppression of the weak by the strong, with whatever obstructs "Liberty, Equality, Fraternity." For this, all oppressed peoples now turn their eyes hitherward.

Who that hates slavery, and has clear eyesight, does not see that the work of Abolitionists, for this hour, with prayer and pen, with voice and trumpet-blast, with men and money, with all the weapons, by all means, in all ways, and with the whole soul, is to strike down this rebellion? It totters now, and slavery totters with it. See how it is struck down in the District of Columbia, Western Virginia, Delaware, Maryland, Missouri, and in the Cherokee and Choctaw Nations! See how in Louisiana, North Carolina, Tennessee, Kentucky, Florida, Arkansas, Texas, Northern Mississippi, and Northern Alabama, it reels to-day!

O then, God grant us large vision to see, and high wisdom to do; help us to lay aside every weight — the chronic queries and criticisms, the non-essential ifs and buts that throng the hour — the multiform side issues that so easily beset; and, in His strength, uplift ourselves altogether, to gird anew the Nation's arm, that it may bring down the final blow!

In hope, confidence, deep gratitude, and solemn exultation, faithfully, your fellow-servants,

THEODORE D. WELD,
ANGELINA G. WELD,
SARAH M. GRIMKE.

THE PRESIDENT. The next letter is from our esteemed and gifted friend, O. B. FROTHINGHAM, of the city of New York: —

NEW YORK, Nov. 23, 1863.

MY DEAR FRIEND:

I have received and gratefully acknowledge the kind invitation to your grand intellectual and moral banquet in Philadelphia on the 3d and 4th days of December. I anticipate unusual duties and cares just that week, incident to the opening of my church, and sorely fear I shall miss the treat; not, however, if I can help it. For simply to be there on an occasion so saturated with noble memories, earnest thoughts and pure hopes, so bountiful in sentiment and aspiration, would be an era in one's experience. Never was festival so truly a festival in the fine old religious sense — a season of joy dedicated to the gods. For the spirit of Justice, Truth and Love, the primeval Trinity, will itself preside — invisible thousands of the redeemed will rise in ranks around the hall — a cloud of witnesses too numerous for admission, if spirits filled any points of space — and the angels, too, of the great redeemers, will glorify the house from floor to ceiling. Only to sit in silence amid such an assembly, and let the tears of gratitude flow from one's eyes, would be a sacramental observance; and with all that, to hear the speaking, and on all that again to press the hands that have wrought at this great task for thirty years, and to look into the faces in which so proud a moral triumph is reflected! Well, I won't try to say what that would be, but only try to think it will be mine to enjoy in actual fruition and in long memory.

You know, dear Mr. GARRISON, that I shall be with you at any rate, even though my presence bodily may be here. You know that I am always with you in your work and in your prayer. You know that I am ever gratefully yours,

O. B. FROTHINGHAM.

THE PRESIDENT. Here is a letter from the Hon. OWEN LOVEJOY, who expresses the hope of being with us to-day. What Mr. LOVEJOY has done, in his place in the United States House of Representatives, for a number of years — how he has had to peril his life from session to session, in the midst of slaveholding wrath and violence — and with what a lion-hearted spirit he has triumphantly met the proud oligarchy of the South, represented in that body, you all know.

PRINCETON, Illinois, Nov. 22, 1863.

MY DEAR SIR:

* * * I have some *hope* of being able to be present at your meeting. In the event of my not being able to attend, will you allow me to say that I am in favor of an act of Congress abolishing slavery throughout the entire limits of the United States, and making it a penal offence to hold or claim to hold a slave?

If we have a right to build a Pacific Railroad to promote the *general welfare*, without any specific grant of power in the Constitution, how much more have we the right to destroy that which is not only opposed to the general welfare, and to the spirit and genius of the Constitution, but is in constant and now bloody antagonism to every avowed purpose for which that organic law was ordained and established? I am aware that the dogma or fiction (for it is nothing more) of State sovereignty will be opposed to this legislation. But to this theory of State sovereignty I oppose the words of the Constitution itself: " This Constitution, and the laws of the United States which shall be made in pursuance thereof, shall be the supreme law of the land, any thing in the Constitution or laws of any State to the contrary notwithstanding." Another mode of reaching the same end would be to take a slave into the United States Supreme Court, and see whether that tribunal dare refuse him freedom under the Constitution. I have never had a doubt that a bench of honest judges would liberate a slave if once in Court. I think that was the chief motive for the atrocious Dred Scott decision. The slaveholder dare not confront his slave in that tribunal, if it could be half decently constituted. I shall therefore be with you in spirit, if not in person. I heartily bid you God-speed in your efforts to secure obedience to the divine command which the fathers traced on the bell, which I think still hangs over Independence Hall, in the city where you meet : " Proclaim liberty throughout all the land, to all the inhabitants thereof."

Yours, for universal freedom,
OWEN LOVEJOY.

Wm. Lloyd Garrison.

The President. The next letter is from one whom we all delight to honor for his invaluable and long-continued services in behalf of the oppressed, in the Congress of the United States, and out of that body — I mean, the Hon. Joshua R. Giddings, of Ohio. (Applause.)

Jefferson, Ohio, Nov. 30, 1863.

My Dear Garrison:

I would most gladly unite with the friends of freedom in commemorating the return of our government to the doctrines on which it was founded. For half a century, the powers which had been ordained to secure liberty were prostituted to the enslavement of mankind ; the powers ordained to secure life were prostituted to the destruction of human existence ; and our *free* government was transformed into a slaveholding oligarchy.

Amid the moral and political darkness which then overshadowed our land, the voice of humanity was at length faintly heard. Its utterance became more and more distinct, until at length the high and holy truth, that all men hold *from the Creator* a right to live, a right to that liberty which is necessary to protect life. acquire knowledge, enjoy happiness, and prepare for heaven, was heard in our congressional halls. A quarter of a century has not yet elapsed, since the duty of separating our Federal Government and the people of the States from all support of slavery was first proclaimed in our National Legislature. The policy was so palpably just, so obviously in accordance with the Constitution, and constituted such a distinct reiteration of the doctrines enunciated by the founders of our institutions, that the advocates of slavery have never attempted to meet it with argument. Threats, intimidation, slander, violence, war and bloodshed have constituted the weapons with which they have attempted to stay the tide of Christian civilization. They have beset the pathway of reform with civil war, with rebellion unequalled in history.

During the last three years, our people have raised, armed and sent to the field a million and a quarter of the best soldiers who have ever fought in the cause of freedom, at an expense of fifteen hundred million dollars. In no age, in no clime, have any people made so great or such willing sacrifice for liberty; while the nations of Europe have stood with folded arms, looking upon this mighty conflict, boasting that they took no interest in this war between slavery and freedom — that they neither encouraged the one, nor condemned the other.

Within the last two years, our people have purified themselves from slavery and the slave trade in the District of Columbia and in the Territories; and the President's Proclamation of Emancipation has repudiated the institution in ten sovereign States, while in four others slavery lingers only in name. Within that time, three millions of degraded bondmen have been legally elevated to the enjoyment of those rights which the Creator bestowed upon them. Heaven itself may well rejoice; and all good men will thank God, take courage, and reëngage in the great work with increased zeal.

I regret to say that, from the length of time and the severity of my own labors, I have fainted, fallen, and been borne from the field of conflict; but as I linger upon the verge of time, I still rest my dimmed vision upon the battle as it yet rages, and my last prayer shall be for the heroes of justice and liberty.

I pray you to express to the members of your Society the assurance of my affectionate regard.

Very faithfully, your friend,

JOSHUA R. GIDDINGS.

THE PRESIDENT. The next letter is from one who entered into the anti-slavery field at an earlier period than almost any of us. Long before my own mind was turned to this subject, he had fully comprehended it, and bravely and faithfully borne an uncompromising testimony for the abolition of slavery. His name deserves to be held in lasting remembrance. I allude to Rev. JOHN RANKIN, of Ohio.

RIPLEY, Ohio, Nov. 19, 1863.

MR. GARRISON:

DEAR SIR,—Your invitation to attend the Thirtieth Anniversary of the American Anti-Slavery Society has been received. I regret that I am not in circumstances that will enable me to be present at your meeting. You and I have ever been united on the subject of immediate emancipation, while we have widely differed in other respects. I feel that my labors must soon close. I am now in the seventy-first year of my age, and, of course, must soon go the way of all past generations. From my boyhood to the present time, I have opposed the abominable system of American slavery. For the liberation of the slaves I have labored long, and suffered much reproach and persecution; but I regret none of the sacrifices I have made for the hapless millions that have been bought and sold as if beasts of the field, and deprived of all that makes existence desirable. Nearly forty years have passed away since I began to warn this nation of the ruin that would result from this horrible system of oppression, but now the day of blood has come. The Son of God has come with his rod of iron, and dashed those slaveholding governments in pieces as a potter's vessel is broken, and has made the General Government tremble on its foundation. "True and righteous are thy judgments, O Lord!"

I greatly rejoice in the President's Proclamation. No other man ever had the privilege of making a proclamation so magnificent. It is to lift more than three millions of people from the deepest degradation and misery to dignified life and station as rational beings. And although it is not broad enough to cover the whole field of oppression, yet it is the fiat that will end the system. He that is higher than the heavens has ordained it, and our brave soldiers in the field are the armies of the living God to enforce it. Let us thank God and take courage; and not relax our efforts while there is a slave in the land.

JOHN RANKIN.

THE PRESIDENT. We have still a large number of letters that you would be pleased to hear, some of which will be read at other sessions, as time may allow. The only additional one that will now be submitted is from Hon. O. W. ALBEE, of Massachusetts, who in the Legislature of that State has done important service to our cause.

MARLBORO', Nov. 12, 1863.

MR. GARRISON:

DEAR SIR,—Your circular of the 12th inst. has been received. I deem it a high honor to be thought worthy of an invitation to the meeting in the city of Philadelphia, to commemorate the Thirtieth Anniversary of the American Anti-Slavery Society; but circumstances will, I fear, prevent my attending it.

In the year 1830 or 1831, whilst a student in Brown University, I chanced to read some sheets printed by yourself in Boston. The sheets were not large, nor the paper very fine; but suffice it to say, they contained facts that settled the question of emancipation with me. Since that hour, I have been an unwavering anti-slavery man;

and if I have done any good service in the glorious cause of emancipation, let God and WILLIAM LLOYD GARRISON be thanked.

Very truly, yours,
O. W. ALBEE.

HENRY C. WRIGHT offered the following resolutions: —

Resolved, That the voice of the people is heard through petitions to Congress; and this Convention earnestly recommend that this voice be raised in petitions for an amendment of the Constitution, declaring that slavery shall be for ever prohibited within the limits of the United States.

Resolved, That a committee of five be appointed to prepare such a petition, and procure the signature of every member of this Convention to the same before its final adjournment.

Mr. WRIGHT stated that this resolution had been suggested to him by one of the leading members of the United States Senate, who would probably, at an early day, introduce the subject in his place in that body.

The resolutions were referred to the Business Committee.

SPEECH OF REV. WM. H. FURNESS.

Mr. PRESIDENT: —

I am reminded of the first time that I had the honor of standing upon the anti-slavery platform with you. You may not remember it; but it was upon the occasion when our friends, FREDERICK DOUGLASS and SAMUEL WARD, so magnificently vindicated the ability of the black man. Then you were surrounded in the gallery behind you by ISAIAH RYNDERS and his crew. If you had been told then, sir, that some few years afterwards you would be standing upon an anti-slavery platform with a file of black soldiers behind you, what would have been your explanation of the prophecy? That the blacks had risen in insurrection, and that you were protected by your friends.

I am not in form a member of the National Anti-Slavery Society. The Society had not long existed before it communicated to me the information that I was already the President of an Abolition Society called a Christian Church; and I have felt myself bound to keep in my own sphere, and to try and bring my little Abolition Society upon the true platform; and that is the reason why I never officially belonged to the American Anti-Slavery Society.

Again, I feel very reluctant to claim to be an Abolitionist, because I think it to be a very high pretension for a man to make. I am perfectly willing to bear the obloquy of the name; but it looks like pride, and may imply a want of self-knowledge, for a man to claim with confidence that he is a genuine, thorough-going Garrisonian Abolitionist. Under these circumstances, I esteem myself honored, inasmuch as I have been invited to read to you the "Declaration of Sentiments" upon which this Society was founded; a Declaration made in this city thirty years ago, and second only in time to the Declaration of 1776.

DECLARATION OF SENTIMENTS.

The Convention assembled in the city of Philadelphia, to organize a National Anti-Slavery Society, promptly seize the opportunity to promulgate the following DECLARATION OF SENTIMENTS, as cherished by them in relation to the enslavement of one sixth portion of the American people.

More than fifty-seven years have elapsed since a band of patriots convened in this place, to devise measures for the deliverance of this country from a foreign yoke. The corner-stone upon which they founded the TEMPLE OF FREEDOM was broadly this—"that all men are created equal; that they are endowed by their Creator with certain inalienable rights; that among these are life, LIBERTY, and the pursuit of happiness." At the sound of their trumpet-call, three millions of people rose up as from the sleep of death, and rushed to the strife of blood; deeming it more glorious to die instantly as freemen, than desirable to live one hour as slaves. They were few in number—poor in resources; but the honest conviction that TRUTH, JUSTICE and RIGHT were on their side made them invincible.

We have met together for the achievement of an enterprise, without which that of our fathers is incomplete; and which, for its magnitude, solemnity, and probable results upon the destiny of the world, as far transcends theirs as moral truth does physical force.

In purity of motive, in earnestness of zeal, in decision of purpose, in intrepidity of action, in steadfastness of faith, in sincerity of spirit, we would not be inferior to them.

Their principles led them to wage war against their oppressors, and to spill human blood like water in order to be free. *Ours* forbid the doing of evil that good may come, and lead us to reject, and to entreat the oppressed to reject, the use of all carnal weapons for deliverance from bondage; relying solely upon those which are spiritual, and mighty through God to the pulling down of strongholds.

Their measures were physical resistance—the marshalling in arms—the hostile array—the mortal encounter. *Ours* shall be such only as the opposition of moral purity to moral corruption—

the destruction of error by the potency of truth — the overthrow of prejudice by the power of love — and the abolition of Slavery by the spirit of repentance.

Their grievances, great as they were, were trifling in comparison with the wrongs and sufferings of those for whom we plead. Our fathers were never slaves — never bought and sold like cattle — never shut out from the light of knowledge and religion — never subjected to the lash of brutal taskmasters.

But those for whose emancipation we are striving — constituting, at the present time, at least one sixth part of our countrymen — are recognized by the law, and treated by their fellow-beings, as marketable commodities, as goods and chattels, as brute beasts; are plundered daily of the fruits of their toil without redress; really enjoy no constitutional nor legal protection from licentious and murderous outrages upon their persons; are ruthlessly torn asunder — the tender babe from the arms of its frantic mother — the heart-broken wife from her weeping husband — at the caprice or pleasure of irresponsible tyrants. For the crime of having a dark complexion, they suffer the pangs of hunger, the infliction of stripes, and the ignominy of brutal servitude. They are kept in heathenish darkness by laws expressly enacted to make their instruction a criminal offence.

These are the prominent circumstances in the condition of more than two millions of our people, the proof of which may be found in thousands of indisputable facts, and in the laws of the slaveholding States.

Hence we maintain — that in view of the civil and religious privileges of this nation, the guilt of its oppression is unequalled by any other on the face of the earth; and, therefore,

That it is bound to repent instantly, to undo the heavy burden, to break every yoke, and to let the oppressed go free.

We further maintain — that no man has a right to enslave or imbrute his brother — to hold or acknowledge him, for one moment, as a piece of merchandize — to keep back his hire by fraud — or to brutalize his mind by denying him the means of intellectual, social and moral improvement.

The right to enjoy liberty is inalienable. To invade it is to usurp the prerogative of Jehovah. Every man has a right to his own body — to the products of his own labor — to the protection of law — and to the common advantages of society. It is piracy to buy or steal a native African, and subject him to servitude. Surely the sin is as great to enslave an AMERICAN as an AFRICAN.

Therefore we believe and affirm — That there is no difference, *in principle*, between the African slave trade and American Slavery:

That every American citizen, who retains a human being in involuntary bondage as his property, is, according to Scripture, (Ex. 21: 16,) a MAN-STEALER:

That the slaves ought instantly to be set free, and brought under the protection of the law·

That if they had lived from the time of Pharaoh down to the present period, and had been entailed through successive generations, their right to be free could never have been alienated, but their claims would have constantly risen in solemnity:

That all those laws which are now in force, admitting the right of Slavery, are therefore, before God, utterly null and void; being an audacious usurpation of the Divine prerogative, a daring infringement on the law of nature, a base overthrow of the very foundations of the social compact, a complete extinction of all the relations, endearments, and obligations of mankind, and a presumptuous transgression of all the holy commandments—and that, therefore, they ought instantly to be abrogated.

We further believe and affirm—that all persons of color who possess the qualifications which are demanded of others, ought to be admitted forthwith to the enjoyment of the same privileges, and the exercise of the same prerogatives, as others; and that the paths of preferment, of wealth, and of intelligence, should be opened as widely to them as to persons of a white complexion.

We maintain that no compensation should be given to the planters emancipating their slaves;

Because it would be a surrender of the great fundamental principle, that man cannot hold property in man;

Because SLAVERY IS A CRIME, AND THEREFORE IS NOT AN ARTICLE TO BE SOLD;

Because the holders of slaves are not the just proprietors of what they claim; freeing the slaves is not depriving them of property, but restoring it to its rightful owners; it is not wronging the master, but righting the slave—restoring him to himself;

Because immediate and general emancipation would only destroy nominal, not real property; it would not amputate a limb, or break a bone of the slaves, but, by infusing motives into their breasts, would make them doubly valuable to the masters as free laborers; and

Because, if compensation is to be given at all, it should be given to the outraged and guiltless slaves, and not to those who have plundered and abused them.

We regard as delusive, cruel and dangerous, any scheme of expatriation which pretends to aid, either directly or indirectly, in the emancipation of the slaves, or to be a substitute for the immediate and total abolition of Slavery.

We fully and unanimously recognize the sovereignty of each State to legislate exclusively on the subject of the Slavery which is tolerated within its limits; we concede that Congress, *under the present national compact*, has no right to interfere with any of the Slave States, in relation to this momentous subject:

But we maintain that Congress has a right, and is solemnly bound, to suppress the domestic slave trade between the several States, and to abolish Slavery in those portions of our territory which the Constitution has placed under its exclusive jurisdiction.

We also maintain that there are, at the present time, the highest obligations resting upon the people of the Free States to remove Slavery by moral and political action, as prescribed in the Constitution of the United States. They are now living under a pledge of their tremendous physical force to fasten the galling fetters of tyranny upon the limbs of millions in the Southern States; they are liable to be called at any moment to suppress a general insurrection of the slaves; they authorize the slave-owner to vote on three fifths of his slaves as property, and thus enable him to perpetuate his oppression; they support a standing army at the South for its protection; and they seize the slave who has escaped into their territories, and send him back to be tortured by an enraged master or a brutal driver. This relation to Slavery is criminal, and full of danger: IT MUST BE BROKEN UP.

These are our views and principles—these our designs and measures. With entire confidence in the overruling justice of God, we plant ourselves upon the Declaration of Independence and the truths of divine revelation as upon the Everlasting Rock.

We shall organize Anti-Slavery Societies, if possible, in every city, town and village in our land.

We shall send forth agents to lift up the voice of remonstrance, of warning, of entreaty and rebuke.

We shall circulate, unsparingly and extensively, Anti-Slavery tracts and periodicals.

We shall enlist the pulpit and the press in the cause of the suffering and the dumb.

We shall aim at a purification of the churches from all participation in the guilt of Slavery.

We shall encourage the labor of freemen rather than that of slaves, by giving a preference to their productions: and

We shall spare no exertions nor means to bring the whole nation to speedy repentance.

Our trust for victory is solely in God. *We* may be personally defeated, but our principles never. TRUTH, JUSTICE, REASON, HUMANITY, must and will gloriously triumph. Already a host is coming up to the help of the Lord against the mighty, and the prospect before us is full of encouragement.

Submitting this DECLARATION to the candid examination of the people of this country, and of the friends of Liberty throughout the world, we hereby affix our signatures to it; pledging ourselves that, under the guidance and by the help of Almighty God, we will do all that in us lies, consistently with this Declaration of our principles, to overthrow the most execrable system of Slavery that has ever been witnessed upon earth—to deliver our land from its deadliest curse—to wipe out the foulest stain which rests upon our national escutcheon—and to secure to the colored population of the United States all the rights and privileges which belong to them as men and as Americans—come what may to our persons, our inter-

ests, or our reputation — whether we live to witness the triumph of
LIBERTY, JUSTICE and HUMANITY, or perish untimely as martyrs in
this great, benevolent and holy cause.
Done at Philadelphia, the 6th day of December, A. D. 1833.

I am informed that of the sixty persons and upwards, who appended their names to this Declaration, only fifteen have died, when the anticipation here expressed has been realized. The large body of the signers "live to witness the triumph of liberty, justice and humanity."

You all know what have been the weapons of our friends in the great war in which they have been engaged. If our country had responded to these sentiments thirty years ago, as they responded to the tidings of the attack upon Fort Sumter, slavery would have been utterly abolished by this time, without the shedding of a single drop of blood. But there is a homely proverb, that it is in vain to talk about what might have been, or what should have been. Blood is running like water, and the consolation and reward of our friends is, that when the South broke out in brutal assault upon the life of the nation, that the nation was so well prepared for the hour was due in great part to the fidelity with which they have redeemed the pledges they gave in this Declaration, in forming Anti-Slavery Societies throughout all the North, and in sending every where anti-slavery information.

I confess there are very strong points of resemblance between the Abolitionists of the North and the conspirators of the South. Our friends at the North, thirty years ago, undertook to fire the Northern heart, insensible to the fact that they were in danger of firing the Southern heart at the same time. So, also, a few years ago, the leading conspirators at the South undertook to fire the Southern heart, never dreaming what a tremendous fire they were going to kindle in the Northern heart. So that, in this respect, the Abolitionists of the North and the Fire-eaters of the South resembled each other; with this difference — that the Abolitionists undertook to kindle the Northern heart with fire from heaven; the Fire-eaters undertook to kindle the Southern heart with fire from — the other place. (Applause.)

SPEECH OF WILLIAM LLOYD GARRISON.

On the Fourth of July, 1776, our fathers put their names to the Declaration of American Independence. They testified before the world, in that manner, to their acceptance of certain "self-evident truths" contained in that Declaration; and, therefore, that there could be no violation of them without guilt. Now, it is one thing to speak the word of liberty, but a very different thing to keep it. Our fathers proclaimed the truth. Did they adhere to it? Did they proceed to carry out honestly and impartially their own Heaven-attested sentiments? No; they were content to leave in bondage, as a matter of compromise, 600,000 slaves, who have since multiplied by natural generation to 4,000,000. They did not dare wholly to trust in God; and hence they were left to enter into a covenant with slaveholding, which in 1860 naturally broke out in bloody rebellion.

Thirty years ago, the Declaration to which you have just listened was issued by a small body assembled in this city, and the signatures of the members present were appended to the instrument. The result was, the immediate formation of the American Anti-Slavery Society, which adopted the Declaration as the basis upon which all its action should rest. Has the Society been true to its principles and sentiments? I feel I can truly say that it has been faithful and uncompromising from the beginning till now; that we have not yielded one jot or tittle of any of our demands; that in all trials, in all discouragements, in the hottest persecution, we have been faithful to our cause, and to the victims whose advocates we profess to be.

Is there any thing in this Declaration that any honest man can object to? Is there any thing in it opposed to the principles of justice, mercy, or brotherly love? How has it come to pass, then, that the proclamation of those sentiments has filled the land, for a whole generation, with violence and persecution? How is it that, during all that time, the Abolitionists have been held up as fanatics, madmen and incendiaries, who ought not to be tolerated in the utterance of their thoughts? How has the nation been torn and tormented by this anti-slavery agitation! Yet we enunciated no new truths, advanced no strange ideas, made no unreasonable demands. What has just been read to us has been reiterated in substance from age to age, ever since tyranny commenced its reign upon earth. It is a collection of the merest truisms; that man is man, and not a beast; that there is an everlasting distinction between a mere animal and an immortal soul; that the laborer should have his just reward; that all should be protected by equal laws; and that oppression should not be tolerated in any part of our land or world. We have been called "fanatics and incendiaries" for uttering truths like these.

They who have opposed us,—blindly it may be in many instances, wickedly in others,—have been guilty of fanaticism and incendiarism. Justice was upon our side; reason and mercy were with us; and the God of all flesh nerved our spirits to the conflict.

Allow me to take this opportunity to say, that there is one interpolation in the Declaration of Sentiments which I did not like at the time, and which I have never liked since. An esteemed friend in the Convention thought it would take off the edge, a little, of one of the allegations, if we would verify it by a reference to Scripture. As originally written, it stood thus:—

"That every American citizen, who retains a human being in involuntary bondage as his property, is a man-stealer."

But this was amended so as to read:—

"That every American citizen, who retains a human being in involuntary bondage as his property, is (according to Scripture, Exodus 21:16) a man-stealer."

That weakens instead of strengthening it. It raises a Biblical question. It makes the rights of man depend upon a text. Now, it matters not what the Bible may say, so far as these rights are concerned. They never originated in any parchment, are not dependent upon any parchment, but are in the nature of man himself, written upon the human faculties and powers by the finger of God. It matters not, though all the books in the universe, claiming to be never so sacred and holy, should declare that man has not a natural and an inalienable right to himself. Those books would only deserve to be given to the consuming fire. (Applause.) We do not base this cause upon any book. We base it upon man, upon God in man; and it will stand invulnerable, whether we can prove or not, by mere texts of Scripture, that a man has a right to his own body and his own soul.

I believe that if the Bible denounces any one sin more than another, it denounces the sin of oppression; if it represents God as being particularly incensed in his moral nature, it is in view of the treatment of the poor, and the needy, and the outcast. "Wash you; make you clean; put away the evil of your doings from before mine eyes. Cease to do evil, learn to do well; seek judgment; relieve the oppressed; undo the heavy burden; break every yoke, and let the oppressed go free."

I have never refrained from making use of the Bible as a mighty weapon to batter down slavery; but not to settle the question of the right or wrong of slavery by the Bible, or any other book. Slavery is a self-evident wrong.

It will be seen from this Declaration that, from the beginning, as an association, we pledged ourselves to the country that our measures should be entirely peaceful, our appeals to the reason and consciences of men; that we should deal in argument and entreaty, in warning and rebuke, in exposing the iniquity and danger of slavery, and in showing the blessings of liberty. We never contemplated asking of Congress the exercise of any unconstitutional power. We never attempted to stir up a slave insurrection, nor to do any thing more than this—to reason and remonstrate with the holders of slaves, and to leave it to their consciences to break the yoke, and set their victims free. Yet, had we been the vilest of the vile; had we been a band of incendiaries and assassins, whose only purpose was to " cry Havoc, and let slip the dogs of war," and have chaos come again; we could not have aroused against us the indignant opposition of this nation more thoroughly or more effectively than it has been during our long protracted struggle.

But " Wisdom is justified of her children," and the nation is getting to be now clothed, and sitting in its right mind. The Anti-Slavery cause is, at last, receiving a fair and honest verdict; and the approving judgment of posterity is sure. It will be admitted, in the future, that the Abolitionists only asked what was self-evidently just and reasonable, humane and Christian; and that the imputations cast upon them were vile and wicked, and made for a most villanous purpose.

How strange it always seems, in looking back through the course of history, and seeing the various struggles along the pathway of time to aid and bless the human race, that there should have existed any hostility to those reforms! What did the prophets say that was not worthy of all acceptation? Yet, how were they subjected to every form of persecution! Go back to the days of JESUS. Is it not now a matter of universal astonishment that any fault should have been found with him who went about doing good, who was harmless and undefiled, who was willing to lay down his life for his enemies? How could his brave and heroic apostles, going forth to save and bless their fellow-men, have been stigmatized as "pestilent and seditious fellows, seeking to turn the world upside down," and as " the filth of the earth and the offscouring of all things,"? And is it not amazing when we come down to Wickliffe and Luther, to George Fox and William Penn, to Roger Williams and John Wesley, who stood forth as the champions of religious liberty, that the people of their generation should have seen in them any thing evil?

Will it not be so, in the judgment of posterity, in regard to the Anti-Slavery struggle? While I will not say that the Abolitionists have committed no errors, nor that they might not have done their work in some respects better, I believe that there never was a body of reformers better kept in spirit, or in a sound understanding as to the best way of doing their work, than the Abolitionists in their efforts for the overthrow of slavery.

Signers of the Declaration of Sentiments! when we put our names to that instrument, how little did we understand the nature and power of slavery, or the actual condition of our country under its corrupting influence! How little we comprehended the trials through which we should be called to pass! We knew that the nation was slumbering, and that trumpet voices were needed to arouse it from its sleep of death; but did we not go to our own familiar friends, to kind neighbors and honored fellow-citizens, and expect to obtain their approval and coöperation? Did we not go to our cherished religious denomination, or to our political party, and expect, as soon as our appeals were made, it would give a patriotic or Christian response? How were we disappointed in every direction! How, instead of meeting with sympathy and encouragement, we had to face the frowns even of those who had formerly been our near and dear acquaintances! We have been " in perils of waters, in perils of robbers, in perils by our own countrymen, in perils in the city, in perils in the wilderness, in perils among false brethren"; buffeted, mobbed and outlawed; in some instances, a price has been set upon our heads; we have been regarded as those who were unfit to live. Yet we have ever tried to approve ourselves and our sacred cause " in much patience, in afflictions, in necessities, in distresses, in tumults, in labors, in watchings, in fastings; by pureness, by knowledge, by suffering, by kindness, by love unfeigned, by the word of truth, by the power of God, by the armor of righteousness on the right hand and on the left, by honor and dishonor, by evil report and good report." And may we not, without vaunting, ask, " Where is the wise? where is the scribe? where is the disputer of this world? Hath not God made foolish the wisdom of this world?"

But thanks to God that we were early called to this great cause!

To Him be all the glory. That a most wonderful work has been achieved is now admitted even by our enemies. We might have been as multitudinous as the sands on the sea shore, as the stars in the midnight sky; yet, had we been in the wrong, we should have been defeated, and ground to powder. We were few, poor, uninfluential, obscure; and yet a mighty work has been performed. Is it of the Abolitionists? No; it is of God. It is because truth is mighty, and no weapon that has ever been or ever can be fashioned, can prosper against it. It is because, in a righteous movement, "one shall chase a thousand, and two put ten thousand to flight." It is because "ever the right comes uppermost, and ever is justice done."

We were told, all along, that if our principles should be reduced to practice, and our measures carried out, there would be the most terrible consequences both to the master and to the slave; that society would be overturned, and every part of the South red with blood and conflagration. What has been the result? The work of emancipation is going on, not in a peaceful state of society, but in the midst of civil war, the worst time in which to try such an experiment — civil war upon a colossal scale. Yet as the slaves emerge from the house of bondage, how docile and peaceable is their conduct! They are behaving not only as well as we said they would, but transcending even our anticipations and prophecies. (Applause.) Wherever they have been tried, whether merely in digging ditches, trenches and rifle pits, or whether "armed and equipped as the law directs for military duty," they have discharged their responsibilities in the most faithful manner. In my judgment, it stamps them as a remarkable people; so remarkable, that I really have in my mind great doubts whether any other people upon the face of the earth could go through the same sufferings and degradation, and come out with so much credit to themselves. (Applause.)

Danger in giving men justice? Danger in protecting cradles from the kidnapper? Danger in allowing the husband and wife to be safe together? Danger in paying the laborer honestly for his work? How insane the nation has been! Slavery demonizes those whom it possesses. It calls good evil, and evil good; it puts light for darkness, and darkness for light. They who are possessed by it are rendered lunatics. There never was a man yet who could reason sanely in favor of slavery. It is not practicable to frame a sound argument in favor of wrong-doing. God does not allow that to be possible. If Gabriel himself should try it, he would only be morally foolish in proportion to his intellectual powers.

By the help of God we have continued to this day; and we have great reason to be thankful. But our work as Abolitionists is not yet done. The question is doubtless in your minds,—Is this the time, or will the next annual meeting of the American Anti-Slavery Society be the time, for dissolving our association? That remains to be seen. I do hope in God that this coming session of Congress will enable us, in May next, to dissolve the American Anti-Slavery Society. (Applause.) If that body will only abolish slavery, I pledge the country that there shall be no more anti-slavery agitation. As everybody seems to desire to get rid of this kind of agitation, the shortest method is to abolish slavery, which is the sole cause of the agitation. (Renewed applause.)

But if, on coming together next May, slavery shall not have been abolished, then our work will not have been completed; and we are pledged by the Declaration, and by our relations to God and to those in bonds, not to give up until every slave in the land is set free. Then our anti-slavery societies will, in the nature of things, terminate. We are organized to abolish slavery; when slavery is abolished, of course our mission ends, in that particular. But our work for humanity will not end. We shall put forth strenuous efforts to give light and knowledge to the emancipated, and to make their freedom a blessed boon to themselves and the republic.

How many times, in anti-slavery meetings, have I read,—so descriptive of the imperative duty and the cheering results of emancipation,—the 58th chapter of Isaiah, in which God expresses his abhorrence of a sham fast, and announces the true fast! It is not to bow down the head as a bulrush, nor to put on sackcloth and ashes, but to undo the heavy burdens, break every yoke, and let the oppressed go free. How many times have I read the promises connected with obedience to this command! Now we are in the midst of the breaking of yokes, and we are to see whether God will be true as to the promised results of emancipation. I aver that those promises are being fulfilled literally, and in the most remarkable manner. First—"Then shall thy light break forth as the morning, and thy darkness shall be as the noon-day." No cutting of throats; no firing of plantations; but the substitution of light for darkness. Now, what do we see? Following close upon the army, almost in the midst of shot and shell and Greek fire, the way being opened, we have an army of missionaries and teachers going down to the South, to scatter light among those who have been so long sitting in darkness, and in the region and shadow of death. Most speedy and marvellous fulfilment of the promise!

Next — "Then shall thy health spring forth speedily." Do you suppose there is not to be a great improvement in their physical condition when these imbruted millions are snatched away from the slave-driver's lash? But look at this promise from another point of view. You know that the rebels congratulated themselves upon the thinning out of our forces at New Orleans and at Vicksburg by "Yellow Jack," as they call the yellow fever. Yet the result has been that, since "the Yankees" have gone down there, with Gen. BUTLER and Gen. GRANT to lead them, there has been no Yellow Jack! Liberty has gone into sanitary measures, and the fever has disappeared.

Finally — "Then shalt thou call, and I will answer; thou shalt cry, and I will say, Here I am. Thou shalt be like a watered garden whose waters fail not; and they that shall be of thee shall build the old waste places; thou shalt be called, The repairer of the breach, The restorer of paths to dwell in; for the mouth of the Lord of hosts hath spoken it." It is only a question of time, — and time not far distant, — for all these promises to be literally fulfilled. The highest justice is the path of safety, and the best political economy.

The meeting adjourned to 3, P. M.

FIRST DAY — AFTERNOON SESSION.

J. M. MCKIM called attention to the fact that upon the platform was a veritable slave Auction-Block, captured from the Alexandria slave-prison.

THE PRESIDENT. The first letter to be read this afternoon is from Hon. B. GRATZ BROWN, of Missouri, who, for a number of years, has taken his life in his hands, and been an uncompromising advocate of the abolition of slavery in that State. He has been hated, proscribed, ostracised. Who ever dreamed that Missouri would eventually elevate him, a radical, thorough-going Abolitionist, to the Senate of the United States? (Applause.)

ST. LOUIS, Nov. 21, 1863.

MY DEAR SIR:

Your very kind note of the 12th inst. was received some days since, and would have been responded to earlier, and more at length, but for a sad domestic bereavement that has very much prostrated me. It will be necessary for me to be in Washington city two or three days before the session begins, but I will endeavor to take Philadelphia in my route, and be present with you for a brief period, if it be possible. So far as my feeling is concerned, I can assure you that I appreciate, more than most persons so far away, the great influence of the Anti-Slavery Society in arousing this nation to a sense of the sin of slavery that was bending it beneath the yoke, and in confirming our people in the resolution to do away with it at every hazard. God in his great Providence seems to have shaped this Revolution to carry forward that resolve, sharply by the edge of the sword; but more potently and enduringly by the vast augmentation of moral power and the deep stirring of national instincts which have been called forth by the struggle. For our own State of Missouri, I believe I may now say that the work of deliverance is well-nigh done—would have been done long since but for the interposition of federal influence, civil and military, to sustain slavery and the slave dynasty. But even these things cannot long be—the end of all sham doing is at hand, and, in the long hereafter, Missouri, be assured, will sternly keep her faith with freedom.

I remain, Sir, very truly, yours,

B. GRATZ BROWN.

WM. LLOYD GARRISON, Boston, Mass.

THE PRESIDENT. The next letter is from another Senator of the United States, whose name will be his own highest eulogy—CHARLES SUMNER, of Massachusetts. (Applause.)

BOSTON, 1st December, 1863.

MY DEAR SIR:

I shall not be able to take part in the proceedings to which you kindly invite me; but wherever I may be, I shall unite in your thanksgivings that God has already allowed so much of the good work to be accomplished, and by visible assurances enabled us to see clearly that slavery will soon be at an end.

It is sad to think that this infinite good is reached only through the fiery processes of war—so contrary to all your desires and to all mine. But we have not been choosers. The alternative has not been ours. To save the Republic—to save civilization—to save our homes from degradation—to save ourselves from participation in unutterable crime and baseness—it has been necessary to rally the country against a rebellion, *whose single object is the exaltation of slavery.* Never before in history was there a war so necessary and just as that which we are compelled to wage, and never before was there a war which promised such transcendant results.

It is only when the rebellion is seen in its true light, as *slavery in arms,* seeking dominion and recognition—at home and abroad—

that we can find the true measure of our duties. Of course, every concession to the rebellion—all parley with it—is a voluntary assumption of its guilt.

You and your associates have stood firm for many years. Such pious fidelity must have its reward in an approving conscience; but it cannot be forgotten hereafter on earth or in heaven.

And may God continue to bless the good cause, and to bless you, who have labored so nobly!

Believe me, my dear Sir, with much regard, very faithfully yours,

CHARLES SUMNER.

Wm. Lloyd Garrison, Esq.

The President. The last letter to be read this afternoon is from one of the signers of the Declaration, Simeon S. Jocelyn, now of New York. I became acquainted with him almost as soon as I entered into the Anti-Slavery cause, and found him one of its warmest and truest friends. He has labored from that hour to the present unceasingly in its behalf. I found him preaching to a small congregation of colored people in New Haven; his sympathies having been drawn out at a very early period towards that class of people in our land.

NEW YORK, Dec. 2, 1863.

Wm. Lloyd Garrison:

Dear Sir,—Your invitation to me to be present at the Third Decade of the American Anti-Slavery Society was duly received, for which please receive my thanks.

I have hoped to be present on the occasion so deeply interesting to those of us who, thirty years ago, under circumstances of great solemnity, adopted the memorable Declaration of Sentiments and Purposes, (drawn up by your own hand,) and consecrated ourselves to the work of securing, under Divine Providence, the liberty of the millions of our colored brethren in this land under the most terrible bondage known upon earth.

I find it impossible for me to be present on the first day of the convocation, and at this late hour, I can but feebly hope that I may be with you on Friday, such is the pressure of duty here this week connected with the cause among the freedmen at many points.

May the season be to all one of precious remembrances, devout thanksgiving, and the most earnest renewal of purpose and effort for the complete extirpation of slavery, and thereby the overthrow of the rebellion, the salvation of the country, and the relief, instruction and perpetual elevation and blessing of the millions rushing from the house of bondage, now opened by the God of the oppressed, who has "made bare His arm" for their deliverance!

I have the utmost confidence that the decree of freedom for three millions of the enslaved in the rebel States, by President Lincoln, will never be revoked, but that the proclamation of liberty " to all the inhabitants of the land " is early in order. But the h, ¬a-headed monster will struggle to the death; and the object contemplated by the meeting and the Society, to move the whole people, and through them the government, to the issue, together with every possible labor of all the friends of God and humanity, will all be demanded. With judgments and repentance, the desired results will be attained.

But, with gratitude, courage and joy, let us still " press the battle to the gate." May the Divine favor attend your deliberations, and crown the doings of the Convention with untold blessings upon the oppressed and their benefactors!

Truly, yours,   S. S. JOCELYN.

SPEECH OF J. MILLER McKIM.

I comply cheerfully with your request, Mr. Chairman, though the task it assigns me is not in all respects an easy one. To look back upon the origin of this Society, and run the eye down its course to the present time, and then submit the reminiscences suggested, and to do it all in the space of a single short speech, is a task requiring powers of condensation beyond my pretensions.

There is another difficulty about it. To give an account of a movement with which one's own personal history — at least in his own mind — is inseparably identified, without violating one of the first rules of good taste in a speaker, demands a degree of phraseological skill which but few possess. The word *I* is perhaps the ugliest as well as the shortest in the English language. It is a word which careful parents teach their children never to use — either in the nominative, possessive or objective case, except on compulsion; yet it is a word without which *I* cannot possibly get on in the duty you have assigned me.

But having accepted my part, I accept also its conditions. And this I do all the more readily from certain advantages likely to accrue from it. " From one learn all," the adage says. The history of one Abolitionist, howsoever humble, even though it be for a day, is the history, to that extent, of every other Abolitionist — and of the cause. There are people here, doubtless, who are ignorant of the character of Abolitionism and Abolitionists. Let us for once, Mr. Chairman, give them an inside view. Let us lay aside reserve, and speak with a freedom which in other circumstances would hardly be justifiable.

Thirty-one years ago, this witness was a student at Andover Theological Seminary. While there, a desire, which, for more than a year, had consumed him, culminated into a purpose. In the depths of his soul and before God, he consecrated himself to the work of a missionary among the heathen. What his precise motives were, it is not necessary here to inquire. That they were of a mixed character, partaking not a little of the ardor and romance of youth, subsequent reflection has left no room to doubt.

There was another student at the Seminary, whose views and feelings were in harmony with my own, and who joined in this vow of self-consecration. His name was Daniel E. Jewett. I mention him for reasons which will presently be obvious.

I had been at Andover but a short time — less than two months — when a severe domestic affliction — the death of my eldest brother — called me away; and I returned to my home in Carlisle, in this State, where I had been born and bred.

For two or three years previous to the period now referred to, the country — a very considerable portion of it — had been in a state of high religious excitement. Every where people's attention was directed with unusual earnestness to the subject of personal religion. Since the days of Whitfield, it was said, there had been no excitement equal to it in depth and intensity; but toward the latter part of 1833, this excitement began to subside. The "revivals," as they were called, which followed this period, and which were got up by the machinery of "protracted meetings" and other appliances, were, for the most part, mere imitations — simulations; without depth and without earnestness.

With the subsidence of this religious excitement in the country, the feelings of the sincere and enlightened who had shared in it began to take a new turn. Their attention was called away from themselves to the condition of others. They had made sufficient progress in the divine life to understand that cardinal injunction : " Let no man seek his own, but every one his neighbor's weal."

About this time I happened one day, in a barber-shop, to pick up a newspaper, the columns of which I found filled with discussions of the subject of slavery. It was a question to which my attention had never before been directed. The paper interested me exceedingly. Its vigor of style and the boldness of its argument were striking. It was the *Liberator*. I took it home with me, read it carefully, and came back the next day to talk about it. An argument arose between me and the barber, in which that gentleman had greatly the advantage. He gave me a book to take home with me: it was a thick pamphlet, of about the size and appearance of the *Atlantic Monthly*, and was entitled "Thoughts on Colonization." Its author was WM. LLOYD GARRISON. I read it at one sitting. The scales fell from my eyes. The whole truth was revealed to me. The evil of slavery, the vulgar cruelty of prejudice against color, the duty of the country and of every man in it toward the black man, were as plain as if they had been written out before me in letters of fire. From that time to this, I have been an Abolitionist. From that time to this, I have regarded my friend JOHN PECK, the colored barber, as one of my best benefactors.

In the latter part of 1833, I learned that there was to be a Convention in Philadelphia, for the purpose of forming a National Anti-Slavery Society. This information I derived from my Andover friend, DANIEL E. JEWETT. He wrote to me, begging that I would come to the meeting. He dwelt feelingly upon the condition of the two and a quarter million (that was the figure then) of our unoffending fellow-men held in bondage, and urged me not to be insensible to their claims. "How do you know, my brother," he said, "that this may not be the work to which you have, unconsciously, dedicated yourself? How do you know that this is not the very field which your yearnings have been foreshadowing?"

I laid what he said to heart, and determined to attend the Convention. The little band of pronounced Abolitionists in Carlisle — all of whom were black, except myself — appointed me a delegate, and I set off for the city. It was in the day of stage-coaches, before the new era of railroads, and I was two days in coming. I stopped at the "Indian Queen," in 4th street, then considered one of our best hotels. The style of caravansera known as the "first-class hotel" was not then known — out of Boston. Your "Tremont House," I believe, was at that time in the full tide of successful experiment. I lost no time, the next morning after my arrival, in presenting myself, according to directions, at the house of Friend EVAN LEWIS, in 5th street, above Cherry. Mr. LEWIS was editor of a Quaker anti-slavery journal, called *The Advocate of Truth*. He was a faithful friend of the cause, as well as one of the most prominent at that time in Philadelphia. With friend LEWIS I went to the Convention. It met in the Adelphi Building, in 5th street, below Walnut. Its proceedings were not secret, though they were, nevertheless, not thrown open by advertisement to the public. There were some sixty or seventy delegates present, and a few spectators, who had been especially invited. A small number, it will be said, for a National Convention. But at that time, it must be remembered, the movement was in its incipiency. The cloud of Abolitionism was not even so big as a man's hand. Now it covers the heavens!

When I entered the hall — which was on the morning of the second day — the proceedings had begun; though, as I soon learned, there was no specific business before the meeting. A Committee had been appointed the day before, consisting of WM. LLOYD GARRISON, SAMUEL J. MAY, EDWIN P. ATLEE, and others, to draw up a Declaration of Sentiments; and the Convention was now expecting their report. While waiting, Dr. ABRAHAM L. COX read a poem addressed to Mr. GARRISON, written by JOHN G. WHITTIER, at that time a young author, comparatively unknown to fame. You remember the piece:

> "Champion of those who groan beneath
> Oppression's iron hand,
> In view of penury, hate and death,
> I see thee fearless stand.
>
> *   *   *   *   *   *   *
>
> "I love thee with a brother's love;
> I feel my pulses thrill
> To mark thy spirit soar above
> The cloud of human ill."

After the poem, LEWIS TAPPAN arose, and delivered a glowing eulogy upon Mr. GARRISON. He related two very striking anecdotes, which, though I remember them distinctly, I shall not, in this presence, repeat. He concluded by saying that it had not been his purpose to eulogize Mr. GARRISON; that what he said was said in no spirit of panegyric, but as a matter of fidelity to truth and to the cause. Mr. GARRISON had been struck at as a representative of the cause. It was our duty, he said, to repel these assaults; to vindicate our faithful pioneer from the calumnies and misrepresentations of the enemy, and to stand by him "through evil report and through good report."

This was the first specimen I had had of what has since been called "mutual admiration." And here let me say that the charge implied in the use made of this phrase is without just foundation. When Abolitionists praise their representative men, it is for the reason suggested by Mr. TAPPAN. It is to defend them against the shafts of pro-slavery malice and calumny. It is from a sacred regard to truth and the interests and honor of the cause; and in no spirit of adulation, "mutual" or otherwise.

And—if you will allow me still further to digress—I will add that the charge against us of using needlessly hard and denunciatory language is equally without foundation. Why, sir, last night, while Mr. GARRISON was speaking, several gentlemen—new converts to the cause—left the house because the speaker was too tame! Their hate of slavery and slaveholders, and all that belongs to the system, is so intense, that Mr. GARRISON's terms of condemnation were not strong enough to relieve their minds. They are of a class whom the speaker sometimes meets, one of whom on a certain occasion represented himself as belonging to the "Five Nations." He was a gentlemanly, mild-looking person—any thing but a savage in appearance—and being asked what he meant by so styling himself, he explained by saying he was for giving the rebel slaveholders " confiscation, emancipation, ruination, extirpation and *damnation*." Parson BROWNLOW, also a new convert to the cause—the same that once persecuted the saints—is of this class. He is represented as saying that he is "for giving the slaveholding rebels 'Greek fire' in this world, and *hell fire* in the next." Now, Mr. Chairman, this is not the language nor is it the spirit of the old Abolitionists. The charge of using hard and acrimonious language lies not properly at our door.

But to return from my digression. Mr. TAPPAN's speech was interrupted by the announcement that Mr. GARRISON and the rest of the Committee were coming in with their report. They had prepared a draft of a Declaration, and it devolved upon Dr. EDWIN P. ATLEE to read it. After the reading, followed criticism of its contents—or, rather, criticism of some of its phrases; for, as a whole, the paper commended itself at once to all who heard it. THOMAS SHIPLEY, that good man and faithful friend of the slave, objected to the word "man-stealer" as applied indiscriminately to the slaveholders. To this it was replied that the term was an eminently proper one; that it described the exact relation between the master and the slave. It was urged that things should be called by their right names; that LUTHER had said he would "call a hoe a hoe, and a spade a spade." Besides, it was added, it was a scriptural phrase, and the chapter and verse were quoted in which it was used. This mollified friend SHIPLEY, though it did not set his mind entirely at rest. At length, some one suggested that the term should be retained, but that it should be preceded by the words, "according to Scripture." This met the difficulty, and the paper was amended so as to read: "Every American citizen who holds a human being in involuntary bondage as his property, is, *according to Scripture*, (Exodus 21 : 16,) a man-stealer."

Among the speakers, while the Declaration was under discussion, were two who interested me particularly. One was a countryman dressed in the plainest garb, and in appearance otherwise not particularly calculated to excite expectation. His manner was angular, and his rhetoric not what would be called graceful. But his matter was solid, and as clear as a bell. It had the ring of the genuine metal, and was, moreover, pat to the point in question. When he sat down — which he did after a very brief speech — the question was asked: "Who is that?" and the answer came: "THOMAS WHITSON, of Lancaster county, in this State."

The other speaker was a woman. I had never before heard a woman speak at a public meeting. She said but a few words, but these were spoken so modestly, in such sweet tones, and yet withal so decisively, that no one could fail to be pleased. And no one did fail to be pleased. She apologized for what might be regarded as an intrusion; but she was assured by the Chairman and others that what she had said was very acceptable. The Chairman added his hope that "the lady" would not hesitate to give expression to any thing that might occur to her during the course of the proceedings.

This debate on the Declaration took place in Committee of the Whole. After one or two slight verbal changes, the Committee arose, and reported the document to the Convention. It was adopted unanimously, and ordered to be engrossed. The next morning, being the last session of the Convention, it was brought in engrossed and ready for signature. Before the work of signing began, it was agreed that it should be read once more. The task was assigned to our friend, SAMUEL J. MAY, who performed it with much feeling. At times his emotion was such as to prevent him for awhile from proceeding. The same feeling pervaded the audience. Then followed informally the ceremony of signing. Each one, as he came up to put his name to the instrument, showed by his manner, and, in some instances, by his words, that he was doing a very solemn thing.

By this time I had come to be tolerably well acquainted with the Convention, both as a whole, and in its individual members. My part in the proceedings had been, and was to the end, a silent one. The only distinction I enjoyed was that of being the youngest member of the body.

Looking back upon this interesting occasion, the whole thing comes up before me with the distinctness of a picture. I see the Convention just as it sat in that little hall of the Adelphi Building. I see the President, BERIAH GREEN, of Oneida Institute, sitting on an eminence in the west end of the hall; at either side of him the two Secretaries, LEWIS TAPPAN and JOHN G. WHITTIER.

Mr. GREEN, though as it proved one of the best men that could have been had for the office, was not the person originally contemplated for Chairman. The Abolitionists at that time, like other people, had an idea that a Convention would not be a Convention without a man with a great name to serve as Chairman; therefore, when the delegates came to Philadelphia, the first thing they did was to cast about for some man of distinction to preside. They called on THOMAS WISTAR, a venerable and wealthy member of the Society of Friends; but he declined. Then they waited upon Mr. ROBERTS VAUX, an aged and highly respected citizen, whose social position and reputation as a philanthropist indicated him as a proper person to preside over the meeting. He received the Committee politely, and listened to them courteously. He sympathized with them in their general object; he was opposed to slavery, and would be glad to see it abolished; but—and then followed the usual objections; and, in short, while grateful for the honor rendered him, Mr. VAUX begged leave respectfully to decline.

Discouraged in their attempts to find a great man for Chairman, the delegation concluded to select for this purpose one of their own number; and the choice fell upon BERIAH GREEN. A better man could not have been selected. Though of plain exterior and unimposing presence, Mr. GREEN was a man of learning and superior ability; in every way above the average of so-called men of eminence.

Mr. TAPPAN, who sat at his right, was a jaunty, man-of-the-world looking person; well dressed and handsome; with a fine voice and taking appearance. WHITTIER, who sat at his left, was quite as fine looking, though in a different way. He wore a dark frock coat with standing collar, which, with his thin hair, dark and sometimes flashing eyes, and black whiskers—not large, but noticeable in those unhirsute days—gave him, to my then unpractised eye, quite as much of a military as a Quaker aspect. His broad, square forehead and well-cut features, aided by his incipient reputation as a poet, made him quite a noticeable feature in the Convention.

These were the officers of the meeting; the rest were all upon a dead level of equality. There were no distinctions tolerated among the members. At an early stage of the proceedings, it was determined that no titles should be given or received; no Honorables, Doctors, or Esquires. Men were to be recognized as men, and all factitious distinctions discarded. It was a *levelling* Convention, in the best sense of that word.

It is impossible, Mr. Chairman, to look back upon those days without noticing that Time, with his remorseless scythe, has been at his inevitable work. Death has thinned our numbers. Some of the best members of that Convention have gone to their rest. Among these was good THOMAS SHIPLEY, whose departure WHITTIER has so beautifully commemorated :

> "Gone to thy Heavenly Father's rest,
> The flowers of Eden round thee blowing,
> And on thine ears the murmurs blest
> Of Siloa's waters gently flowing.
>
> *   *   *   *   *   *   *
>
> "O loved of thousands! to thy grave,
> Sorrowing of heart, thy brethren bore thee;
> The poor man and the rescued slave
> Wept as the broken earth closed o'er thee."

EVAN LEWIS, another of the Philadelphia delegates, took his departure soon after the holding of the Convention. He was an able and faithful friend of the cause, and performed his part well. Though dead, he yet speaketh. She who was the partner of his toils while he lived, remains to finish the task which they had jointly undertaken; and the mantle of the father has, in a good measure, fallen upon the shoulders of his children.

Dr. EDWIN ATLEE, the younger, another Philadelphia member of the Convention, passed early from the scene of conflict. Faithful and true to the cause while he lived, he left, in his good name, an inheritance of which his children may well be proud, and which should ever be a stimulus to them in works of well-doing.

Of the members of the Convention who remain, I shall not speak. Quite a number are here to speak for themselves. Among them I may be excused for mentioning the three who are respectively the President and Vice-Presidents of the Pennsylvania Anti-Slavery Society; JAMES MOTT, ROBERT PURVIS, and THOMAS WHITSON.

Mr. Mott, when I saw him at the Adelphi Building, thirty years ago, was in the prime of manhood. He was tall, and as straight as an arrow; his sandy hair untouched by the frosts of time. Thomas Whitson was also in the prime of life; tall, hearty, and progressive. His full shock of stubborn brown hair showed that he had not yet reached the climax of his vigor. He was stalwart in body and robust in mind, and ready for a tussle with any opponent. Mr. Purvis was in the full bloom of opening manhood; ardent, impetuous, and overflowing with enthusiasm. You will remember the speech he made, Mr. Chairman — so exactly like himself. Impassioned, full of invective, bristling with epithets, denouncing " that diabolical and fiendish system of atrocity, American slavery, and that equally rapacious, and, if possible, still more detestable scheme, the infamous Colonization Society."

At that Convention there were no adjournments for dinner. We sat daily from ten o'clock A. M. till dark, without recess. We had meat to eat which those who have never been "caught up into the third heaven" of first principles wot not of. The last hours of the Convention were especially impressive. I had never before, nor have I ever since, witnessed any thing fully equal to it. The deep religious spirit which had pervaded the meeting from the beginning became still deeper. The evidence of the Divine presence and the Divine approval were palpable. Had we heard a voice saying, " Put off thy shoes from off thy feet, for the ground whereon thou standest is holy ground," our convictions could scarcely have been clearer.

Those who were there will never forget the address with which President Green closed the Convention. The concluding part of that address was somewhat as follows:

" Brethren, it has been good to be here. In this hallowed atmosphere I have been revived and refreshed. This brief interview has more than repaid me for all that I have ever suffered. I have here met congenial minds; I have rejoiced in sympathies delightful to the soul. Heart has beat responsive to heart, and the holy work of seeking to benefit the outraged and despised has proved the most blessed employment.

" But now we must retire from these balmy influences, and breathe another atmosphere. The chill hoar frost will be upon us. The storm and tempest will rise, and the waves of persecution will dash against our souls. Let us be prepared for the worst. Let us fasten ourselves to the throne of God as with hooks of steel. If we cling not to Him, our names to that document will be but as dust.

" Let us court no applause; indulge in no spirit of vain boasting.

Let us be assured that our only hope in grappling with the bony monster is in an Arm that is stronger than ours. Let us fix our gaze on God, and walk in the light of His countenance. If our cause be just — and we know it is — His omnipotence is pledged to its triumph. Let this cause be entwined around the very fibres of our hearts. Let our hearts grow to it, so that nothing but death can sunder the bond."

As Mr. GREEN finished, he lifted up his voice in prayer; and such a prayer is rarely heard. Its fervency and faith seemed to illustrate what the speaker had said about "taking hold of the throne as with hooks of steel," and "gazing upon the very face of God."

But, Mr. Chairman, I have been speaking for three-quarters of an hour, and have as yet scarcely touched the threshold of my subject. Reminiscences! They come upon me so thick and fast that the whole time of this Convention would not suffice to give them expression. Here I have been lingering over a few of the incidents of the first three days of the great anti-slavery epoch: what shall I say of the whole thirty years which have followed, every day of which has been freighted with an event — every hour with some striking incident!

I must now stop, and give place to others. I have already consumed more than my fair share of the time. We have more than a score of able speakers here, every one of whom has a prescriptive right to be heard. So, without further words, I abruptly close.

At the request of Mr. GARRISON, the signers of the Declaration of Sentiments arose, and the following were found to be present: ISAAC WINSLOW, ORSON S. MURRAY, WILLIAM LLOYD GARRISON, SAMUEL JOSEPH MAY, ROBERT PURVIS, BARTHOLOMEW FUSSELL, ENOCH MACK, JAMES MILLER MCKIM, THOMAS WHITSON, JAMES MOTT, JAMES MC-CRUMMELL.*

SAMUEL J. MAY. There were others who were members of the Convention, whose names were not signed to the Declaration; and I look back with a feeling of shame to the fact, that there were four or five women — LUCRETIA MOTT, ESTHER MOORE, LYDIA WHITE, SIDNEY ANN LEWIS — who did us good service; who spoke, and spoke always to the purpose; and I remember that, in one or two instances, they relieved us from difficulties into which we had got ourselves in

---

* See Appendix B.

the discussion. Perfectly well I remember them. Why were their names not signed to the Declaration? It shows that we were in the dark on the subject. But their names should always go down to posterity as active members of the Convention; and I desire that they should be remembered as having taken an active and important part with us.

MARY GREW. Why were their names not signed?

Mr. MAY. Because we had no conception of the rights of women. Because it would then have been thought an impropriety; a thought at which we all laugh now.

Mr. GARRISON. To show the spirit which prevailed in that Convention, of unusual liberality certainly for those times, let me read two resolutions therein adopted:

Resolved, That the cause of Abolition eminently deserves the countenance and support of American women, inasmuch as one million of their colored sisters are pining in abject servitude—as their example and influence operate measurably as laws to society—and as the exertions of the females of Great Britain have been signally instrumental in liberating eight hundred thousand slaves in the Colonies.

Resolved, That we hail the establishment of Ladies' Anti-Slavery Societies as the harbinger of a brighter day, and that we feel great confidence in the efficiency of their exertions; and that those ladies who have promptly come forth in this great work are deserving the thanks of those who are ready to perish.

You remember that in 1840, our friend, then Miss ABBY KELLEY, was placed on our Business Committee, and the American Anti-Slavery Society was broken asunder, and almost entirely shipwrecked. But we have got bravely over it; and now there is no question in any part of our country that is free, in regard to the right of woman to speak as freely as man speaks, and to be as freely heard.

LUCRETIA MOTT. I deem it but just to state, that although we were not recognized as a part of the Convention by signing the document, yet every courtesy was shown to us, every encouragement to speak, or to make any suggestions of alterations in the document, or any others. I do not think it occurred to any one of us at that time, that there would be a propriety in our signing the document. In the evening, at our house, I remember a conversation with our friend

Samuel J. May, in the course of which I remarked, that we could not expect that women should be fully recognized in such assemblages as that, while the monopoly of the pulpit existed. It was with diffidence, I acknowledge, that I ventured to express what had been near to my heart for so many years, for I knew that we were there by sufferance. It was after the Convention had gathered on the second day, that the invitation was sent out. Thomas Whitson came to our house with an invitation to women to come there as spectators or as listeners. I felt such a desire that others than those assembled at our own house should hear, that I wanted to go here and there, and notify persons to go; but I was asked not to use up the whole morning in notifying others, for we must try and be there ourselves. When I rose to speak, with the knowledge that we were there by sufferance, and it would be only a liberty granted that I should attempt to express myself, such was the readiness with which that freedom was granted, that it inspired me with a little more boldness to speak on other subjects.

When this Declaration, that has been read to us here to-day, and that we have so often delighted to hear, was under consideration, and we were considering our principles and our intended measures of action; when our friends felt that they were planting themselves on the truths of Divine Revelation, and on the Declaration of Independence, as an Everlasting Rock, it seemed to me, as I heard it read, that the climax would be better to transpose the sentence, and place the Declaration of Independence first, and the truths of Divine Revelation last, as the Everlasting Rock; and I proposed it. I remember one of the younger members, Daniel E. Jewett, turning to see what woman there was there who knew what the word "transpose" meant. (Laughter.)

It has been honestly confessed that there was not, at that time, a conception of the rights of woman. Indeed, women little knew their influence, or the proper exercise of their own rights. I remember that it was urged upon us, immediately after that Convention, to form a Female Anti-Slavery Society; and at that time, I had no idea of the meaning of preambles and resolutions and votings. Women had never been in any assemblies of the kind. I had only attended one Convention—a Convention of colored people in this State—before that; and that was the first time in my life I had ever heard a vote taken, being accustomed to our Quaker way of getting the prevailing sentiment of the meeting. When, a short time after, we came together to form the Female Anti-Slavery Society, which I am rejoiced to say is still extant, still flourishing, there was not a woman capable of taking the chair, and organizing that meeting in due order; and we had to call on JAMES McCRUMMELL, a colored man, to give us aid in the work. You know that at that time, and even to the present day, negroes, idiots and women were in legal documents classed together; so that we were very glad to get one of our own class (laughter) to come and aid us in forming that Society.

SPEECH OF REV. SAMUEL J. MAY.

I have also been asked for reminiscences. May I be permitted to commence a little further back than the formation of this Society? The greatest event in my moral or spiritual life occurred on the evening when I first heard our friend WILLIAM LLOYD GARRISON, in Boston, in the Fall of 1830. I was so impressed by his words, that a resolution was formed in my soul, from that moment, to dedicate myself to the cause of the slave. I was called on to preach in the city of Boston the following Sunday. I am ashamed to say that I had nothing at all, in any of the sermons I had taken with me, bearing in the least on this great subject. But, fortunately, I had a sermon on Prejudice. So I appended to that hastily, in pencil, an application of the doctrine of the sermon to the condition of the colored people in our country. I delivered the sermon. I will not stop now to describe to you the effect that it had upon the audience. The reminiscence is called to my mind merely by what has been said this afternoon respecting the early influence of woman. The excitement was very great. The minister of the church was exceedingly angry, and spoke to me in terms of stern reproof, and said I should never enter his pulpit again. As I passed out of the house, I saw on all hands that an unusual emotion had been awakened throughout the congregation. When I arrived at the vestibule of the church, I found it well-nigh filled with persons talking busily together about the strange utterance to which they had listened. A woman, pressing through the crowd, stepped up to me, her countenance suffused with emotion, the tears trickling down her cheeks, and had the courage to stretch forth her hand to me, and say, "Mr. May, I thank you. What a shame it is that I, who have now been for nearly thirty years attending meeting in what are called Christian churches, have never before heard an earnest appeal on behalf of the wronged and outraged colored people of our country!" I shall never forget that woman. It was an event that sent deep into my soul that reverence which I now feel for woman. (Applause.)

The first letter that you read this morning brought to my mind another reminiscence which antedates the meeting that formed this Society. Early in the Spring of that year, a noble woman, PRUDENCE CRANDALL, in the town of Canterbury, Conn., in the simplest and most unostentatious manner, led to it by an event which she neither courted nor sought to avoid, proffered her school, which had attained some reputation, to the children of colored persons, and such others as pleased to send their children with them. The excitement can better be imagined than described. The people rose almost in a body, and the poor woman was overwhelmed with expressions of abhorrence and determined opposition. Of course, I went to her, and proffered her such aid as I could give. Without entering into the narrative at all, I will merely say that, in a day or two, I found myself solemnly pledged to test the question of that woman's right under the law to open a school for colored persons — a right which they called in question. I had pledged myself to ANDREW T. JUDSON, afterwards one of the Judges of the Supreme Court of the United States, who was her principal persecutor, to try that question from the lowest court in Canterbury to the highest court in the United States. He said tauntingly to me, "Ho! ho! Do you know what you undertake?" "Perhaps I don't," was my reply. "It will cost you money — a vast deal of money." "It may," said I. I had not consulted an individual, excepting only my friend, that most excellent man, GEORGE BENSON, the father of Mrs. GARRISON. Said I, "So sure am I that the aim of this movement will be justly appreciated by philanthropists throughout our country, that I shall have all the money I want." I confess, however, to a little trembling after a time, when not an individual offered me a dollar to sustain me in that trial. A few days, however, brought me a letter from that true philanthropist, ARTHUR TAPPAN. The story had got into the newspapers, and was noised abroad. ARTHUR TAPPAN I had known in my childhood, but had not seen him for many years. He had then become a very wealthy man, wielding, it was said, something like seventeen hundred thousand dollars. It was a very cordial letter, saying, in substance, "I have heard of what you have undertaken; I heartily approve of it. If I am not mistaken, you have not the means to carry on the trial that you have invoked. I therefore beg

you to consider me as your banker, who will honor all your drafts."
(Applause.) I confess, Mr. President, I could hardly keep on my
feet, walking with seventeen hundred thousand dollars in my bank!
But I will not go on with the story; it is very long. I will merely
say, that after two years of controversy, that cost over $600, which
was readily paid by Mr. TAPPAN, the result of that controversy was
in favor of Miss CRANDALL. (Applause.)

Mr. GARRISON. I happen to have here a volume from which I
will read a paragraph: —

"THE BLACK LAW OF CONNECTICUT. We neglected, in our last,
to mention that Miss CRANDALL, for a violation of the notorious statute of Connecticut, in continuing to instruct colored children, had
been arrested and carried before a Justice of the Peace, by whom she
was committed to jail, to take her trial at the ensuing court. She
was confined in the same room which was occupied by the murderer
WATKINS during the last days of his life."

Mr. MAY. I must confess to a little management in that matter.
Of course, if any one of us had come forward, and given bonds for
Miss CRANDALL, she would not have been incarcerated. But I went,
assisted by my friend Mr. GEORGE BENSON, diligently around among
my friends, and instructed them that no one should give bonds. The
law was an *ex post facto* one. It was enacted by the Legislature of
Connecticut after the school was commenced. Nevertheless, they
prosecuted her under that law, and I received due information that
the trial was to take place. I said, "Very well; you can let it go
on if you will." Presently came a messenger, informing me that the
Judge had found her guilty, and that they wanted some one to give
bonds. "Very well, you can give bonds; there are enough of you
in Canterbury to do it." Then they wanted to know if I would not.
"Certainly not," said I; "I have something else to do besides giving
bonds." Miss CRANDALL understood what was to be done. I wanted
to let the people know how odious the law was; and if her bonds had
been but a cent, I should not have given them. They came to me a
second time; but I said, "It is useless; I shall give no bonds."
Presently the report came that the Sheriff was approaching the town
where I lived, and where the jail was, with Miss CRANDALL. Meanwhile, I had had the cell, where WATKINS had been lately confined,
nicely cleaned and whitewashed, and had a comfortable bed put in it,
and one of Mrs. GARRISON's sisters, Miss ANNE BENSON, consented to go

and spend the night with Miss CRANDALL. So the Sheriff brought up Miss CRANDALL, and I found opportunity to say to her, "Are you afraid?" "No," said she, "I am trembling lest they should n't put me in." (Applause.) Then they came to me again, and said, "It is only five miles; if you will get some one to give bonds, we will go and get the Judge." "My dear friends," said I, "if the Judge was here, and the bonds were three cents, I should not give them, nor would any body else, if I could prevent it. If you want to avert the imprisonment, you have only to give bonds yourselves. Let A. T. JUDSON, or somebody else, give bonds for her." But they were too stuffy for that, and foolishly said, "Put her in." She was put in; and when the key was turned, and taken out of the lock, the game was in my hands. Of course, it was announced in all the papers that, for keeping a school for colored girls in the State of Connecticut, that boasted itself more than all the States of its large appropriations for the universal education of the people, a noble young woman had been incarcerated in the cell of a murderer. You manage a newspaper, brother, and you know how such things sound. The tale went the country over.

The next day we let Miss CRANDALL out, by giving bonds, and I took my horse and chaise, and my wife and children, and went off and refreshed myself with a little journey, knowing that the matter would work exactly as I intended it should.

That is a reminiscence. I am thirty years older than I was thirty years ago, and getting a little into that period of life when we are apt to become garrulous; so you must stop me if I say too much. But I wished to do this justice to ARTHUR TAPPAN. I do not know that the part he took in it was ever publicly announced before. Think of it! He sent me word to employ the best counsel; and so I did. WILLIAM W. ELLSWORTH, afterwards Governor of the State, was one of my counsel; and CALVIN GODDARD, formerly one of the Judges of the Supreme Court, was another. They were among the most distinguished lawyers of the State. They were very generous. They did not charge me what they might have done. Nevertheless, the expenses on the whole amounted to over $600, all of which were paid by Mr. TAPPAN.

Nor is that all. The papers of the county all refused, although filled with the most egregious misrepresentations of Miss CRANDALL, of the purposes of her school, and of the intentions of her patrons and friends, to allow me a line for explanation. Even the editor of one of the papers, whom I had assisted in getting up his publication, told me that he could not; that it would be the destruction of his paper to admit any thing upon the subject, excepting what our opponents might send. Of course, I was somewhat disturbed at this. I wrote a letter to Mr. TAPPAN, saying that I would come and see him if I could escape from my engagements long enough, but the pressure on me was very heavy. Two days after, who should enter my study but ARTHUR TAPPAN, leaving his immense business, his large monetary concerns in New York, to come and see me, because I could not go to see him! After I had laid the matter before him, he said to me, "Start another paper." It so happened that there were types and an unused press in town; and I went as soon as he had left, and engaged them for a year, and started my paper, called *The Unionist*.

And here comes another reminiscence. I had been so happy as once to hear our friend CHARLES C. BURLEIGH speak in a public meeting, and to hear him once was enough to know there was a great deal in him. I was then not only in charge of a parish which required the full exercise of the little ability that I had, but I was also conducting a religious paper, into which, unfortunately, in the prospectus, not foreseeing what would occur, I had pledged myself that there should be nothing of personal or local controversy admitted. So that, although I was editing a paper, I could not defend myself in it against these assaults of my enemies, consistently with my prospectus; therefore Mr. TAPPAN told me to start another paper. But I could not carry on two papers. So I bethought me of this young man, CHARLES C. BURLEIGH, and harnessed my horse and went after him. It was on Friday, in the midst of haying time. A very busy week he had had of it, and although he then believed in shaving, he had not shaved himself since the haying season commenced. I went to the house of his excellent father, and inquired for CHARLES. "He is in the hay field, as busy as he can be." Nevertheless, I must see him; and I sent for him, and up he came; and I am sure he looked as much like the son of JESSE, when he came to SAMUEL to be anointed, as DAVID did himself. Nevertheless, I saw it was CHARLES BURLEIGH, and I told him what I wanted. He engaged to be with me the next Monday morning, and he was. He did good service in the cause. He wrote himself into a reputation that has been, I believe, increasing ever since, as a writer and as a speaker.

You see, Mr. President, you tapped rather a full cask. That is a reminiscence I had no thought of bringing up. But now, to come back to the Convention, where you wanted me to begin. I said to my brother JOHNSON, while brother McKIM was speaking, that I thought his introduction was a little too long; mine has been longer, so he must forgive me. And now I will give you a reminiscence about him. He came all the way from Andover to the Convention —

Mr. McKIM. No, I came from Carlisle; I was only six weeks at Andover.

Mr. MAY. At any rate, he was a Simon-pure, blue Presbyterian, I suppose. But his heart was moved in the cause of humanity, and that turned the sourest of his dogmas to sweet. After we had been in session two days together, and were coming out of the Convention in the evening, I felt a grip on my arm, and heard brother McKIM ask — "Brother MAY, are you a Unitarian?" "Yes," said I, "I am as much of a Unitarian as I am of an Abolitionist." "Well, I never expected to feel towards a Unitarian as I do towards you." (Laughter.) I believe the hearts of all present at that meeting were drawn together with an affection that can never die out, so long as we live. The countenances of the friends who were there then cheer my heart as no other countenances in this world could. They bring back to my recollection that meeting, in the midst of the most malignant opposition. When I read the *Press* this morning, speaking so kindly, cordially, admiringly of Mr. GARRISON, I could not help thinking of the announcement in the papers on the morning of the day that our Convention commenced, thirty years ago. We were spoken of singly, some half dozen or more of us, and to each name was appended some epithet, intended, doubtless, as it was adapted, to awaken the malignant hatred of the community. The Police gave us to understand that they could not protect us in the evening, and that our meetings must be held during the daylight. So we met in the morning at nine, and adjourned at sundown. I very well remember that my name was announced as the "Rev. Dr. MAY, of Connecticut, the leader of the amalgamationists." That title was assigned me in consequence of a discussion which I had had in Connecticut with ANDREW T. JUDSON, which had been reported in the papers, and in which he thought, in the presence of a large assembly, to put me down by asking, "Sir, I want to know whether you are willing that your daughter should marry a nigger?" Of course, the audience were as silent as possible to hear my answer. Said I, "I am not willing that my daughter, my only daughter, should marry any unfortunate man. I regard the colored men of our country as most unfortunate men; and therefore I should not be willing that she should marry one." There was a chuckling in the audience, and a smile of triumph on many faces. Said I, "Stop! I have given you only half the answer. If you wish me to say whether I would rather my daughter should marry a man every way adapted to her, the only objection to whom should be his complexion, or should marry a man whose only recommendation to her should be his complexion, of course I should say, let her a thousand times rather marry the blackest man that you could find." (Applause.) It was because of that answer, which went through the papers at the time, that I was trumpeted here as the "leader of the amalgamationists." That is another reminiscence.

I gave so full an account, ten years ago, of my recollections of our meeting at the formation of the Society, that I am afraid I shall repeat myself if I go on much longer in this strain. I wish I could remember one of the brothers who rose in the midst of the Convention, and said, in reply to a suggestion for the softening of some of our measures, "Can you draw out Leviathan with a hook, or the great sea-serpent with a pin-hook?" Of course, that settled the question!

But I will not detain you longer. I will only set myself right on the woman question. When I first heard that ANGELINA GRIMKE was lecturing in New York, I was a minister in South Scituate, Mass. She was lecturing to crowded audiences of men and women indiscriminately, and, of course, I was very much shocked. But in connection with the account of her large audiences, and the composition of her audiences, were statements of the immense power with which she spoke. I took the two facts with me into my study, and sat down and looked them fully in the face. A woman was addressing promiscuous audiences *with immense power*. Said I to myself, Whence came that power? Is a God-given power in woman, any more than in man, to be unused? Does He give her talents to be wrapped in a napkin or buried in the ground, any more than to man? Certainly not; and the difficulty was dispelled from my mind. So I sat down, and wrote her a letter:—

"DEAR MISS GRIMKE: I hear you have been addressing promiscuous audiences. I am astonished; it is in such utter violation of all that we have considered proper and decorous and becoming in your sex! Nevertheless, I am satisfied that it is a prejudice, and I beg you to come to my home, and assist me as soon as possible to trample it under my feet."

She came. Meanwhile, I had given notice in different parts of the town and county where I lived, that she would address a meeting in my meeting-house first, and in another meeting-house afterwards, and so through the county. I took her and her sister all through the county, lecturing wherever a meeting-house could be found in which she could be heard; and an impression was made in that county which I trust is perceptible to this day. Is there a county in the State of Massachusetts that is more truly anti-slavery than Plymouth county? If there is, I know it not. I remember at one of the meetings some gentlemen living in Hingham had said very hard things about me. They appeared at the door, and presently they came further in. I watched them. Very soon their attention was arrested, enchained. They drew nearer and nearer, and I saw their countenances lighted up with emotion; and I was satisfied that they had felt the power of the speakers. When the meeting was over, they came bristling up to me: "What are you going about the county with these women for, setting at nought all the usages and proprieties of society? But we wish you to bring them to Hingham as soon as you please!" And so a meeting was held in Hingham, the most important town in the county excepting Plymouth; and there Miss Grimke made one of her grandest speeches; which, however, I am sorry to add, caused her a long fit of sickness, and obliged her to suspend her invaluable labors.

An allusion has been made to-night to the mob of October 21, 1835, in Boston. It is a fact of which you may not all be aware, showing the almost complete universality of the feeling which permeated the people of our country in regard to the Abolitionists as the enemies of the public, that, on that very day, Beriah Green, Gerrit Smith, and several others of the leading Abolitionists of New York, were undergoing at Utica the same treatment almost that Mr. Garrison received. And on that same day I was myself mobbed, my person attacked, and my life threatened, in the village of Montpelier, the capital of Vermont. On one and the same day, in three different States of the Union, at the North, Abolitionists were mobbed, simply for proclaiming the glorious truths of the

Declaration, and insisting upon their application to all men. And this reminds me of one more reminiscence, with which I will close.

For several years after I became acquainted with those "pestilent men" who have turned the world upside down, so that it now stands right side up, I devoted the greater part of my time to lecturing; and there is a fact I should like to have you all remember, to show you how naughty we were in the outset of our movement. More than a dozen times, as I approached a village to lecture, I would meet some prominent man, or after I got there he would call upon me at the hotel, and say: "Mr. MAY, you have come to deliver a lecture on slavery in our village?" "Yes, sir, I propose to do so." "Do you not know that this question of slavery was considered by the framers of the Constitution of our country, and that they adjusted it?" "Sir," I replied, "did you ever read the Constitution of the United States?" "You don't pretend to deny, Mr. MAY"—— "Did you ever *read* the Constitution of the United States?" "Why, sir, every body——" "Did *you* ever read the Constitution of the United States?" And certainly more than a dozen times I found men, holding high positions in society, who acknowledged that they had never read the Constitution! I reported it to the managers of our Society, in Boston, and one of the naughty things that we did at that time was to publish a cheap edition of the Constitution of the United States, and circulate it as one of our anti-slavery tracts. Did we not deserve all the harsh epithets and ill treatment with which we have been visited? (Laughter and applause.)

The Society adjourned, to meet the next day, at 10 A. M.

SECOND DAY—Forenoon Session.

The Society assembled promptly, and in the absence of the President, J. M. McKim was called to the chair. It being announced that the Rev. Henry Ward Beecher was present and could remain but a few minutes, (being under the necessity of returning immediately to New York,) he was invited to address the meeting. Upon coming to the platform, he was greeted with enthusiastic cheers.

SPEECH OF REV. HENRY WARD BEECHER.

It gives me great pleasure to meet you this morning, and none the less because we meet in circumstances of peace and of prosperity. After a long battle, with weapons not carnal but spiritual, it seems as if at last a victory was beginning to dawn upon us. I have lived for more than twenty-five years on faith, and have learned to subsist upon it tolerably well; though I confess that a little sight now and then helps one's faith very much. But there are a great many who have not been able to live on this diet of faith, and now that they are being fed on sight, they are falling into line, and beginning to train in the great anti-slavery army.

I do not stand here this morning so much to go into any analysis or measurement of shades of opinion, as to recognize the great services that, for a long period, without weariness, against every human discouragement, have been rendered to the cause of patriotism, of religion, and of humanity, by those that are represented in this Association. There have been, of course, all this time, differences of opinion among the friends of freedom; but I think that all honest men will agree, that for sincerity, profound conviction, heroism and moral courage, the members and adherents of this Anti-Slavery Society have stood preëminent. And when the history of this struggle shall be written, no inconspicuous place will be given to those that shall then have passed away; and we shall see, what we see in every age of the world, men mobbed when they lived, but splendid tombs built for them when they are dead. But you care little for that. The spirit in which you have worked is one which works for the sake of the work, for the sake of God who inspires it. I doubt not you have taken your remuneration as you went along, and could have afforded to die with your testimony on your lips, without having seen the sight, or, like Moses, having seen it only at a distance. But better things are in store for us. All the signs of the times look as though God meant emancipation in earnest, and meant it now. Whatever may have been men's ideas in respect to immediate emancipation, as the term is usually employed, I think that war has but one doctrine upon the subject, and that we are coming to it — that we, if we live a few years longer, shall see our country disembarrassed and uncursed by this monstrous evil, this gigantic iniquity.

Last night, Governor Curtin said that the doctrine enunciated in my remarks, namely, that we had no right to lay down the sword, having taken it up, until we had utterly exterminated the cause of the war, Slavery, was the doctrine of Pennsylvania. Undoubtedly he has been in circumstances to know the pulse and the feeling of this people. North of Pennsylvania, I think I may say I know it to be the doctrine of the people. It seems as though in the Providence of God, the underground work having been done, and the foundation having been brought up to the surface, and the building going up in the sunlight, its proportions of beauty becoming more and more apparent, we can have workmen now whom we could never have invited into the trench under ground. My wish is, more and more, that we should, for the sake of the great cause, lay aside the things in which we differ, and work together for the things upon which we are agreed, God working in us to will and to do of his own good pleasure.

For myself, I have vowed that if a man will now set his face towards emancipation, I will never look an inch behind him to see what he thought yesterday or the day before. I will not scan his record unless he becomes a critic of mine. But I will put my shoulder beside the shoulder of any man who will march in the ranks now. I will not ask who shall be leader; only that there shall be a leader, and that he shall lead in the right direction. I only ask to be in the ranks, to work as every other man works, not for himself, not for any party, but for the sake of God and the country, for the cause of Christ as it is embodied and represented in this era of our national history, for the sake of those that are in bondage, and must be in bondage as long as there is a slave in this land; for you are slaves as long as there is a slave; you are bound as long as others are bound. According to the apostolic injunction, every man is in fetters as long as one man is fettered.

I congratulate you this morning. On my return from Europe, after an absence of a few months, I looked for growth, but I hardly knew where were the buds and where the branches. I find the buds branches, and on the branches fruit. It is as if, in the month of May, one should be carried a month to sea, not knowing he had been gone an hour; when he returns, he finds himself in the bosom of Summer. Things are germinating, and every where springing into marvellous growth and fruitfulness.

The last time I was in Philadelphia, I was escorted into the Hall between files of policemen, who defended my right of speech by the municipal power of the city. Last night, it was not necessary to have policemen. I find myself accepted now by the men who, three years ago, would not have opened their doors to me, nor uttered my name except as an offence. They say I have changed. Very well; let it be so; I am content; I am entirely changed; I have abandoned my old doctrines; I have become conservative; I have smoothed off all the hard edges, and rounded all the corners! They are steadfast and immovable; they have always been right. Let it go so; I am quite content. I will be considered as having changed every week, as much as you please; only take the principles, only work for the slave, and work in good practical earnest, it is very little matter what men say of you, where they put you, what they call you. It is the cause, and not men, that is important. It is the incarnation of God in our time, the reappearing of Christ in his own providences, the shaking the foundations of things, that they may be moved, which is important. All our personal matters, however strenuous the opposition to us may be, are but chaff, which the wind should drive away. If now the men of wealth, of intelligence, and of standing, in Pennsylvania, are willing to lay one hand on the Bible and the other on the charter of their liberties, and say, "Let the oppressed go free," they may call themselves MOSES and AARONS from the beginning, and I will never say nay to it.

So, too, in New York, and so in Boston; the leaven is working. Let us, then, give thanks to God; thanks for the past, that we were permitted to work in it; thanks that we are permitted to live to see the consummation which we expected to see over pearly battlements, but now shall see in the land of the living.

During my visit to England, it was my privilege to address, in various places, very large audiences; and I never made mention of the names of any of those whom you most revere and love, without calling down the wildest demonstrations of popular enthusiasm. I never mentioned the name of Mr. PHILLIPS, or Mr. GARRISON, that it did not call forth a storm of approbation. It pleased me to know that those who were least favored in our country were so well known in England. And the name of President LINCOLN was never pronounced without a torrent of approbation, even in the stormiest meetings. It is true that a man is not without honor save in his own country; and I felt that I had never had before me, in an audience here, such an appreciation of the names of our early and faithful laborers in this cause as there was in that remote country, among comparative strangers.

I am thankful for the privilege of looking on so many noble and revered faces, and so many young and enthusiastic persons, united together by so sacred a bond as that which unites you. I feel, not that I agree with you in every thing, but that I am heart and soul with you in the main end. Toward that end, we may take different paths, very likely, but when we come together at the end, we shall all be there. It is the end that crowns the beginning, rather than the beginning the end. I therefore feel that I am honored in being permitted to stand before you this morning, to utter these few words of sympathy and of greeting. Your cause is dear to you — just as dear to me. Your names, honored among yourselves, will never lack some wreaths, if I may be permitted to pluck any to place upon them. I thank God that he called you into existence. An uncanonical Church you are, a Church without ordination, but in my judgment, a Church of the very best and most apostolic kind, held together by the cohesion of a rule of faith, and an interior principle. Your ordinances are few and simple, but mighty through God. Your officers are not exactly elected. Whoever has the gifts, and the inspiration behind those gifts, he is your teacher and your leader. That is the truest form of the Church. I stand here in the midst of a part of God's great spiritual, earthly Church, happy to be in your midst, asking the privilege to call myself a brother only, asking the privilege of calling you that are advanced in years fathers and mothers, and asking the privilege also to work according to the light that is given me, and where I differ from you, of having still your confidence that I mean right. I will never work against you, as I never have. I will work with you as far as you will let me; and we shall all be supervised by a higher Love and a diviner Wisdom, and where mistakes are made, they will, after all, work together for the good cause. We shall meet, if not again on earth, in that land where no struggles are needed, where we shall rejoice and give thanks to Him who called, and guided, and crowned us with victory.

On motion, by Rev. SAMUEL MAY, Jr., a Committee was appointed to superintend the publication of the Proceedings of this Third Decade Meeting, with authority to incorporate therewith such documents as should seem to them appropriate. The Committee was subsequently named, as follows: WILLIAM LLOYD GARRISON, MARY GREW, OLIVER JOHNSON, SAMUEL MAY, Jr., JOHN T. SARGENT.

On motion of STEPHEN S. FOSTER, in view of the large number of persons who desired to address the meeting, speakers were requested not to occupy the floor more than fifteen minutes at a time: and the President was requested to remind each speaker when his time should have expired.

ORSON S. MURRAY, of Ohio, one of the signers of the Declaration of Sentiments, occupied fifteen minutes in reading part of a series of resolutions, written by himself, upon which he said he neither asked nor deprecated the action of the meeting. No action was taken upon them.

On motion of EDWARD M. DAVIS, the Honorable HENRY WILSON, United States Senator from Massachusetts, was invited to take a seat upon the platform. He was greeted, as he did so, with hearty applause.

A Committee on Finance was appointed as follows: JAMES N. BUFFUM, THOMAS GARRETT, MAHLON B. LINTON, ABBY KIMBER, AARON M. POWELL, WENDELL P. GARRISON.

SPEECH OF STEPHEN S. FOSTER.

It gives me great pleasure, fellow-citizens, to be with you on this occasion. It is one of the most interesting of the whole period of my life. I love to look into the faces of my old and early anti-slavery friends. I have new friends, but they are not like the old friends, the friends of my youth and early manhood. There is no gratification I ever received, or ever expect to receive in this life, so great as that of meeting those with whom I have stood shoulder to shoulder through many a hard fought battle in this and other pro-slavery States of this Union. And yet the pleasure of this meeting is marred by one consideration; and that is, that there are two or three million of our countrymen yet clanking their heavy chains. While we are happy, they are sad and sorrowful. While we are free, and protected by the government of our country, they are still struggling in chains! Their fate is yet all uncertain. Their sky of hope is brightening

They are sustained by the faint promises of hope; but still all is uncertain.

I have feared, since I have been with you upon this occasion, that we have become over-confident in regard to the success of the movement with which we have so long stood identified. The conviction seems to have become fixed, in the mind of every man in the ranks of the Anti-Slavery Society, that this war is the end of slavery, that we have already given it its death-blow. But so thought the friends of freedom in the Revolutionary War. They settled down in the confident belief that they had given the system a fatal stab, and that they should live to see it quickly pass away; and therefore they thought it unnecessary to incorporate in the Constitution of the country a provision for ever prohibiting the toleration of slavery. How much more are we secure now of the abolition of slavery, upon the heels of the war, than were our revolutionary fathers in their day? Is the country in a better state upon the question of human liberty than it was then? Are we more deeply penetrated by a sense of the sinfulness of slavery than were our fathers? [A VOICE— "Yes."] Why, then, are slaves dragged from the capital of your country back to their masters in the loyal States of this Union? Why is ABRAHAM LINCOLN, to-day, holding the military and naval power of this land, and shaking it in the very teeth of the slaves of the loyal States of this Union, telling them that if they rise and strike for freedom, they shall be crushed with the iron hand? ["He is n't doing it."] Not doing it? Has not he sworn, according to his own idea, to maintain slavery in the loyal States? ["Exactly the contrary."] Has not Hon. B. GRATZ BROWN told you that the people of Missouri would have abolished slavery but for Federal interference? Where is that sacred regard for constitutional obligation which for years was talked of on this platform? Has Mr. LINCOLN said to his agents, "In case the slaves strike for freedom in the loyal States, join them against their loyal masters"? Has the military protection of the slave system in the loyal States been withdrawn?

We assume too much, far more than our *political* friends assume in this matter. The Hon. Senator from Massachusetts on my left (Hon. HENRY WILSON) would tell you, if you were to ask his opinion, that ABRAHAM LINCOLN to-day holds himself constitutionally bound to maintain the institution of slavery in every loyal State of this Union, as he was in all the States prior to the rebellion; and to the execution of the Fugitive Slave Law in the District of Columbia, to-day, as much as ten years ago. The Bench of that District, every member of which was appointed by ABRAHAM LINCOLN, has allowed slave after slave to be arrested in the District of Columbia, and sent into slavery in the State of Maryland.

It seems to me that, in this state of the case, we have no reason to be very confident. If the nation is anti-slavery, why does it not say so? In the name of common sense, when the whole civilized world would applaud the declaration, why do they not say, by some authoritative act, that there shall be no slave on American soil henceforth? Nothing would be easier, nothing better for our cause; nothing would save so much the shedding of human blood as that simple declaration. How can you say the nation wants it done, when the nation will not do it? The President has set free a portion of the slaves— he has abolished slavery nowhere. Where he had not power to give liberty to the slaves in fact, he gave them liberty by law. Where he had power to give them liberty in fact, he did not give them liberty by law. He thus shamefully marred that act, which, if properly done, and placed upon moral grounds, would have sent his name down to posterity beside the name of WILLIAM LLOYD GARRISON. But he has declared, from beginning to end, that he has emancipated slaves, in no single instance, because he had any regard for them, but always out of regard for the white man, and for the perpetuity of the Federal Government. I would not trust my own, I would not trust any body's liberty in the hands of such a Government. Never, until I hear the Government of the United States pronounce authoritatively in all its departments, executive, legislative, judicial, the fiat which dooms slavery to everlasting perdition, will I lay off my armor. Lay off yours if you are tired of fighting, if you are weary and careworn, and feel that you cannot longer carry on the warfare; but I am a veteran soldier; I am here to-day to reënlist for the war; and, God being my helper, not one particle of my armor will I lay aside until the last fetter is broken. Not one jot or tittle of my stern demand for justice will I abate until the nation, as a nation, declares that slavery is for ever abolished in this country. (Applause.)

I feel that I ought to speak more strongly to-day than ever before, because the nation is more guilty to-day than ever before. According to their interpretation of the Constitution, never had the nation, until recently, the constitutional power to abolish slavery. To-day it has it, and is therefore the more guilty for not doing it. Never before was the question put directly to the nation, whether it should set free the slaves, and thereby promote universal liberty and end this war, or whether it should hold the slaves still longer, and cause the shedding of oceans more of human blood; for all admit that a proclamation of freedom would help the loyal cause, and bring the war the quicker to a close. There is a double guilt resting upon this Administration; first, for holding the slave in his chains, and secondly, for taking your sons and mine, tearing them away from the peaceful pursuits of home life, to go down to the South and meet the bristling bayonets of Southern rebels. The war might be ended at once by an act of justice. The nation refuses to perform that duty, but chooses rather to murder your sons and mine, and to prolong the bloody strife. The guilt of the nation accumulates every hour that we hold a slave in his chains. God is demanding every day that the oppressed shall go free; and the Government says, "No, we will try a little longer; we will not give up yet; we will have more plagues yet before we will let the people go." And we shall have them. Proclaim emancipation to the slaves, to the men whom God appoints as the true soldiers of this land; then, if they fail to do the work, I will volunteer, non-resistant as I am; and I will go down to Carolina, and face the rebel armies; with the sword of the spirit, however, and not with the sword of steel. I will lead your armies, if you want them led, unarmed. I will not shrink from my share of the danger. Place me between you and the enemy. Only let me have an army of Liberators, and that is all I ask. I will do all in my power to swell the ranks of the Union army, if you will make the war a war for freedom; but so long as, by the Constitution and the laws of the country, the Executive is compelled to use the army to put down an insurrection in any loyal State of this Union, God forbid that I should enlist, or invite any body else to enlist! For one, God being my helper, I shall go forward, whoever may falter.

SPEECH OF CHARLES C. BURLEIGH.

I doubt not that I speak the sentiment of every friend of our cause when I say, that we are all determined to go forward, and not to falter until the last fetter is struck from the limbs of the last slave. (Applause.) It seems to me that the error of our friend FOSTER is in assuming that his position is actually different from ours upon this point. We agree with him in purpose, and we agree with him mainly in regard to the propositions which he has stated, but dissent from some of the inferences which he draws. When he would exhort us not to be over-confident, we would say amen. It is a danger which should always be guarded against. But when he holds up to us, as a reason why we should not be over-confident, what all impartial observers will regard as an exaggerated and disjointed view of the facts of the case, rendering the picture darker than the truth, and making it, therefore, exert a discouraging rather than an encouraging influence, we dissent from the course which he pursues, and doubt the wisdom of his recommendation. We say, "Do not despair," as well as "Do not be over-confident." We say, Do not regard the difficulties more than they are, nor the progress made less than it is; lest the effect should be to deter some from further effort, from the apprehension that it is altogether in vain that we labor. Looking back upon a thirty years' struggle of Abolitionists, who have wielded the weapons of truth, the sword of the spirit, sharper than the two-edged steel, piercing even to the dividing asunder of soul and spirit and of the joints and marrow, what would they say, if they were to be told that we are in a worse position than when we began; that we have not advanced towards the attainment of our great object, but on the contrary have receded, and are further from the end than at the period immediately following the Revolution? Far, very far from that is the truth. We are far in advance of the revolutionary period. In the first place, accepting the premises upon which all moral enterprises proceed, we should infer that we must have advanced, from the very fact that a handful of faithful men have been laboring for thirty years past, by argument, appeal, persuasion, remonstrance—all the weapons of the moral armory—earnestly and diligently. But what is the fact? Just after the revolutionary period, the best and most clear-sighted anti-slavery men of the country would not have dared to advocate immediate emancipation, would not have dared to inscribe upon their banner immediate and unconditional freedom to the bondman. Is it nothing that we have converted the very best intellect of the country to that doctrine? Is it nothing that, whereas not even the wisest and most just of our fathers imagined it to be practicable, it is now conceded on all hands to be demonstrated as the best course, except by those who are determined to uphold slavery, and the continually diminishing class of conservative politicians, who have been left in the dark because, groping by candle-light before the sun rose, they turned their backs upon the growing dawn, and have forgotten that it is mid-noon?

Moreover, at the time immediately succeeding the revolutionary period, even those who called themselves anti-slavery men recognized, not the absolute justice of slavery, it may be, but a certain sort of right in the masters still to retain their slaves. I wish that I could have foreseen the course of this argument, that I might have slipped into my pocket a pamphlet containing the proceedings of the Abolition Societies of the period immediately following the Revolutionary war; for I would have compared their doings with those of this gathering to-day, and then asked you, if such a handful of the choice men of that day dared to go no further than they did, and if to-day our Declaration of Sentiments can receive the applause of this assembly, which is only the representative of multitudes of people all over the land, have we made no progress? (Applause.)

Our friend alludes to the fact that the Government still sustains slavery in the loyal States. True; and the more shame to the Government. Every word he says against the pro-slavery position of this Government, I heartily respond to; but how could he have had an opportunity to find fault with the Government for not making a clean cut, if it had not made a jagged one? The Government in the olden time never abolished slavery in the District of Columbia, never issued a proclamation of freedom to more than three million slaves, never recognized the black man in any of its measures, even so far as ABRAHAM LINCOLN and WILLIAM H. SEWARD and THURLOW WEED have already done. He has been recognized as a citizen, in defiance of the DRED SCOTT opinion, by the Attorney-General of the United States. Yes, we have official authority, from a Missourian Attorney-General, for the doctrine that the black man is a citizen of the country.

We have been told of the efforts of the Government against the Emancipationists of Missouri. Then, I say, the more shame to the Government for that. But at the time just after the Revolution, there could have been no act of interference needed by the Federal Government to prevent the abolition of slavery in any Slave State of the Union. Let me also, in justice to the man whom I have criticised, perhaps as freely as my friend FOSTER, remind you that if he went against the Radicals in Missouri, he went in favor of the Radicals in Maryland. (Applause.) We have a man at the head of the Government who is not altogether according to my taste, or in accordance with my feeling or my policy; but let us do him justice all the more assiduously, because we do not like his position.

I hold, then, that we have reason to be encouraged. The very ground we take is that of our friend Foster, that we will not give up until the work is accomplished; but we will labor all the more earnestly, and with all the more energy, because we see the signs around us of the progress we are making. We see the black man recognized among the defenders of the country, and see him regarded as a citizen, allowed as a citizen to appropriate the lands of the West, as well as to defend his newly-acquired liberty. Even States which we regarded as incorrigible Slave States— even Border-Ruffian Missouri — tread upon the very verge of emancipation, and at the next step are likely to go over. Shall we not thank God and take courage, not laying down our arms as if the victory were won, but shouting with all the more vigor, in the language of the great Captain of Scotland, when he saw the wavering of the foe:

> "Press on, brave sons of Innisgail,
> The foe is fainting fast,
> One blow for children and for wife,
> For Scotland, liberty, and life!
> The battle cannot last."

SPEECH OF AARON M. POWELL.

Instead of the third meeting of this kind which is celebrated by many who are present, it is the first one in my own experience. But it is to me as valuable, I apprehend, in my own appreciation, for the length of time in which I have been familiar with this movement, as to you who have labored longer, and in the more trying and darker periods of the struggle. I want to stand here a moment this morning, and to express personally my own sense of gratitude for having been permitted, even for ten years, to share somewhat in this contest. I cannot think even of the shorter period over which my own mind can pass in review, without the deepest gratitude in my own heart at having been permitted to labor in the Anti-Slavery cause, in that hour when we were obliged to walk by faith wholly, and not by sight occasionally. It is, I think, an occasion for the special gratitude of every Abolitionist to have been permitted to live in a time such as we have passed through, and such as we see at the present hour. I do not wish to dwell upon the past, or to indulge in any of the more recent reminiscences. I share the feeling which has been expressed this morning, that we are in the midst of great responsibilities. I think that we are surrounded by new and glorious opportunities for completing our labor. But the completion of it yet remains to be done. I am glad to stand here with the older members of the American Anti-Slavery Society, on this Thirtieth Anniversary, and to see in all the evidences of this hour, war-time as it is, the glorious moral method, which has been its method, vindicated as it is. We stand to-day vindicated in the wisdom of our position, and with every encouragement still to stand upon the platform of absolute right and impartial justice, as the only correct basis of effort in grappling successfully with oppression. As the New York *Tribune* of yesterday very truthfully remarked, there may be a connection between the meeting here thirty years ago, and the Presidential administration of this period. So it remains as true to-day, that if we adhere to this platform of absolute right and impartial justice, we shall see this work carried on in a new Union in the future, which shall be a true Union, dedicated to impartial liberty.

But, my friends, if by any mistaken counsel, which I do not believe is to prevail, if by any lack of conscience, which I trust there may not be, that type of politicians should prevail, represented, not by the Hon. Senator upon our platform, but by the editor of the New York *Times*, there will be no Union such as we hope for. But I believe that the HENRY J. RAYMOND school of politicians will not prevail, if there can be still impartial criticism of leading public men and public measures, in the light of impartial justice and absolute right. I mention the New York *Times*, because, speaking for the body of so-called Conservative Republicans, after GRANT's victory, which seemed to render it more certain that the North was to triumph, that paper says, in a column and a half editorial, that "masterly inactivity" is the policy now which should be pursued in regard to slavery. If that political counsel prevails, it is not statesmanship—it is a sham; it is selfishness under the name of conservatism. If that doctrine be allowed to prevail, then these battles, with tenfold increased horror, must in the future be fought over again. But if the American Anti-Slavery Society shall continue its labor earnestly and faithfully unto the end, then shall the line of political conduct based on the right find a moral support among the people which will enable them to go forward, and reconstruct the Union upon the basis of liberty for all men throughout the land. I stand here this brief moment, then, that I may utter an exhortation to you who are the immediate members and friends of this Society, to continue your efforts, recognizing the new opportunities, and remembering our increased responsibility to make one last, best effort for the complete overthrow of the common enemy of the country, human slavery. If there is that fidelity which there ought to be; if there is an appreciation of the importance and significance of this hour, this transition period, there will be engrafted into the Constitution of the country the simple amendment, when slavery has been abolished by a general emancipation act, that there shall be neither slavery nor involuntary servitude in any State or Territory of this Union, as explicit as the ancient prohibition in the Territories of the Northwest.

At the outset of this rebellion, there was assembled at Washington a Peace Congress, supposed to contain the wisdom and statesmanship of the country, outside the Halls of Congress. And what was that wisdom in that hour? How was it proposed that we should avert this great calamity of national war? CHARLES FRANCIS ADAMS, to the disgrace of that noble name, offered a resolution proposing an amendment to the Constitution—an amendment in the interest of slavery. And now, with three hundred thousand graves between us and slavery, with the industry and economy of the country disarranged, and with mourning and lamentation in every household in the land, in Heaven's name, may we not end this conflict by amending the Constitution, so that it may be as explicitly in the interest of liberty as in the beginning it was proposed to make it in the interest of slavery? (Applause.)

SPEECH OF LUCRETIA MOTT.

When I see these young men and strong coming forward with acknowledgments of their indebtedness to the cause, and rejoicing that they have been among its later advocates; and when I look around upon this platform, and see here a LUCY STONE, an ELIZABETH JONES, and a THEODORE TILTON, all laboring so effectively in the field, I feel that we older ones may indeed retire, and thank God that he who has blessed us all our lives long is now blessing the lads; for there is surely no greater joy than to see these children walking in the anti-slavery path.

I feared yesterday that we were dwelling too much upon the past. We were so deeply interested in the earliest movements of this Anti-Slavery Society, that we did not go back, except by mere incidental mention, to BENJAMIN LAY and RALPH SANGERFORD, who dwelt in caves and dens of the earth, of whom the world was not worthy, to ELIAS HICKS, THOMAS CLARKSON, and all those earlier laborers; we did not go back as far as that. I feared, however, that we were not enough leaving the things that were behind, and pressing forward toward those that were before. Although I did not entirely agree with our friend FOSTER, and was glad that he was answered as he was—for I have so large Hope that I always take encouraging views of things when I can—yet I felt that there were duties to be performed in our case in regard to freedmen as well as in regard to those still held as slaves in our land. It is of little consequence to us now what we have suffered in the past, what obloquy, reproach and contumely we have endured in our religious societies, and in other relations in society. We might, as women, dwell somewhat upon our own restrictions, as connected with this Anti-Slavery movement. When persons interested in the cause were invited to send delegates to the London Convention of 1840, and some of those delegates were women, it was found out in time for them to send forth a note declaring that women were not included in the term "persons," but only men; and therefore, when we arrived in London, we were excluded from the platform. Yet, let me say, in justice to the Abolitionists there, that we were treated with all courtesy, and with a good deal of flattery in lieu of our rights. But all those things we may pass by.

Last evening, when we were listening, some of us, to the eloquent and earnest appeals made by HENRY WARD BEECHER, we saw in the assemblage some who, a few years ago, rushed from their seats in the church, because they could not bear to hear WILLIAM FURNESS speak so plainly on the subject of slavery, and who warned friends from abroad that they must not come to our houses because we were Abolitionists. When Madame PULSKY and her friends came, and were asked to go with me on a visit to the Penitentiary, and the carriage was at the door, word came that they were discouraged from coming, because we were Abolitionists! When I see those men coming forward now, and joining in the applause for the thorough anti-slavery sentiments of HENRY WARD BEECHER and others, so far from blaming them, or setting them at nought, I would rather welcome them at this eleventh hour, and I hope they may receive their full penny, if they work diligently to the end. I have felt sometimes almost, with the Apostle, willing to be accursed of my brethren for this cause's sake; but willing afterwards, when they come forward and mingle with us, to give them the right hand and invite them upon the platform, and glad to hear them, if they have any thing to say on the right side. When I sa v these things last evening, I remembered the remark of RAY POTTER, one of the signers of the Declaration, who, in a speech in Rhode Island, said that Abolitionists had the great Temple of Liberty to rear, and must do all the rough and hard work; but when it was near the top, he said, then would come forth people to lay their little fingers upon it, and say, " We have got it up!" I could not but remember this last evening, and also a few weeks ago, when I rejoiced to see the crowds listening to the words that proceeded out of the mouths of PHILLIPS BROOKS and others upon this very platform. When I heard some of the members of the Freedmen's Association, in this meeting, talking about the objections that were met and answered again and again by the Abolitionists years ago, of the duties connected with the liberation of the slave which we must perform, I felt that, after all, we were but unprofitable servants, and had not done as we ought to have done in regard to doing away with that deep-rooted prejudice which is the concomitant of slavery, and which we know can never be removed while slavery exists. Some of us women can perhaps more fully sympathize with the slave, because the prejudice against him is somewhat akin to that against our sex; and we ought to have been more faithful than we have been, so that when we hear the words applied to us, " Come, ye blessed of my Father," we might be ready to ask, " When saw we thee an hungered, or athirst, or in prison, and ministered unto thee?" It seems to me, therefore, as has been recommended here to-day, that we should keep on our armor. It may not be necessary to continue our operations in precisely the same way. But it will be necessary to multiply our periodicals, and scatter them, as we have done heretofore, with good effect. When our friends were talking of what was done, and how we were received in the beginning, and when Church and State were, as our friend GARRISON showed so clearly, arrayed against us, I remembered that then, just as in olden times, the common people heard us gladly. In truth, the original good heart of the people—excuse my theology—cannot resist the wisdom and the power with which Truth speaks to their understanding; and therefore it was that we were gladly received among them. Many have come and made their acknowledgments, that when we were mobbed, when Pennsylvania Hall was burned, they were in the wrong, they were in the mob; but now they say, " Whereas I was

blind, now I see, and I am willing now to be faithful to what I see."
Let us welcome them, hail them in their coming, and gladly receive
them. And with all these coadjutors, the work will go on, emancipation will be proclaimed, and we may be just as confident and earnest as we were before our friend Foster reproved us. I think we may rejoice and take courage. I like a little addition to the rejoicing of good old Simeon: "Now lettest thou thy servant depart in peace, for mine eyes have seen *of* thy salvation;" for the whole salvation has not come, but we have seen *of* the salvation.

SPEECH OF REV. SAMUEL MAY, JR.

Although I cannot claim to be one of the original members of this Society, I am happy to look back upon twenty-five years of connection with it, and upon such services as I have been able to render it. I should be sorry, therefore, to go away from Philadelphia without uttering one word in behalf of our good cause. Let me first reassure our good friend, S. S. Foster, on the subject of our future warfare upon slavery, as I have been in a position to know something of the minds of the different members of this Society. The number of those who believe that our work is done, or who entertain the least thought of laying down their arms, is so exceedingly small that they can be counted on the fingers of a single hand. Neither this Society, nor any one of its Committees, has made any announcement affording ground for the least shadow of a suspicion that we mean to disband, or cease from our work, while a single slave treads the soil of our native land. There is no such purpose. We have known too much of the privilege and blessing of being enlisted in this good cause ever to desert it while a single slave clanks his chains. I think, too, we understand our duty too well for this. I know there are a few, a very few, who think we may cease our *associated* labors. I know of one eminent lady who thinks so. She is not with us to-day. She has ceased to coöperate with our Executive Committee, of which she was so long a member. She thinks that our work, as an associated body, is at an end; and it is not for us to condemn her for that opinion. There is no desertion of the Anti-Slavery cause on the part of Maria W. Chapman, whose name I mention, because it ought to be named in this Society with respect and honor. If she withdraws from us before we think our work is done, let us remember how much earlier than most of us she enlisted in its ranks; how early her clear foresight saw the danger; how eloquent were her pen and her voice in dispelling the cloud of darkness which overshadowed the land; how clear was her faith; how brave was her heart. And if she now leaves the Society (not, I am sure, the anti-slavery work) sooner than we think she should do, may we not suppose there may be given to her now a foresight of the future better and clearer than ours, such as she had thirty years ago, when she was among the first to take up the great cause, and when, with brave and unflinching heart, she faced that Boston mob and all its terrors? We can have no blame for such a servant of the cause as that. Nevertheless, adhering to our own convictions of duty, nearly every other member of the Society, and of its Committees and officers, maintains his ground. So I think our friend Foster need not be troubled.

As we look back through the last thirty years, perhaps the most painful object in our survey is the opposition which the Anti-Slavery cause has had to encounter from the churches of the land. With here and there an exception, the great body of religionists, who took upon themselves the name of Christ, and dared to organize in the name of him who ever went out to the lowliest and humblest and most oppressed of men, threw themselves in the way of our Society and its object. We will not stop to utter words of reproach to-day. The Church could not see the palpable truth that Anti-Slavery was the "Gospel for the day." It proved itself a blind leader of blind followers. And what a judge and divider over it did the Anti-Slavery cause become! Powerful ecclesiastical bodies and mighty religious associations fell asunder at its touch, and arrayed themselves in opposing ranks. The Church fell upon this great rock of Truth and Justice, instead of building upon it, and was broken! But there were winnowed out of every sect those that knew this cause was Christ's own cause in the land. Many, misled and deceived by false-hearted leaders, entertained the belief that anti-slavery was infidelity. I wish to express, therefore, the great satisfaction I felt this morning, when that eloquent speaker, Henry Ward Beecher, came among us in his kind, courteous, and fraternal spirit, and, from his position as an accredited preacher of the Christian religion, recognized upon this platform the great services this Society has "rendered to patriotism, to religion, and to humanity." That, in my mind, is a sufficient offset to columns and pages of scurrilous denunciation. Not that *we* needed any such testimony from Mr. Beecher or any body else; not that it makes any difference to us what he or any one else says upon that point;

but it neutralizes the objurgations and false assertions of so many in the clerical profession. We know on what foundation we have built. We need not the testimony, although we rejoice in it. And we are glad to-day to recognize, amidst other changes, some change in the churches and religious bodies of the land. No longer content with sending the Gospel to distant lands, they are beginning to recognize the poor, the needy, and the ignorant freed slaves of our own land. The Christian bodies of to-day which receive the most hearty sympathy are those that are ministering to the spiritual and physical wants of the freed slaves of the country. To-day, the Sanitary Commission, and that other body which, not satisfied with the simple title of Sanitary Commission, takes upon itself the name of *Christian* Commission, go forward to bless the suffering soldier and the ignorant slave, to recognize the freedom of the colored man, and to meet him in the army, on the plantation, or in the hospital, with Christian kindness, instruction, and supplies. This is now recognized as eminently *Christian* work by the churches; and herein may we be glad.

Upon one other point of my friend FOSTER'S remarks, I wish to say a single word. Although I have no apologies to offer for what has been wrong, timid, slow, doubting, in Mr. LINCOLN'S position or policy, yet, with Mr. BURLEIGH, I say, let us do justice; and when Mr. FOSTER said that the President had issued his great Proclamation with an entire disregard and indifference for the rights of the slave or the colored man, and only for the benefit of the white man, it seems to me that he did the President great injustice. (Applause.) Did not Mr. LINCOLN expressly say that he " sincerely believed " that great measure " to be an act of justice "; and did he not, upon this very ground, " invoke " for it " the considerate judgment of mankind and the gracious favor of Almighty God "? Does not all that is best in the land respond to it as such, and is it not upon that basis that we all feel it most secure?

Mr. FOSTER. Did not the President declare to the civilized world that he would prefer to put down this rebellion without disturbing the power of slavery?

Mr. MAY. I think there was nothing about "preference," but that he was determined to put down the rebellion; and, as President of the United States, he was bound so to act.

HENRY C. WRIGHT. Has the President of the United States, as President, any right to free a single slave, purely as a matter of justice, or for his good? His only power, as President of the United States, is to free the slave as a military necessity. (Applause.)

The President. The next speaker is one who has devoted a large portion of her life, since she came to years of intelligence, to the cause of the slave. There is no one, in the Old World or the New, who has labored more devotedly, more self-sacrificingly, or more wholly given all that she is and all that she has, to be put upon the altar of bleeding humanity, than Abby Kelley Foster.

SPEECH OF ABBY KELLEY FOSTER.

I agree with almost every thing that has been said here this morning in relation to the present aspects of our cause and our present duty. Yet there is one thing that remains for us to be reminded of. Although we all feel and know that, of necessity, there must have been an immense change in the public sentiment, in consequence of the action of this Anti-Slavery Society, yet we should not be too confident as to the character of the wonderful change since the war commenced. Although brought up in the Orthodox Church, I do not believe exactly in the doctrine of instantaneous conversion; but I believe in the fall from grace. I want to remind you that we had labored for twenty-seven years previous to the terrible mobs of 1860. Do we remember the Fall of 1860 and the Winter of 1860 and '61? Do we remember that never was a more bloodthirsty mob organized in the city of Boston than was organized in the Fall of 1860?

Charles C. Burleigh. When the Devil came down in great wrath, because he knew he had but a short time.

Mrs. Foster. Let us see whether he knew he had but a short time. Have we forgotten that bloodthirsty spirit which went from Boston, all along through Albany, on the line of the Central Railroad, through the entire West; which came down here into Pennsylvania, and pervaded every part of the North — the spirit of determination that free speech should utterly be crushed out? — a spirit that responded to what was proposed by the Peace Convention at Washington, viz: that we should give slavery free course to run and be glorified through this country; that, notwithstanding our twenty-seven years of anti-slavery agitation, free speech should be crushed, as we knew it must be, if those peace resolutions had been accepted by the South. If they had been, we should truly have been crushed out, as we believed, at that period. Truly would free speech have been trampled under foot, and slavery would have been triumphant, but for the fact that the slaveholders would not accept the offer. No thanks to the governing masses of the North that that consummation of diabolism did not succeed. No, no. Did Slavery think it had but a short time to live? No, it was blind. Sin is always blind. The North did not dream it; politicians did not dream it. They believed that, notwithstanding the flood of light, they could crush us all down, and that Slavery could have a longer lease of life, not for its own sake, but to promote what they believed to be their pecuniary and political well-being.

And now, whence comes this sudden change? A Pentecost, forsooth! Is it by the pouring out of the Holy Ghost, or the pouring out of human blood? Is it because the great mass of the people have come to believe, and have received grace into their hearts? God knows I do not willingly stand here to bring scorn, opposition, contempt or hatred upon those who have turned right-about-face, when I charge that it is not from the highest but from the lowest motives, and that therefore it is not from motives upon which we can rely, and which should make us jubilant. They have taken this course, as every body knows—the Government takes it and the commercial man takes it—because it is their only safety. Senator WILSON knows that the Government proposed, and the Secretary of State issued letters of instruction to all our ministers plenipotentiary abroad, declaring that the rebellion would be put down without changing the status of an individual. It was the intention and determination to do so. We have not Secretary SEWARD to thank, we have not President LINCOLN to thank, we have not the Government of the United States to thank, we have not the commercial men nor the churches to thank; but we have JEFF DAVIS and the terrible persistency of the rebels to thank, that there has been this change of conduct in the North. It was a matter of military necessity, and therefore we have it. And having been induced by military necessity, for the sake of self-preservation, we cannot rely upon it. It has been said by a leading paper, that if the rebels should lay down their arms to-day, Secretary SEWARD—although his Gettysburg speech differed somewhat from his Auburn speech, because his language is the echo of public sentiment always, as far as it goes and he can get it, and the one was made before and the other after the last election in Pennsylvania, and the other States which were so doubtful—would gladly, and the Government would gladly, receive them back like the prodigal son, and kill for them the fatted calf, and JEFF DAVIS might be candidate for next President of the United States. [A VOICE—"Never!"] I trust he never will, because I trust that the rebels will still persist. I believe that they are given over to a reprobate mind, to believe a lie, and their damnation is sealed; and their damnation being sealed, the salvation of the country may be secured.

If in 1860 there could be such a spirit manifested throughout the length and breadth of the North, I do not believe that the change since that time has been any thing more than the result of selfishness, and therefore unreliable. It is only by labor, incessant labor, in season and out of season, that we can create such a public sentiment as we need; and we never could have attained it, if success had attended the Union arms. I was thankful for MEADE'S disaster, as it is called—his withdrawal. I should be sorry to have too much success; we want just little enough to keep up the North to the sticking point, until it shall be obliged to go on and abolish slavery for its own safety.

Our friend MAY says that he can count upon his fingers all those who think the mission of the Anti-Slavery Society is finished. I cannot do that. I know that one State Anti-Slavery Society was disbanded, ostensibly for other reasons, but from private conversation I know that that Society was abandoned, and their anti-slavery paper was put down, because their leading and most self-sacrificing men thought that we had done our work in the Anti-Slavery cause. At the time that Fort Sumter was attacked, they declared that the mission of the Anti-Slavery cause was fulfilled, and that South Carolina was now doing the work we had formerly done. Count on my fingers? No; this house would not contain the numbers. Many of them have laid down their lives upon the battle-field. They thought the army was doing the work of the Anti-Slavery Society. From Pennsylvania, hundreds of young men have gone to the battle-field with that conviction; and I know there are old men and elderly women, who have labored for thirty years in the Anti-Slavery cause, who have that conviction, and therefore have laid down their arms.

Let us not, therefore, be too confident. Do not let us dwell too much on what has been done. NAPOLEON spoke a great truth, when, receiving the congratulations of his Generals on the eve of his invasion of Russia, he said, "I want you to remember that nothing is done while any thing remains to be done." St. Helena witnessed the truth of that sentiment. Nothing is done while any thing remains to be done, so far as the death of American slavery is concerned. Not that I believe that one iota of moral truth that has ever been uttered, any more than one atom of physical matter that has ever been created, can be lost. But, so far as the accomplishment of the overthrow of slavery is concerned, were success to attend the Federal arms to-day, I feel confident that slavery would linger, God knows how long; and I am willing, therefore, to wait another ten years, if need be, in order to insure its destruction now.

Mr. GARRISON. It seems to me that it is not at all our province to undertake to determine the motives by which the people are animated, who have recently come into sympathy and coöperation with us for the abolition of slavery; that it is not our province to accuse them of being hollow and hypocritical. Thank God that a general change has taken place, a most miraculous change! Whoever will come up now, and speak a word for freedom, I will hail as a friend and a brother, and will leave his motives to God, to whom alone he is responsible.

SPEECH OF SUSAN B. ANTHONY.

Among the early lessons which I learned upon the abolition platform was this: That it was our distinctive work to educate the heart of the people of this nation into a full recognition of the humanity of the black man; that we were to so educate the people of the North that they would refuse to aid the Government in holding the black man in chains; and I suppose that is precisely our work to-day. I remember that I had thought fugitive-slave work was very important and really anti-slavery; and I also remember that one of the first lessons I had to learn was, that the fugitive slave would be aided by common philanthropy and benevolence, and that we, who called ourselves Radical Abolitionists, should give our attention, our thought, our efforts, to the removal of the cause which compelled the fugitive, with bleeding feet, to cross the Free States of the North to the British domain. It seems to me that the Sanitary Commission work, the Freedmen's Association, the Freedmen's Educational work, are to-day common charity, common benevolence, and the world will look after it. Here, in this third decade of the American Anti-Slavery Society, are assembled, from different parts of the Free States, the representatives of a little handful of men and women over the country, who have for these thirty years been working to undermine the law of the nation which allows the holding of property in man. Precisely this is the work which I think we should abide by at this hour, leaving to the grand masses of the world, whose attention is now called to the question of liberty—to the question of saving this nation, to the question of emancipation even—leaving it to them to take care of the freedmen, to take care of the sick and wounded upon the battle-field. Let us go on with our primitive and fundamental work of removing the laws which allow of the existence of slavery.

That is the specific work to which the Association of which I have been a member for the last six months (the Woman's Loyal League) has specially devoted itself. We aim to circulate throughout the entire North a petition, to be presented to the next Congress, asking that body to enact a law of Universal Emancipation. As women, we felt that it was especially fitting for us to work in this way, because as women we could have no voice as to what should be the basis of reconstruction of this government, save through the one right which the nation has left to us, the right of petition. Women can neither take the ballot nor the bullet to settle this question; therefore, to us, the right to petition is the one sacred right which we ought not to neglect. I appeal to women here to-day to set themselves about this work when they shall return to their homes; to circulate this emancipation petition themselves, and to urge upon their neighbors and friends to engage in the work.

I know there are women here who would like to know something of the progress of this petition movement. I am sorry not to be able to make an enthusiastic and encouraging report; but the fact is, that wherever our petitions have been sent, from vastly too many places the responses have come back, "What do you mean by asking us to circulate a petition for emancipation? Is not the work already done? Has not the President proclaimed freedom? Is he not doing the work as fast as he can?" This has been the one great obstacle, the one great discouragement, which we have had to meet. Those who have hitherto occupied the highest places in our estimation have seemed the most indifferent, and to feel as if this was really an unnecessary work. Why should we, who have been at work for these long years, endeavoring to move slavery out of the way, when it has been the cause of all the national disasters and national strifes and discords which we have had, be afraid, in this last struggle, of doing too much?

The petitions to-day are being returned rapidly. Day before yesterday, one mail brought four or five thousand signatures. I only hope that the people, at this hour, will begin to feel that there is need of a public expression. There is an important question to come before the next Congress — the question of reconstruction. I have no doubt that Senator WILSON himself would say to you this morning, if he were to speak, that the signatures of a million of the men and women of the North, poured in upon Congress, will do much to encourage the members to stand fast by their principles. The Congress needs to know that the people, their constituencies, stand by them, and will demand of them the strictest faithfulness to freedom, and will not abide the slightest compromise of principle. It is for us to make them feel this.

THE PRESIDENT. We shall now hear from one who represents a phase of this struggle most significant of the success of our movement. We have burned the bridge behind us, and there is no more going backward. We have passed the Rubicon; and we are going on, conquering and to conquer. You may read the utter overthrow of slavery in the arming of such a mighty host of the colored population of our country at the present time. I have the pleasure of introducing to you Col. WAGNER, of Camp William Penn.

SPEECH OF COL. WAGNER.

MR. CHAIRMAN, AND LADIES AND GENTLEMEN:

When I received, at the hands of the Chairman of your Business Committee, an invitation to attend your meeting, I feared that my duties at the camp would not permit me to be present. In coming here this morning, I did not expect to make a speech, and for two reasons: I am not able to make you a speech; and if I were, I would not assume to come here, and preach abolition doctrines to those who learned them many years ago. I am not a member of this Anti-Slavery Society, unless I may be permitted to style myself a believing member — one who has never joined your Association, but who has in some little measure contributed towards the abolition of slavery. I have graduated in that school where those who study become most thorough-going and emphatic Abolitionists. My Abolitionism is but of recent growth. When I entered the army, I determined to do what I could to crush this rebellion. I believed, with hundreds of thousands of others, that it could be done without interfering with slavery. But I had been but a short time in the army when I saw that, to crush this rebellion, it was necessary to eradicate slavery. I had been there but a little while before I met "our erring brethren" on the field of battle, and, falling into their hands wounded and a prisoner, I was able to obtain information which I never possessed before. It was then and there that the conviction forced itself upon me that slavery must be abolished; and, friends and fellow-citizens, I tell you it *will* be abolished. (Applause.)

I am sorry that some of your members are quarreling with the means for accomplishing the ends for which you have labored so long and so faithfully. For my part, I am willing to accept the assistance and receive the help of all who are willing to accomplish this great end of freeing our country from what has been a curse to it, and has stained and defaced our escutcheon. I hope none of the members of this Society will think of laying down their armor; but if they do, I am sure there are those who are ready and anxious to work until not a slave remains on our soil. I do not suppose, for a moment, that one who has been a member of this Association for thirty years will think now, when the work is so nearly accomplished, of withdrawing, while yet so much remains to be done. A great deal remains to be done in the army, and a great deal by you who are at home. It is for you to uphold the hands of those who are administering the law at our capital. Faithfully have you performed it in years past; I am confident that faithfully you will perform it, until the work for which you are associated shall be ended, and the rebellion shall be crushed.

I agree with you, Mr. Chairman, that one of the great means adopted by the Government of this country in crushing this rebellion is the arming of the negro race. I believe that the arming of that class of our citizens will be the means of administering the last and crushing blow to slavery. At the South, we are arming those who have been made free by the Emancipation Proclamation of our President. We also arm those who are still held in bondage. In Maryland, in Delaware, in Kentucky, and in Tennessee, we are receiving those who are not included in that Proclamation into the armies of the United States, and thereby giving them freedom.

I am not one of those who hope without reason, but I am confident that this war is drawing to a close. I am equally confident that it will never end until the last slave is made free. There was a time when I imagined the colored man was not equal to the white man in intelligence. But if he is not—I do not say that he is not—give him for a few generations the opportunities that you enjoy, and he will make himself what it was intended by God that he should be, a man, in all respects, such as we are. (Applause.) I look at this matter from a military stand-point. I look upon the soldiers of our own color, and upon those of a darker complexion. I have had some little experience with both; and my dispassionate opinion is, that the one is equal in every way to the other. The colored man makes as good a soldier as the white man. He obeys orders as promptly and as intelligently; he acquires the drill as perfectly, if not more so, than the white soldier. His valor he has proved on many a bloody field; his courage he has shown on the battle-field and in the hospital. And the day will come when he will show those that now look down upon him with contempt and reproach, that he is a man, willing to do and to dare all that other men do and dare, in striking for freedom and for the right.

Mrs. MOTT inquired what had been the character of Camp William Penn, as to depredations upon property, as compared with camps of white soldiers.

Col. WAGNER. I am pleased to be able to say, that no depredations of any kind have been committed by the soldiers of Camp William Penn. The friends of the colored soldiers have been pleasantly and agreeably surprised to find them in this respect far superior to white soldiers in a similar position. I have never yet seen a camp of white soldiers where depredations were not committed; but at Camp William Penn there have been no depredations. It is not owing to a more rigid discipline there; we have no other rules than those that govern white camps. But the men seem to feel the dignity and responsibility of their position. (Applause.) They seem to realize that the world is looking at them, and watching the progress of their camps, and of those of their color who have taken upon themselves the duty of fighting for the country and the flag. They come to the camp, many of them, ragged and dirty; but when they put on the uniform, they feel that they are men, and that they can hold up their heads among men. They are glad to see that even they have now an opportunity of doing something for our flag and for our nation. Say what you please about the degradation of the negro, it is all nonsense. Give him an opportunity of showing what he is, and he will show himself a man.

The President. I can bear the same testimony with regard to the conduct of the colored regiments at Readville, in Massachusetts, where the 54th and 55th regiments were stationed. It is the universal testimony of the neighborhood, and the whole region round about, that never before was there a regiment stationed in that neighborhood without depredations being committed; but since the colored regiments have been there, there have been no depredations.

SPEECH OF OLIVER JOHNSON.

Looking back upon more than thirty years of personal identification with the Anti-Slavery movement, there is much that I could say if I felt at liberty to occupy these precious moments. But I know there are many around me who are anxious to address you, and therefore I will be brief.

Since I came to this meeting, one thought has possessed me — one thought, hour by hour, and almost moment by moment; and it is the thought of what I, as an Abolitionist, owe to the Anti-Slavery cause. Something has been said here of sacrifices made for that cause. Sacrifices have indeed been made and sufferings endured by many true-hearted and noble-friends — sacrifices and sufferings of which it does not become me to speak lightly; but I appeal to you all, even to those who have suffered and endured most, to say if the personal benefits derived from the advocacy of the slave's cause do not outweigh, a thousand-fold, all the trials which you have been called to endure on its account? Nay, if those trials themselves have not, through the overruling interposition of God, been turned into blessings? Such at least is my own experience; and I am here to-day with no memory of sacrifices made, but with a heart penetrated by a sense of gratitude for benefits received. The cause owes me nothing, but I am indebted to it beyond all power of payment, or even of computation. It has enhanced for me every joy of life, transmuted pain to pleasure, brought light out of darkness, and crowned me with blessings indescribable and inestimable. There are no delights to be compared with those which we may earn by an unselfish devotion to a great and noble cause. My heart swells with thankfulness to God that he called me early to this work; that while I was but a boy, on my native hills in Vermont, I heard and heeded the trumpet-call of Garrison, and, through sympathy with his spirit, learned to love him before I ever looked into his face. How vividly do I remember now the days of his imprisonment at Baltimore, and how my heart was thrilled in reading the noble lines which he inscribed on the walls of his cell, showing how, "in innocence, he was great and strong"! How did I exult when he was released; with what interest did I watch his progress northward, and when at length he arrived in Boston, with what eagerness did I embrace the first opportunity to take his hand, and hear him plead the cause of the oppressed! From that moment I was an Abolitionist, and I look back now upon more than thirty years of earnest labor in the cause, regretting only that I have not been more entirely devoted to it, and have done so little in its behalf. It is little indeed that any of us have done for it, compared with what it has done for us. In laboring to break the chains of the slave, we have found deliverance from the fetters of superstition and priestcraft, and felt our minds and hearts expanding in the sunlight of God's highest truth. Reproached as infidels by a pro-slavery Church, we have found by experience that those who devote themselves to the cause of humanity "walk with God," and in the fellowship of his saints.

I entreat the young men and the young women here assembled, if they would enrich and ennoble their lives by the acquisition of whatever is most worthy of their ambition, to give themselves unreservedly to the work of reform — to take the side of the oppressed and the wronged, to cast their influence on the side of truth, however unpopular, and to allow no temptation of wealth or fame to swerve them by so much as a hair's breadth from the principles of justice and righteousness. The final triumph of the Anti-Slavery cause is, we hope, near at hand; but much remains to be done before we can lay off our armor. And when slavery has been abolished, other moral issues will be presented, other reforms arise, to test the courage and devotion of the new generation. The men and the women who have conducted the Anti-Slavery movement from its small beginning almost to the day of its triumph will soon pass away; but the principles they have advocated will not perish, but live to inspire the devotion of succeeding generations to the end of time.

I listen always with satisfaction to those who exhort us to fidelity, to those who set before us the work to be done, and exhort us to faithfulness in its performance. In all that our friend FOSTER has said here to-day upon that point, I have sympathized with him. But let me say, in all frankness, that there is one particular in which I cannot agree with him. Through his whole speech ran the assumption, as it seemed to me, that his fellow-laborers here are ready to lay off their armor, regarding their work as done. Has any thing been said here to justify such an assumption? I think not. Has he proposed any work for the performance of which we are not, one and all, ready to strike hands with him? We are girding ourselves anew for the work before us, and we will not throw down our weapons till the last slave is free. (Applause.) But I, for one, find hope the best stimulus to labor. I shrink instinctively from the dark shadow which some of our friends would throw over us, when they affirm that, notwithstanding all that we have done for thirty years, the country is in a worse condition, in regard to the principles of universal liberty, than it was at the close of the Revolutionary war. If I believed that, I should utterly despair of the cause. "We are saved by hope," says an apostle, and I believe it. The cheering signs which greet us on every hand, betokening the speedy triumph of our cause, fill me with hopefulness, augmenting my power to work and my joy therein.

Have we indeed done nothing in these thirty years? Are we no nearer the end than we were at the beginning? Is this nation to-day in no better position than it was thirty years ago, when this Society was first formed? How can any body think so, in view of the facts by which we are surrounded? Take the press of this city for illustration. Thirty years ago, the men who formed this Society assembled in this city almost by stealth, and held their meetings in the daytime, warned by the Police that they could not be protected at night. There was not a newspaper here that would report their proceedings — not one that did not denounce them as "fanatics" and "amalgamationists," as men who were bent on the destruction of their country. How is it to-day? Every press in the city sends its reporters to our platform, and our proceedings are reported fairly and honorably. In this circumstance alone, we have an indication of a wonderful improvement in the public sentiment.

It is said that, after all, the people are selfish — that they have not relinquished their hostility to the Anti-Slavery cause from pure love of principle, but for their own interest. But is it not a sign of progress when men who have long resisted our movement have at last discovered that its claims are coincident with their worldly interest? Saints—perfect people—do not travel in regiments; and if I thought the slaves could not be emancipated before the mass of the people are brought up to the standard of absolute justice and righteousness, I should expect them to grind in the prison-house for centuries. No good cause has ever triumphed except through influences and motives as various and mixed as those now operating in our country for the overthrow of slavery. If men preach the Gospel of Freedom, even though it be for strife and contention, shall we not rejoice? If they have formed a purpose to abolish slavery rather from a regard to their own interest than from love to the slave, shall we not thank God and take courage?

CHARLES C. BURLEIGH. What does it indicate in regard to the position of our cause, that selfishness should incline any man to seem to favor it? Is it not a sign of progress and triumph?

SPEECH OF JAMES N. BUFFUM.

You assigned me the duty of collecting the money, instead of speaking, but I am inclined to endorse the last speech, and to say Amen to brother JOHNSON. Perhaps my experience as a business man is worth something. You know, sir, that I have been deeply interested in this cause for the last thirty-two years. Although it was not my privilege to sign the Declaration, I have often wished it had been. I was only prevented by illness. I glory in the fact that I was an Abolitionist before the signing of that Declaration; and I would give the best hundred dollars that I possess if my name were there. As I go about among business men who formerly hated me, I find them cordial, and expressing their approbation of my sentiments, and avowing themselves Abolitionists. I feel encouraged, and it is a marvel to me to see the change.

While our friend ABBY KELLEY FOSTER was speaking this morning, there were a thousand facts rushing into my mind showing progress. One I may mention, of an individual who, about two years ago, stood upon the platform of a JOHN BROWN meeting with a pistol in his hand, threatening death to the Abolitionists. A few days ago, he came out in a letter, in which he gloried in this war because, first, it was to save the nation's life; secondly, because it was going to end in a higher civilization; and above all, he gloried that the African was now able to vindicate his freedom in arms.

I met a venerable man, a short time ago, one of our wealthiest citizens, who always contended against the principles which I entertain, and he said to me, "Mr. BUFFUM, are you aware that every body is coming up to your platform?" "No, I was not aware of that; but I know they will do it." "Well, it is a fact, and the nation has got to carry out your principles, and there is no other salvation for it." I was equally astonished the other day, in going down State street, in Boston, to meet a gentleman who, a short time ago, as he confessed, was in favor of putting down the Abolitionists, and he said, "Did you know that there was a great anti-slavery meeting held at the Merchants' Exchange?" "No." Well, now, the Merchants' Exchange is the headquarters of all the wealthy merchants of Boston, and there they are holding anti-slavery meetings, and they have turned the place into an anti-slavery lecture room! FREDERICK DOUGLASS was delivering one of his strongest anti-slavery lectures, and this man was among the audience listening.

I say, it is marvellous how this Anti-Slavery cause is going on. I look at it, and thank God and take courage.

THE PRESIDENT. Those who think we have not made much progress remind me of the story of the man in the Deluge, who, after every thing had been submerged, as the ark came floating by, came splurging up in the midst of the waters, and tried to get in. Failing in this, he said with disgust, "Go to thunder with your old ark; it is not much of a shower after all!" But now the fountains of the great deep are broken up, and slavery is going under, and the Ark of Liberty is floating triumphantly, and soon it shall rest on Mount Ararat, and those who have kept the covenant shall come forth rejoicing, and the land shall be redeemed for ever.

SPEECH OF LUCY STONE.

It is because there is anti-slavery work left to be done that any of us should be speaking here to-day, or asking for help in the work. I believe that those who have spoken upon the two sides, that much is to be done, and that much has been done, are both equally right. It cannot be that those who have toiled thirty years in such a work as this, who have stood on this platform until they have grown old and gray, and especially in the midst of a strife where our fathers and brothers, husbands and sons are being slaughtered by thousands, will cease to labor while that strife goes on, though it may not seem to require much labor on our part to make the last death-rattle of slavery sound in its throat. When I sat here yesterday, and heard the speakers giving an account of the first meeting of the Society, and heard one speaker say of JAMES MOTT, that in that early day his hair was untouched by the gray, I thought I have only known him since his head was covered with white, but thank God I have known him so long! And Mr. GARRISON'S hair was not then thinned, making him to look like the prophet ELISHA. But these men were all young and earnest when they pledged themselves to go on with this work, and never to cease. I thank God for them; and I concur in the ground that they take, that much remains to be done. Prejudice against the negro is to be overcome; for slavery is let down deeper in the hearts of the people of this country than they themselves know. We see a great deal of opposition to slavery, and it is wonderful to see the change. But it is very much like the water in Niagara river, which goes along because it cannot help it, and not because it wants to. It may be because I live in New Jersey, in the midst of a nest of copperheads, where my next door neighbor believes that men ought to be bought and sold, and tells me frankly to my face that he believes it; but I cannot help feeling that there is a great deal of pro-slavery sentiment yet to be rooted out. We all need to work for it.

And when we see what our friends SUSAN B. ANTHONY and Mrs. STANTON are doing in New York, almost without aid; seeing that there is need of a law to abolish slavery, lest there should be any misunderstanding; seeing that the Constitution, rightly interpreted, meant anti-slavery, while the Supreme Court said there was no anti-slavery about it; asking for a law so plain that it cannot be mistaken, declaring that there shall be no slavery nor involuntary servitude any where in all these United States; when we see our friends trying to obtain a million of names to a petition for such a law, is there nothing to be done on the part of woman? Men may vote; but I shall never forget, unless it ceases to be a fact, that women have no such possibility of expression. We are not allowed to vote; but we may petition, and by and by they will hear. Send these petitions by hundreds and thousands into your villages and hamlets, and let the returns be as numerous as they ought to be; for I know there are a great many young girls who may not have an opportunity to work in other ways, and boys not old enough to vote, who will be glad to have the opportunity to do something, and they can circulate these petitions. I remember that an old man told me once that if I came to him again with such a petition, (it was for a law allowing colored people and whites to intermarry,) he would ride me on a rail. I went every year, was never carried on a rail, and his wife always signed the petition. By and by we can put all these petitions together, when we have got all the names we can, and carry them in a large roll to Congress; and there will be men there brave enough and true enough to be willing to present them. And if what we do shall bring about the result we seek, in aid of the President's proclamation, and there shall be a law passed, that there shall be neither slavery nor involuntary servitude in any part of the United States, how thankful we shall be! The youngest boy and the youngest girl, as well as the oldest man and woman, may thank God, and rejoice that they have assisted in making this a free country.

SPEECH OF MRS. FRANCES D. GAGE.

LADIES AND GENTLEMEN:

On my lone little isle of the sea, (Paris Island, S. C.,) I have hardly had the opportunity of reading newspapers, or knowing what course the current of events at the North was taking; and I confess that I have listened to the remarks here, yesterday and to-day, with some surprise. I did not suppose there was any one interested in anti-slavery at the North, that had not faith enough to see through all that is going on to-day, and to believe that slavery is coming to an end. Why, old SOPHY, at her cabin door, would teach you better faith than I have heard here from some to-day. She came to see me after the battle of Fredericksburg, where some of my kindred fell, and found me weeping. "Missis, what makes you cry, honey? This isn't a nigger war; it isn't a secesh war; it is GOD's war; it will all come out right." And old SOPHY, and the great hearts of the race, have taught us faith, until it is now unwavering. We need not listen for the words of Mr. SEWARD, or to learn what the men at Washington are doing. We can learn a better wisdom, while they are thinking of it; and when we speak our hearts strongly enough, they will respond. Let us be like the Western boys on the Lookout

Mountain; when our commander at Washington tells us to take the rifle-pits at the bottom of the mountain, and we have taken them, let us, with enthusiasm, with our knapsacks on our backs, move onward and upward until we take the batteries at the top, without waiting to talk about having nothing to do. We have a grand work to do. If, as some of our friends say, Mr. SEWARD makes a better speech after the election than before it, let us compel him to continue to make better speeches until he makes them right. (Applause.)

I have seen better evidence than any thing here that slavery is coming to an end. I have stood surrounded by black men and women, not picked men, but black men crushed down as low as South Carolina could crush them, and that is saying as much as any one can say; I have seen them self-sustaining, putting money into their banks, to supply their own needs. And I have seen the women staying behind to till the cotton and the corn, and sending their husbands and sons to the battle-field to fight for liberty. And do you think this great hope is ready to roll back? As well attempt to put the oak back into the acorn, or turn Niagara back upon its fountains. I tell you nay. Whatever the politicians may do, if the people are faithful, the end must come, and that end shall be universal freedom.

And now, with regard to these petitions that have been presented to you to-day, sign them and circulate them with a hearty good-will. If you can do nothing else in your neighborhood, you can circulate these petitions. And when the women of this country shall give expression to their private home feelings through these petitions, there is no power at Washington strong enough to resist the influence. A million of women, asking for the emancipation of all the slaves of this Union, will be a larger power than this country has been in the habit of thinking women possessed. Work faithfully, earnestly, unfalteringly, and the end will come, and we shall sing hallelujahs over a country redeemed, where no slave sighs in bondage, and no mother gives birth to a slave.

THE PRESIDENT read a letter from JOHN JOLLIFFE, Esq., formerly of Cincinnati, now of Washington, written in the expectation that he might not be able to attend the meeting. Having read the letter, the President continued: The name of Mr. JOLLIFFE must be very familiar to a large number in this audience. He has been a distinguished lawyer of Cincinnati, and for a number of years he has interposed at all times, whenever needed, in behalf of the fugitive slave. His life has been imperilled; he has been hunted by the bloodhounds of slavery; and he has won for himself the esteem and love of the friends of freedom every where. Yesterday I was told that he would not probably be with us, but I am happy to-day to be able to introduce him to you.

SPEECH OF JOHN JOLLIFFE.

I did not come here with any expectation of speaking, but to have my heart cheered by what I should hear. I am glad, however, to have an opportunity of standing here to speak to this audience. If every slave were to be emancipated to-morrow, we should have enough work to do to keep us busy for a hundred years. The effects of slavery will remain long after every slave has been emancipated. This people have all to be educated up to the standard God intended they should occupy in his creation. This is our hardest work. It is missionary work, as much so as that of any foreign missionary enterprise ever conducted in this country. I have no faith, as a general rule, in politicians. They are only the exponents of the public will. This little band of twenty or thirty men have done this mighty work. ABRAHAM LINCOLN'S proclamation was not one that came, as I believe, from his heart. It was one that he was impelled to issue by the force of public opinion behind him. And if we want other proclamations of freedom, or other great enterprises successively, we must labor with renewed diligence, and they will be accomplished. If so much has been done by thirty or forty people in Massachusetts, and scattered in different parts of the United States, how much more can be done when we have a hundred thousand Abolitionists to aid in the work? The whole army of the Northwest are Abolitionists, and they speak against slavery in words so harsh that Mr. GARRISON would never utter them.

Mr. GARRISON. I was told that, last evening, one man, who had always been conservative, left the meeting in consequence of the tameness of my remarks. He could not stand it! (Laughter.)

J. MILLER McKIM, from the Business Committee, reported the following resolution and memorial, which were adopted by a unanimous vote; the memorial to be signed by the President and other officers of the Society, and forwarded to the bodies to which it is addressed: —

Resolved, That, as the voice of the people is heard through petitions to Congress, this Convention earnestly recommend that this voice be raised in petitions for an amendment of the Constitution, *for ever prohibiting slavery* within the limits of the United States.

MEMORIAL

To the Senate and House of Representatives, in Congress assembled.

The American Anti-Slavery Society, assembled in its Third Decade Meeting, in the city of Philadelphia, respectfully petitions your honorable body so to amend the Constitution that slavery shall be for ever prohibited within the limits of the United States.

SPEECH OF REV. SAMUEL J. MAY.

I occupied the time yesterday with reminiscences, because the meeting was in the humor for such things. But I am not disposed to look back, in the great work which we undertook thirty years ago, for I see how much remains to be done. My eyes are intently fixed upon that which is before us. Far from putting off the anti-slavery armor, I feel that we must buckle it closer to our bodies, our hearts and souls, resolving that we will not cease from the labor we have commenced until not only slavery is abolished, but until all that can be done to repair the damages caused by slavery to the population of our country, black and white, shall have been done. That is the work to which we are called. There seems to be discouragement in the minds of a few, because, I think, they do not fully appreciate what has been already accomplished, and are not earnest enough in behalf of what yet remains. Of course, I have not been satisfied with all our good President has decreed or proposed; but I consider what he was at the commencement of his administration, and perceive that he has made great progress. His interpretation of the Constitution has trammelled him. But I believe he has always been honest. At first, he was on a very low plane—almost as low as the slaveholder's. But he has risen—recently, has risen faster than the people. I believe he is ready, willing, eager to rise as far as righteousness shall demand; yes, to the summit of the requirements of impartial justice. Has he not said something to this effect?—" I am the servant of the people. If the people want emancipation, why do they not demand it?" Who for a moment believes that our President, notwithstanding the incubus that hangs upon him in the persons of some of his Cabinet, will not do all he may think that he ought to favor the progress of liberty? He must, he will, in all good conscience, do only what at the time shall seem to himself to be right and proper. I have watched his course; and though I have been impatient with him, yet have I never seen any thing that has impaired my confidence in his good intentions. I am persuaded that he desires and intends to do right. Let us, then, persevere in the work we commenced thirty years ago,—educating the people, and the officials of the people,—the President himself, if he needs instruction,—until they and he shall be brought to see, in its original brightness, the truth, the glorious truth, that was radiated upon our nation at its birth, and which our fathers declared to be *self-evident;* that truth, which, alas! has been so obscured that some of our prominent statesmen and divines have dared to pronounce it "a rhetorical flourish"—"a glittering generality"—"a palpable exaggeration"—"an obvious lie"; aye, aye, and the people have been so politically depraved as not to be horrified by such utterances, and rise, as they should have done, with one accord, to denounce such impious traducers of the Declaration of Independence.

We put our hands to a great work, thirty years ago; greater far than we then supposed. Although much remains to be done, let us praise God that he has enabled us to do what we have. Although we did not succeed, as we earnestly endeavored to, in averting what we clearly foresaw and foretold to be inevitable, if slavery could not be abolished by moral and religious instrumentalities—*a civil and servile war;* although we have not been so successful in our labors as to avert that horrible calamity, may we not rejoice that God, in his long-suffering and exact justice, is still with our nation,—a nation guilty beyond all other nations, because our opportunities, our privileges, our light, have all been greater than theirs? How has he overruled our mistakes, enlightened our counsels, and led us, by the necessities of the case, to adopt the measures which alone can lead to our redemption! There is no part of the history of our race, in all time past, that seems to me to indicate the hand of Almighty God more distinctly than we see it in his dealings with our nation to-day. For nothing do I ever give thanks to the Most High more heartily than for this, that he will not permit the children of men, nationally any more than individually, to sin with impunity. Never do I offer a prayer that the consequences of our sins may be averted from us. I only ask that we may be brought to forsake our sins, and abhor them. If we throw them not off under the pressing influence of his goodness, then do I thank God for the chastisements by which he compels us to renounce them. So that now, while I am filled with grief, and my heart is continually harrowed by the reports which come to us of the sufferings of our fellow-men, our neighbors, our relatives, who have been sent into the battle-field, yet, nevertheless, do I give thanks, that having sinned as we have done, beyond the day of grace, God is now, in the day of his visitation, helping, compelling the people of our land to do the work meet for repentance; and that now, without much longer delay, every yoke is to be broken, and the millions of our enslaved countrymen are to be set free. The work which we, with such singleness of purpose and earnestness of heart, commenced thirty years ago, but found too hard for moral suasion and ecclesiastical discipline to accomplish, will now be done, thoroughly done, by the sterner instruments which the Almighty, in his righteous displeasure with us, has permitted to be applied.

Let us, then, now that the blindest are coming to see that the sin of slavery is the cause of our nation's woe, let us now go, by hundreds and thousands, and tens of thousands, and demand of our legislators the entire abolition of slavery throughout the land. Now is the day, and now the hour. Necessity demands what justice and mercy have long begged for in vain. Necessity knows no law, no constitution, but is a law unto herself. Necessity will compel our rulers not merely to give liberty to those who have been the subjects of rebels, but to give liberty to all within our borders; for our terrible experience has taught us that slavery, tolerated any where in the country, will be a root of bitterness that will ere long produce fruits certainly not less evil than those which we have eaten of during the last three years. Let us go, then, to the Government of our country, and assure the legislative, the judicial, and the executive officers of it, that, never while we live, or while those live whom we have inspired with feelings like our own, never shall the anti-slavery agitation of our country cease, so long as there is any slavery in the land. Let them see that we say this not as a mere threat, but as our solemn conviction of duty. We did not espouse the cause of the oppressed as a matter of choice. We were impelled to it by a deep sense of moral obligation; and that obligation cannot cease to urge us, until the unparalleled iniquity of American slavery is entirely and for ever abolished in every part of these United States, and our country has indeed become " the land of the free, and the *asylum of the oppressed.*"

ONSON S. MURRAY expressed his belief that Mr. and Mrs. FOSTER had been misapprehended by those who had spoken in reply to them. A great work was to be done to build up a correct public sentiment at the North; and while we turn our attention so much to what has already been accomplished, there is danger of overlooking the great work yet to be done.

SPEECH OF ANDREW T. FOSS.

I feel very unwilling to ask you, after listening so long to excellent speeches, to hear what I have to say; and yet I want to say a few words. If there is any thing in this world I am covetous of, it is anti-slavery fame. I do not care about any other, but I want that. I want my name to stand connected with the Anti-Slavery movement, as far as possible. If I have no other legacy to leave the only child that is spared me, I want to leave an anti-slavery reputation. I was not a signer of the Declaration of Sentiments made in this place thirty years ago; but I can say, with friend BUFFUM, that I wish I had been. He thinks he would be willing to pay a hundred dollars. I would give ten years of my life, and that is about all I have to hope for, if I had been a signer of that Declaration. But although I was not a signer of that Declaration, I was in the field before that.

The first thing I ever heard of anti-slavery was Mr. GARRISON'S pamphlet, "Thoughts on Colonization." I had at that time a colonization agent in my house, whom I was expecting to preach for me the next Sunday; but I was compelled to say to him, "What shall I do? I agree entirely with the views of this pamphlet." But I told him — "I will let you preach for me on one condition; and that is, that you will let me reply to you. On no other condition will I consent, for from this time henceforth I am an immediate, unconditional Abolitionist." I believe I was born so; for I have no knowledge of any conviction or of any conversion. The moment I heard this Gospel of Truth, I accepted it. But I did not feel like entering directly upon this as the great work of my life. That was the ministry to which I had been ordained; but I intended to preach the everlasting gospel, and as much anti-slavery as the gospel would afford. So I wrote me an anti-slavery sermon, I believe the first ever delivered in New Hampshire, and delivered it with the hope that it would be popular. I prepared the sermon with more interest than I had ever felt in writing a sermon before; and I waited the next

Sunday morning with the utmost impatience for the bell to ring; and when it rung, it seemed to me it would ring for ever. The words of the Lord were shut up like fire in my bones, and I wanted to give them utterance. I went into my pulpit, and had a crowded audience. I expected to get a hearty response from them. I had a Judge of the Supreme Court of the State sitting in the broad aisle, and I thought that when I got along a little way, I should look down and see the Judge nodding his head, and looking smilingly upon me. But in about fifteen minutes I looked down, and the Judge, instead of smiling approbation, looked as if he was about to pass sentence of death upon me. I was disappointed; but I said, "I have put my hand to the plough, and I will plough this furrow out, at any rate." And so, from that day to this, I have been trying to do what I could for anti-slavery. For twenty years I tried to bring the Baptist Church, its Bible Societies, Missionary Societies and Tract Societies, upon the true ground on the anti-slavery question, until I gained the reputation of being a disturber of Zion. But at last I came to the conclusion that I could free the Baptist Church, and all other churches, faster outside of them than I could in them. It seemed as if I could get a better hold of them outside; and so, for the last ten years, I have been outside of the Church. And if the Church stands higher to-day than she did thirty years ago, I lay the unction to my soul that I have lifted some ounces towards getting her up. I am full of hope and expectation. I may be disappointed, as I have been two or three times in my life; but I have never been disappointed when I have placed my faith in Almighty God, and I shall not be now. We are to see slavery end at some time, and the only question is how soon, and by what instrumentality? I believe it will end by the hand of this war. I believe that when the last rebel is either dead or subdued — and God grant that one or the other may take place soon! — there will not be a slave clanking his chain in all this land. It may be assumption for me to say that all this is as clear to me as the sunlight; but if I cannot give any better reason for it, I will give that of MILLY, in Mrs. STOWE'S "DRED," that "I feel it in my bones." I know there is a great work to be done. I feel that I am doing it, and I mean to keep doing until the last labor is accomplished. But I must have this encouragement to bear me up, as I move around in the work, to believe that every blow is effectual, and counts for the truth at last. We are getting near the end, and I expect to live to see slavery abolished. I mean to be at the great jubilee, wherever it is holden; and I suppose that will be all over the land, every where. I said, a little while ago, that I was about ready to die; but a friend says there are a hundred years' work to do, and so I think I will live on and labor on until the last effort that human nature is capable of putting forth shall be finished. Then will be the right time to die; and I promise you that I will die when my time comes.

Now I bid you farewell, and invite you all to be present with me at the jubilee, which is near at our doors.

SPEECH OF STEPHEN S. FOSTER.

If I have not made a good speech myself, I have at least been the occasion of half a dozen good speeches. Last evening, a professed phrenologist came to me, and asked the privilege of putting his hands for a few moments on my head. He wanted to ascertain the cerebral developments of such a peculiar man. I assented, and when I reached my quarters, he was waiting for me. After feeling of my head a while in silence, he said: "Mr. Foster, I am very much surprised. I expected to find Combativeness and Destructiveness very large in your head. On the contrary, I find them exceedingly small." Now, I think that gentleman was not the only one mistaken in this Convention. I have been represented to this audience as living in a cloud. That is news to me. It is news, I am sure, to my wife, who thinks I shall upset every thing, I have so little caution. I always look at things from the brightest side, and I supposed I always lived in the sunlight. Our friend Foss stands here to-day in the sunshine of hope. I never saw a day in which I did not believe I should live to see slavery dead and buried out of sight; because I meant to take such care of my physical constitution that I should outlive this monster. I calculate upon attending the funeral of slavery, and will preach the sermon, if some of my associates do not live to do it. I expect to pronounce my malediction there with a full and overflowing heart.

There is a principle always guiding me to be with the minority. I have always felt that my place is with the minority, defending the weak point. When you were desponding, I preached hope to such an extent that I was called a hair-brained enthusiast. How many times have my friends cautioned me, upon this platform, against such excessive hope! And why? Because nobody else was hopeful. But now, when you are all overflowing with hope, in Heaven's name, is it any harm if one man looks around to see if there are any breakers ahead, and to warn you that it is not yet time to lay off your armor? Suppose there are no breakers ahead, will it do you any harm to be watchful and vigilant? Does my preaching lull you to inactivity? But in the hurry this morning, crowding into fifteen minutes a speech of two hours and a half, I inadvertently said that if any of you were disposed to retire from the conflict, I was not; and that, by implication, was regarded as a censure. In the first place, I did not intend it as a censure. If you can serve the Anti-Slavery cause better off the platform, then go, and my heart goes with you. But for one, I have confidence in the instrumentalities we have used these thirty years, and my motto is still, "No Union with Slaveholders!" No union with the United States Government, so long as a slave treads the American soil! That is my position. If you do not like this kind of armor, lay it off and go somewhere else, and my heart and hand shall go with you. If you are battling with slavery upon the field of blood, you are not on my platform. That is an aggressive weapon, that we repudiated at the outset; and we pledged ourselves never to use it. I cast, therefore, no reflections upon those who have left our platform, or resort to this mode of warfare; but for one, I will continue as I ever have done. I do not censure any one who works not upon our platform; but it ought to be known to us — it was not known to our friend MAY, or he would not have said there was not a member of the Executive Committee, or prominent member of the Society, who was disposed to retire from this warfare — that there are members of the Executive Committee of the American Anti-Slavery Society who are decidedly opposed to carrying on this warfare any longer as we have done, and think that our sending forth anti-slavery agents would do more harm than good. I do not question the anti-slavery integrity of those friends. They have my fullest confidence, so far as their moral and anti-slavery worth is concerned. I only say they differ from me as to instrumentalities. I think that if we are "the sacramental host of God's elect," we should stand together on this platform; but while I prefer to labor here, I will give my heart and hand to any friend who will labor any where else in our cause.

THOMAS WHITSON said: This has been an interesting meeting to me; and the reason you have not heard from me has been, that all I wanted to say has been so much better said by others.

The Society adjourned until 7 P. M.

SECOND DAY—Evening Session.

The Society assembled at 7 o'clock, the Hall being crowded to its utmost capacity.

ROBERT PURVIS, on rising to speak, was received with marked enthusiasm. He delivered an impassioned address, dwelling mainly upon the proscriptive spirit of caste, which, in defiance of the fundamental principles of the American Government, deprives the colored man of his political, educational and social rights, and often exposes him to insult and outrage. We regret that we have no report of his speech, having been disappointed in the expectation that he would himself write it out for publication.

Mr. PURVIS, before commencing his address, read the following memoir of one of the earliest friends of the Anti-Slavery cause in this country:—

MEMOIR OF ARNOLD BUFFUM.

ARNOLD BUFFUM, first President of the New England Anti-Slavery Society, son of WILLIAM and LYDIA BUFFUM, was born at Smithfield, R. I., 1782.

In the house of his father, who was a member of the old Abolition Society, ARNOLD, when a child, often listened to the stories of an old colored man who had once been a slave. After telling of the cruelties and degradations of his slave life, he would proudly say of his youngest son, "PERO loves CUFFEE more than all his children, 'cause he free born!"

From his earliest youth, ARNOLD BUFFUM maintained a faithful testimony against slavery, though his true, loving heart was often deeply wounded by the coldness and enmity of those who had once been his friends. For, at the time when great fortunes were first made by cotton manufacturers in New England, they believed that cotton could only be furnished at profitable rates by slave labor, and they disliked, and sought to silence, all expression against it. Great was his joy to meet WILLIAM LLOYD GARRISON, and the glorious company who formed the first Anti-Slavery Society.

In 1825, ARNOLD BUFFUM visited England, and there enjoyed the society and friendship of ELIZABETH FRY, AMELIA OPIE, THOMAS CLARKSON, JOSEPH STURGE, RICHARD WEBB, and others, who heartily sympathized with him in his love of liberty.

After a life spent in earnest work to promote Education, Temperance, and Emancipation, he departed March 13th, 1859, at the age of 77 years, having earned the title, FRIEND OF MAN, and his end was peace.

The President. There are on the table a considerable number of letters addressed to the meeting by friends of the cause who could not be with us in person. Interesting as they are, and much as we esteem the writers, we are constrained for want of time to omit reading them. They will be published, however, with our proceedings.

SPEECH OF THEODORE TILTON.

Good Friends:

I thank you for this courtesy, and wish I could say something worthy of your good-will. But when the Committee asked me to speak, I pleaded that I might sit dumb; because this is a meeting for retrospect — for old men's tongues and young men's ears. Sitting for two days on this platform, I have not been able to realize, even yet, that this is a *public* meeting. I know the doors stand open to all comers, and many strangers are here; yet, looking over this multitude, I see such a host of my own dear and personal friends — men and women whose names I could name — whose hands I have often clasped in fellowship — at whose board I have partaken hospitality — from whose lips I have had many pleasant words of good cheer — that now, as I look upon you all, gathered here from many different towns, and cities, and States — brought together after many miles of journeying — it seems to me that this meeting is mainly and chiefly a family reünion of fathers and children — and that I am one of the children. And now, though I am summoned to my feet to speak, my mind keeps wandering away from all the intellectual activities that have marked the three preceding sessions of this Convention, and I am thinking at this moment, not of any of the great questions that have been discussed — not of any keen encounter of debate — nor, indeed, of any cunning argument with which to-night I might hope to win you to new allegiance to the good cause — but rather of the devout gratitude to God that fills my heart because of His giving to *me* — the latest and least man among you — one born out of due time — a share, however humble and small, in that sublime work upon which you have now set the crown of thirty victorious years! My heart rises to my lips, and makes me say, May grace and mercy and peace from God our Father abide upon us all to-night!

Sir, I know these people! And I speak the truth when I say

that here before us sit many humble men and women of whom the world is not worthy. And here behind us on this platform are whitened heads, in whose presence I stand reverent and abashed. Who am I that I should stand up among such as these? Shall a pupil discourse to his teachers? Thirty years! Sir, I know not so many. This Society is two years older than I. Before my cradle was rocked, you were already in the world, able to walk alone. (Laughter.)

As you have all been talking personalities, you must let me do the same. On my way to this Convention, I received a curious letter. It was concerning my genealogy. Now, I was never greatly interested in genealogies, and never took any pains to trace my lineage backward into the past — always feeling that I should never be very proud of it. I find now, that I am directly descended from the English nobility — nothing to be proud of, certainly! (Laughter.) Yet there is a redeeming feature in the history. The ancestral nobleman was Sir JOHN TILTON, who spent his fortune on the Gunpowder Plot, and got hung for it! (Laughter.) I knew before, that a later ancestor was PETER TILTON, who hid the Regicides at Hadley, Massachusetts. Later than this, I was born in the very year and month when Mr. GARRISON was mobbed in Boston! Now, these three facts, taken together, give me, I think, a valid title to my agitating tendencies! (Laughter.)

It was a beautiful picture, that drawn by WHITTIER in his letter of yesterday morning, of the small upper room in a black man's house in this city, where, thirty years ago, the architects of this Society went up one after another, and signed their names to their solemn covenant against American slavery. I could draw a picture, not so quiet and pleasant, of the place where I made my own covenant — not with any man, but with God — to spend my life in the same cause. It was in the city of Richmond. This auction-block standing here adds double vividness to my recollection of the scene. Under the red flag of a slave auctioneer, I walked into a slave market, and heard a voice crying, "This woman's name is MARY — how much am I bid for her?" — and there, before my eyes, standing on such a block as this, was a woman holding a babe at her breast, a boy standing at one side, and a girl at the other! Shall I tell you what became of them? The mother and the babe were sold to North Carolina, the boy to Georgia, and the girl to Missouri. My soul flushed into my face like fire, and then and there, in that slave-pen, I said to myself, By the grace of GOD, as Hannibal swore eternal hostility to Rome, I swear eternal hostility to American slavery! (Applause.) This was my first sight of that great conspiracy against human nature, which, breaking out afterwards into an armed rebellion against the Republic, has crowned that capital city with a crown of crime. This, sir, is *my* reminiscence to add to *yours*.

Now, after thirty years, what hath God wrought? The other day I was reading a little memorial of Mr. GARRISON's early labors in establishing *The Liberator*, when the profits of the paper were so small that the editor and his printer lived chiefly on bread and water; "but," said the printer, "when we sold more copies than usual, we bought each a cup of milk." That, sir, was the milk-and-water period of the Anti-Slavery enterprise. (Laughter.) To-day, the good cause feeds on strong meat! My friend, the Rev. Mr. SLOANE, of New York, told me that when he was a boy in Ohio, where his father's house stood always open for hospitality to all anti-slavery itinerants, a lecturer came there one day, whose coat showed that it had been kissed by an egg, and one that had a bad breath. "Let me wipe off the stain," said young SLOANE. "Never mind, my lad," said the hero, "for if you rub it off, I will only catch another at the next town." (Laughter.) But now-a-days, an anti-slavery lecturer may go to the next town, and the next, and the next, and keep a clean coat clean all the way! And now, how sublimely has GOD evolved out of the small beginnings of this enterprise of thirty years ago, the grand results which all men's eyes see to-day! For though the cause is yet in its struggle, it cannot suffer defeat. Its beginners are likely to live to see its glorious end. "Behold how great a matter a little fire kindleth!" Behold how much has been accomplished by the patient labors of a few brave souls, who finally have set all the world to work with them in the same great cause! How few were the originators of this enterprise! They were only a handful! Yes, Jupiter's thunderbolts were only a handful, but they shook the whole world! (Applause.) I think often of that saying of Annie of Austria, "God does not pay at the end of every week, but he pays at last." Now, at the end of a generation, for all the struggle, for all the toil, for all the obstacles and perils, for all the burdens borne in the heat of the day — what a rich reward falls to these early laborers, young then, but now gray! — what retrospect and prospect! — what memories of the past and hopes of the future! In the beginning, the whole power of the Government — its laws, its policies, its bayonets, bore against the slave; now all these, like sharpened arrows, are barbed against the slave's master. The great slave-mongers of History have been Commerce and War. But now Commerce has set her hand and seal to a treaty against the slave trade; and War, no longer an enslaver, has become an emancipator. (Applause.) Mr. PURVIS gave a fit and beautiful designation to the great decree of the President, which crowned that new year with a new policy. What is the significance of that act? A Lombard king who marched through the length of Italy, coming to the south shore, rode on horseback into the water up to the saddle-girth, when, rising in his stirrups, he took a javelin, and, hurling it far forward, exclaimed, as it fell into the sea, "Thus far do I extend the boundary of the Lombard power!" So ABRAHAM LINCOLN, drawing from the War Power the beneficent weapon of Emancipation, has hurled it over nine rebellious States, saying, "Thus far do I extend the boundary of Human Freedom!" (Applause.)

But by whom was this weapon put into the President's hands? I will tell you. DE TOCQUEVILLE, who wrote of this country as it was thirty years ago, said that such were then the prevailing views of Federal rights and State rights, that if a conflict should arise between the Government at Washington and the Government at any State capital, the State would be strong enough to pluck the victory, and the Federal centre would be too weak to do any thing but yield. Now, what if this rebellion, instead of breaking out in 1860, had broken out in 1830? It would then have conquered the Government! Nothing could have saved the Union from the disintegrating blow. Now what, during these last thirty years, has so strengthened the Government that it is now able to conquer, not one, but a dozen rebellious States? It is that change in the moral convictions of a free people, which, more and more unifying Northern opinions and interests against the South, now at last knits and binds all the loyal States into a steadfast allegiance to the Federal Government, and gives to the Executive every weapon needed to crush the rebellion, and to preserve the Republic. The conspiracy, we are told, began about thirty years ago; its antidote began about the same time. While our enemy was secretly fashioning his spear, God inspired a company of good men to set to work immediately to make the shield. It was thus that the anti-slavery agitation arose — the mass of the people not knowing why, and clamoring against it as the disturber of their peace, little dreaming that this very agitation was to create their future safeguard against an approaching conspiracy. I declare, what history will prove, that the unity of the North to-day, in its conflict with the South, is a legitimate result of that moral awakening whose first trumpet-call this Society sounded into the startled ears of the nation thirty years ago. (Applause.) The Anti-Slavery agitation, and this alone, to-day makes it possible for ABRAHAM LINCOLN to stand victor over the slaveholders' rebellion! (Applause.) All honor, therefore, to the early pioneers of the Anti-Slavery movement! The nation owes to these men its present safety; and when it has time to stop and think, it will give them, as the reward due to their labors, the gratitude of the present and of future generations. (Applause.)

The same Divine Providence — for it has not been the work of man — the same Providence that began this sublime work will carry it victoriously to its consummation. I never reflect without pity upon the long unhappy condition of that dusky race of four million of human souls, who, under a free government and in a Christian age, have been chained down to the basest servitude ever known in the world. The strong may take care of themselves, but the weak ought to be helped. That is man's duty and GOD's example. The heavenly Father cares for all, but mostly for those who need most care. The Scriptures take no pains to say that He cares for such sparrows as are strong of wing, but tenderly mention that he cares for such as fall to the ground. If men, therefore, are of more value than many sparrows, will He not lift up that lowly multitude that so long have been bowed down to the ground? One day, while sitting in my office, I received from Mr. GREELEY a hurried note, somewhat as follows: "My friend, read the enclosed, and if you can do any thing for the poor man, I know you will." The enclosed was a little bit of blue paper, sweat-stained, written upon in a scrawling, straggling hand, misspelled, and ran in this wise: "I am a fugitive slave in Canada. I came from Maryland five years ago, leaving my father behind me, an old man, of whom I cannot hear whether he is alive or dead. I have written many letters, but get no answers. What shall I do?" This was the substance. After reading the note, I dropped it on my desk, saying, it is a hopeless case. In a few minutes somebody knocked at my door, and in came an old, weather-beaten black man, white-haired and venerable. He was on his way from Maryland northward — for I never yet found any of that class of people on their way southward. His name was SAMUEL

GREEN. The name in the letter was HENRY GREEN. "Did you ever know a man by the name of HENRY GREEN?" I asked. "I had a son," said he, "by that name. He ran out of slavery five years ago, and I never have heard from him since." "Now listen," said I; and I read the letter to him, and watched his face. "It is my son," said he, "my son HENRY!" And that same evening the railroad train bore him northward, and on the second day afterward he kissed his son's cheek! — a reünion as of two persons rising to meet each other from the grave, after five years of death! Now, my friends, the same Divine Hand that brought together so strangely those two sundered hearts, is stretched out of the heavens for the help of all the sorrowing four million, and will, sooner or later, lead them every one into the "light and liberty of the sons of GOD." (Applause.) For GOD and all good angels are working together for the eradication of slavery from this land. And we are near the day of victory. I am informed that an old man in this State, lying on his death-bed at the beginning of the year, was told by his family that the President had decreed liberty to the slaves. "Read me the Proclamation," said he; and after it was read, he folded his feeble hands, saying, "Now, Lord, lettest thou thy servant depart in peace, for mine eyes have beheld the salvation of my country." Shortly afterward he died — leaving the nation to a new and nobler life. But we must not flatter ourselves that the work is already done, or will be done to-morrow or the next day. It may be that the shadow of war on the land has not yet grown as dark as GOD means it. It may be that we have not yet suffered enough for purification — for we are refined by fire, and disciplined by sorrow. But even though it be by the path of blood and tears, let us thank GOD that, by any path, he is leading the nation forward to liberty.

This Convention has been one of good cheer. It has ministered refreshment to my soul. There has been an Indian Summer in its atmosphere which has warmed my blood, and quickened my pulse. But I have been so over-filled with a strong sympathy that my mind has been robbed and dispossessed of all the thoughts that a better fortune might have thrown into my remarks. I know it is said that "out of the abundance of the heart the mouth speaketh," yet one might make another proverb, and say, "Out of the *over*-abundance of the heart the mouth would hold its peace." And now, my friends, while we are having the baptism of fire and blood in the land, let us have the baptism of the Holy Ghost in our souls. O, sir, when one looks at the magnitude of the cause, its moral grandeur, its infinite importance for humanity, and then looks at his own weakness in its advocacy, what can he do but cry out, " Who is sufficient for these things ? " What manner of man ought one to be who takes upon himself the championship of liberty ! How ought one to purge himself of all that is base and mean ! How clean and pure of soul ought to be the man who dares to rebuke a nation for its sin ! Let us look up into the heavens for the benediction of God upon us and upon our work.

> " Anoint and cheer our soiled face
> With the abundance of thy grace."

Time flies. CLARKSON and WILBERFORCE are in their graves, but their names are precious. The venerable men on this platform shall sooner or later follow, leaving behind them like precious names. For there are some within the sound of my voice whose names shall be as enduring as American history. Yet it makes very little difference who shall be remembered or who forgotten; for when these present storms shall give way to blue skies—when the fields now red with blood shall be green with peace — when every chain shall be broken, and every slave shall offer thanksgiving—all true souls, forgetting the mere human instruments of the Divine will, will cry out, "Not unto us, not unto us, but unto thy name be the victory, O Lord God of Hosts!" (Applause.)

THE PRESIDENT. For one, I am always rejoiced to hear of the success of any candidate, in any part of the country, who represents the idea of liberty. Whatever may be said with regard to his merely echoing public sentiment, one thing I know, that a man sometimes comes into office without losing his manhood, and keeps his integrity. We have such a man with us here to-night, in the person of Senator WILSON. He did not wait till the public sentiment was created, whereby he could safely aspire to public office; but long before he ever dreamed of office, as early as 1836, his interest in the struggle for the abolition of slavery began, and has continued from that hour to this. If he has been Representative and Senator in Massachusetts, Senator in the United States Congress representing Massachusetts, and is there still, it is not because he has played the part of a demagogue, but because he has dared to speak the words of freedom, and to maintain the cause of the slave. (Applause.)

SPEECH OF HON. HENRY WILSON.

Mr. President:

I came here to look into the faces and to hear the voices of the honored men who, thirty years ago, laid the foundations of the Anti-Slavery movement in America upon the rights of human nature and the laws of the living God. Passing on to the post of duty assigned me in the councils of the Republic, I gladly pause to-day to pay the tribute of my sincere respect, gratitude and admiration to the men, and the women too, of the American Anti-Slavery Society, who, for a generation, have vindicated the proscribed cause of the bondmen of Christian America with a fidelity unsurpassed in any age or nation. (Applause.) I came here too, sir, to catch something of that spirit of self-sacrificing devotion to the cause of liberty and humanity that has animated you and the devoted friends who have gathered around you in the struggles of these thirty years. The President of the United States, as he stood the other day among the graves of the fallen brave on the immortal field of Gettysburg, said that the lesson there taught should be an inspiration to greater efforts in the future, in the cause of our perilled country. This anniversary festival, sacred to the memories of past struggles, is to us an inspiration and a hope. I leave you to-night to go to the theatre of public duty, where anti-slavery men are to be tried as perhaps they were never tried before. inspired with the determination to do all that I can to break the last fetter of the last slave in the United States. (Long-continued applause.)

You, Mr. President, were kind enough to say that, in political life, I did not wait for public opinion before committing myself to the sacred cause of equal and impartial liberty. On this occasion, when we may recur to the recollections and reminiscences of the past, I may be pardoned in saying that I was an anti-slavery man years before I entertained any political aspirations, or formed any political associations. In the Spring of 1836, I visited the capital of my country. Passing in the cars from Baltimore to Washington, I saw several slave women toiling in the fields. Turning to a gentleman sitting by me, I expressed the opinion that slavery was an evil and a dishonor, and was told, rather sharply, that I "could not be permitted to express such an opinion in the State of Maryland." That was, perhaps, my first utterance against slavery, and the first rebuke I ever received for such an utterance. I went on to the capital of my country. I saw slavery beneath the shadow of the flag that waved over the Capitol. I saw the slave-pen, and men and women and children herded for the market of the far South; and at the table at which sat Senator MORRIS, of Ohio, then the only avowed champion of freedom in the Senate of the United States, I expressed my abhorrence of slavery and the slave traffic in the capital of this Democratic and Christian Republic. I was promptly told that "Senator MORRIS might be protected in speaking against slavery in the Senate, but I would not be protected in uttering such sentiments." I left the capital of my country with the unalterable resolution to give all that I had, and all that I hoped to have of power, to the cause of emancipation in America; and I have tried to make that resolution a living faith from that day to this. (Applause.) My political associations, from that hour to the present, have always been guided by my opposition to slavery, in every form, and they always will be so guided. In twenty years of public life, I may have committed errors of judgment, but I have ever striven "to write my name," in the words of WILLIAM LEGGETT, "in ineffaceable letters on the Abolition record." Standing here to-night, in the presence of veteran anti-slavery men, I can say, in all the sincerity of conviction, that I would rather have it written upon the humble stone that shall mark the spot where I shall repose when life's labors are done, "He did what he could to break the fetters of the slave," than to have it recorded, "He filled the highest stations of honor in the gift of his countrymen." (Loud applause.)

As I have listened, Mr. President, here to-day to the reminiscences of the past, I have endeavored to realize the condition of the Anti-Slavery cause in America, when you, sir, and your associates, thirty years ago, founded here, in this city of Philadelphia, the American Anti-Slavery Society. When our fathers came out of the fiery trials of the Revolution, they believed that slavery would pass away under our republican institutions and Christian civilization; but the spirit of the revolutionary era passed away as its champions passed from earth. When the American Anti-Slavery Society was formed, in 1833, the conquest and subjugation of the country by the slave-masters who had forgotten the teachings of the fathers was complete. Institutions of learning, of benevolence and religion, political organizations and public men, all bowed in unresisting submission to the iron will of the slave-masters who ruled the governments of the slaveholding States, and shaped the policy of the Republic. When you, sir, and your comrades organized the American Anti-Slavery Society, and proclaimed immediate emancipation to be the duty of the master and the right of the slave, you believed, in the bright ardor of that moment, that Christian America would respond to your noble appeals, would soon break every yoke, undo the heavy burdens, and let the oppressed go free. But the sentinels of the slave-masters sounded the alarm. They demanded that institutions of learning and religion, public men and the public press, should disown the heresy of immediate emancipation, and mark and brand its advocates. They demanded the suppression of freedom of discussion and the liberty of the press. Timid, nerveless conservatism cowered before the imperious demands of Southern slave-masters. The reign of terror was inaugurated, law was prostrated in the dust, and the friends of the slave held property, liberty, and life itself, at the mercy of lawless mobs, who set at defiance the laws of God, and the decencies of civilization.

But, amid scenes of lawlessness, violence, social proscription, and official rebuke, the heroic men who inaugurated the Anti-Slavery movement did not quail or shrink from fearful conflicts, from which the timid instinctively recoiled. Their spirits rose and mantled as the storm of denunciation beat upon their devoted heads. They looked danger in the eye — they hurled defiance at arbitrary power. They saw with clear vision that the conflict was not a war of men, but of ideas and institutions. Like JOHN ADAMS, they saw "through the gloom of the present, the rays of ravishing light and glory." They echoed the hopeful words of one of Freedom's poets —

> "The few shall not for ever sway,
> The many toil in sorrow;
> The powers of hell are strong to-day,
> But CHRIST shall rise to-morrow."

Confident of the future, sir, they reëchoed your defiant words: "We are in earnest; we will not equivocate; we will not excuse; we will not retreat a single inch; and we will be heard!" (Applause.) Few in numbers, strong only in their principles and the potency of their measures, they began that conflict with the advancing hosts of the legions of slavery, which has stirred the country to its profoundest depths for thirty years. Honored then, for ever honored, be the men who, in the days of perilled liberty, when the shadows of slavery were darkening all the land, "cast an arch," in the words of NATHANIEL PEABODY ROGERS, "upon the horizon like a semi-circle of polar lights, and upon it bent the motto, 'Immediate Emancipation!' glorious as the rainbow." (Applause.)

Great movements, affecting the relations of the people and of the nation, cannot be measured by the hours. By years, by epochs alone, can we measure the progressive advancement of a movement so grand and comprehensive as the Anti-Slavery movement in America. What mighty changes have been wrought in the condition of the Anti-Slavery cause in the United States since the American Anti-Slavery Society was organized by representatives of ten States, in 1833! Then a few unknown and nameless men were its apostles; now the most accomplished intellects in America are its champions. Then a few proscribed and hunted followers rallied around its banners; now it has laid its grasp upon the conscience of the nation, and millions rally around the folds of its flag. Then not a statesman in America accepted its doctrines or advocated its measures; now it controls more than twenty States, has a majority in both Houses of Congress, and the Chief Magistrate of the Republic decrees the emancipation of three millions of men. (Applause.) Then, every Free State was against it; now, Western Virginia, Delaware, Maryland and Missouri pronounce for the emancipation of their bondmen. Then the public press covered it with ridicule and contempt; now the most powerful journals in America are its organs, scattering its truths broadcast over all the land. Then the religious, benevolent and literary institutions of the land rebuked its doctrines and proscribed its advocates; now it shapes, moulds and fashions them at its pleasure. Then political organizations trampled disdainfully upon it; now it looks down in the pride of conscious power upon the wrecked political fragments that float at its feet. Then it was impotent and powerless; now it holds public men and political organizations in the hollow of its hand. (Applause.) Then the public voice sneered at and defied it; now it is master of America, and has only to be true to itself to bury slavery so deep that the hand of no returning despotism can reach it. (Great applause.)

Mr. President, you and some others who founded the Society whose thirtieth anniversary you this day celebrate, have lived to see the sentiments embodied in your Declaration of Principles disseminated all over the land, and accepted by the American people. A few months ago, this beautiful city of Philadelphia was believed to be one of the most pro-slavery of the cities of the loyal States; now, Philadelphia is the most loyal, is the most anti-slavery city of the Free States. But a few years ago, an anti-slavery man could hardly utter an anti-slavery sentiment in a political canvass without harm to his political friends. In the last canvass in this Commonwealth of Pennsylvania, in every portion of the State, the champions of the Government clearly and distinctly denounced slavery, and sustained the proclamation of ABRAHAM LINCOLN, emancipating more than three millions of men. (Applause.) Sir, it has been my fortune, during the last three months, to address my fellow-citizens in several of the States, and I am proud to say to you that the supporters of the Government have spoken as distinctly and clearly in favor of the extinction of slavery in America as do the men who surround me on this platform. The people see with clear vision that slavery is the rebellion; that slavery has dug more than a hundred thousand graves of loyal men; that slavery hates the country and its republican institutions; and that mercy to slavery is a crime against our country. (Great applause.)

I am, Mr. President, filled with hope and confidence in the future of my country. I belong not to that class of men who are wont to claim a victory before they have won it. I believe that victory is never sure, so long as there is any thing left undone to win it; and I say to the anti-slavery men, and women too, that, while you have a clear right to be hopeful and confident of the future, you have a duty to perform that will test all your devotion, all your firmness, all your wisdom. We are to be tried — the Government is to be tried. It was suggested to-day that, should the rebels surrender, they would continue to hold their slaves as bondmen. I do not believe it — for I have faith in the American people, and I know they will never permit it. (Great enthusiasm.) But should JEFF. DAVIS and his compeers in treason lay down their arms, you would see the Peace Democracy, that, during the last thirty years, has committed every crime slavery bade it commit — you would see that Democracy whose life is bound up in the existence of slavery, every where demand that slavery should live, and the slave-masters come back again to govern the Republic. And we should see timid men with us, but hardly of us, cowardly shrinking back, consenting to make an inglorious peace, and leave slavery to redden, in another age, as it has in this, the fields of America with the blood of patriotism. Yet, while we are to be tried, I believe we shall remain firm, true and faithful, and that we shall triumph. The way to triumph is to assume that the proclamation of ABRAHAM LINCOLN, emancipating three millions three hundred thousand slaves in the ten rebel States, is the irrepealable law of this land; that this Christian nation is pledged to every slave, to the country, to the world, and to Almighty God, to see that every one of these bondmen is free for ever and for evermore. (Great applause.) Let the loyal men of America assume, as the irrevocable law of the land, that slavery does not now exist in the disloyal States; and that every black man there is free. The President of the United States has pledged the physical power of all America to enforce the Proclamation of Freedom; seven hundred thousand loyal bayonets bear that proclamation upon their glittering points. (Applause.)

When the people of the United States, in November, 1860, thronged to the ballot-boxes, and, in spite of the menaces of the slave-masters, made ABRAHAM LINCOLN President of the United States, slavery cast the shadows of its power over the land. That towering fabric of strength and power is now shivered to atoms. Two questions only were settled by the election of 1860. The people pronounced against the spread of slavery into the Territories of the United States, and against the longer continuance of the rule of the Slave Power. Of slavery in the States we distinctly avowed we had no constitutional power to touch it. We said: "Slavery is the creature of local law; we are opposed to it; we will use our moral influence against it; it shall not be extended; we will not be ruled by it; we will destroy its political power, and we believe that in one or two generations it will gradually pass away." The election of 1860 did not directly affect the existence of slavery in the States, where it stood in all its strength, protected by local legislation. But the slave-masters leaped into the rebellion to perpetuate slavery for ever, and to continue the rule of slave-masters, and the fires of the revolution they inaugurated are melting the chains of the bondman. I can never forget the dark days that followed the election of ABRAHAM LINCOLN. There was BUCHANAN, a poor, weak, imbecile old man, with FLOYD stealing the public arms; with COBB breaking down the public credit; with TOUCEY sending the navy to distant seas; with THOMPSON intriguing to dismember the country; with Democratic leaders all over the North expressing sympathy with the rebel chiefs, assuring traitors that if the contest came to blows, the battle would be fought on Northern soil, with doubtful results.

Timid, nerveless conservatism implored us to accept that wicked proposition—aye, sir, the most wicked proposition ever made in the Congress of the United States—the Crittenden compromise. But amid these scenes of treason, we calmly sat in the Congress of the United States, and bided our time. The President stole into Washington to escape the steel of the assassin. We took possession of the Government. Slavery, in the pride of its power, opened its batteries upon Sumter, brought down the old flag, ran up the banner of rebellion, and proclaimed the dismemberment of the Republic. Two and a half years have passed away, and there stands a proclamation—never to be recalled or modified—making three millions three hundred thousand men in the rebel States free for evermore—(applause)—there stands an act for ever prohibiting slavery in the vast Territories of the United States—(applause)—there stands an act abolishing slavery in the District of Columbia, and I thank God that he gave me the privilege of introducing the bill that abolished the cleaving curse in the capital of my country. (Three cheers for HENRY WILSON were proposed by FRED. DOUGLASS, and given by the audience.) There stands an act annulling the slave codes and black laws of the District of Columbia, making the black man amenable to the same laws, to be tried in the same manner, and to be subjected to the same punishment as white men; and I am thankful that it was my privilege to introduce that measure of justice and humanity. (Applause.) There, too, stands an act, clothing the President with authority to place the sword, the rifle, the bayonet, and the flag, in the hands of black men, to fight the battles of the Republic. There is the recognition of the black Republics of Hayti and Liberia—the treaty for the suppression of the African slave trade—the opinion of the Attorney-General that the black man is a citizen of the United States—and the passport of the Secretary of State, the evidence to the nations of the citizenship of men of the African race. (Applause.) Western Virginia has already pronounced the doom of her slavery. Little Delaware sends an Emancipationist to the House of Representatives. Maryland, under the lead of HENRY WINTER DAVIS—honored be his name! (cheers)—in utterances as clear and distinct as were ever pronounced, speaks for emancipation. Missouri, in spite of malign councils, votes for immediate emancipation, (applause,) and Tennessee, under the lead of ANDREW JOHNSON, is preparing to take her place in the lists of free Commonwealths. Kentucky, alone, bears the banner of slavery proudly and defiantly; her leading influences are against emancipation, but the people are fast ripening for it. They need only bold, earnest and determined leaders and organs to place her by the side of Pennsylvania, New York, and New England, ere another year shall pass away.

The armies of the Republic have in the recent elections proclaimed their undying love of freedom, and their utter detestation of copperhead democracy. The armies are the most potent emancipation societies in America. Our soldiers, in face of rebel legions, are fighting for liberty, speaking for liberty, and voting for liberty. The Government of the United States is indebted to our soldiers in the field for the recent victories of the ballot-box, which have fallen with crushing weight upon the rebellion, and its sympathizing friends in the loyal States. Sir, I saw the other day a letter from General GRANT, who has fought so many battles for the Republic, and won them all, (enthusiastic applause) — the hero who hurled his legions up the mountains before Chattanooga, and fought a battle for the Union above the clouds. (Applause.) The hero of Vicksburg says: "I have never been an anti-slavery man, but I try to judge justly of what I see. I made up my mind, when this war commenced, that the North and South could only live together in peace as one nation, and they could only be one nation by being a free nation. (Applause.) Slavery, the corner-stone of the so-called Confederacy, is knocked out, and it will take more men to keep black men slaves, than to put down the rebellion. Much as I desire peace, I am opposed to any peace until this question of slavery is for ever settled." That is the position of the leading General of our armies. The votes of our soldiers, in the States permitting them to vote, are more than nine to one for the prosecution of the war, and the enforcement of the Emancipation Proclamation of ABRAHAM LINCOLN.

I say to you, sir, and to the anti-slavery men of the United States, who have rejected the subtle policy of concession and compromise, who have repudiated the guilty delusion that the sin of slavery belongs to past generations and repentance to posterity, you who have perpetually sounded into the ear of the nation the sin of oppression and the duty of repentance, go not home with the conviction that your work is done, but go home cheered by the assurance that the battle is going on for you; that you have stormed battery after battery, carried position after position; that you have only to be as true in the future as you have been in the past, to secure a permanent and enduring triumph. If the nation had accepted your doctrine of peaceful, legal, Christian action, this bloody war would never have come upon us. (Applause.) The crimes of two centuries have brought this terrible war upon us; but if this generation, upon whom God has laid His chastisements, will yet be true to liberty and humanity, peace will return again to bless this land, now rent and torn by civil strife. Then we shall heal the wounds of war, enlighten the dark intellect of the emancipated bondman, and make our country the model Republic to which the Christian world shall turn with respect and admiration.

The speaker retired amid the deafening plaudits of the audience.

Frederick Douglass, being seen on the platform, was called for by many persons in different parts of the Hall. As he came forward to speak, he was received with loud applause.

SPEECH OF FREDERICK DOUGLASS.

Ladies and Gentlemen:

I confess, at the outset, to have felt a very profound desire to utter a word at some period during the present meeting. As it has been repeatedly said here, it has been a meeting of reminiscences. I shall not attempt to treat you to any of my own in what I have now to say, though I have some in connection with the labors of this Society, and in connection with my experience as an American slave, that I might not inappropriately bring before you on this occasion. I desire to be remembered among those having a word to say at this meeting, because I began my existence as a free man in this country with this association, and because I have some hopes or apprehensions, whichever you please to call them, that we shall never, as a Society, hold another decade meeting.

I well remember the first time I ever listened to the voice of the honored President of this association, and I have some recollection of the feelings of hope inspired by his utterances at that time. Under the inspiration of those hopes, I looked forward to the abolition of slavery as a certain event in the course of a very few years. So clear were his utterances, so simple and truthful, and so adapted, I conceived, to the human heart were the principles and doctrines propounded by him, that I thought five years, at any rate, would be all that would be required for the abolition of slavery. I thought it was only necessary for the slaves, or their friends, to lift up the hatchway of slavery's infernal hold, to uncover the bloody scenes of American thraldom, and give the nation a peep into its horrors, its deeds of deep damnation, to arouse them to almost phrensied opposition to this foul curse. But I was mistaken. I had not been five years pelted by the mob, insulted by the crowds, shunned by the Church, denounced by the ministry, ridiculed by the press, spit upon by the loafers, before I became convinced that I might perhaps live, struggle, and die, and go down to my grave, and the slaves of the South yet remain in their chains.

We live to see a better hope to-night. I participate in the profound thanksgiving expressed by all, that we do live to see this better day. I am one of those who believe that it is the mission of this war to free every slave in the United States. I am one of those who believe that we should consent to no peace which shall not be an Abolition peace. I am, moreover, one of those who believe that the work of the American Anti-Slavery Society will not have been completed until the black men of the South, and the black men of the North, shall have been admitted, fully and completely, into the body politic of America. I look upon slavery as going the way of all the earth. It is the mission of the war to put it down. But a mightier work than the abolition of slavery now looms up before the Abolitionist. This Society was organized, if I remember rightly, for two distinct objects; one was the emancipation of the slave, and the other the elevation of the colored people. When we have taken the chains off the slave, as I believe we shall do, we shall find a harder resistance to the second purpose of this great association than we have found even upon slavery itself.

I am hopeful; but while I am hopeful, I am thoughtful withal. If I lean to either side of the controversy to which we have listened to-day, I lean to that side which implies caution, which implies apprehension, which implies a consciousness that our work is not done. Protest, affirm, hope, glorify as we may, it cannot be denied that Abolitionism is still unpopular in the United States. It cannot be denied that this war is at present denounced by its opponents as an Abolition war; and it is equally clear that it would not be denounced as an Abolition war, if Abolitionism was not odious. It is equally clear that our friends, Republicans, Unionists, Loyalists, would not spin out elaborate explanations and denials that this is the character of the war, if Abolition were popular. Men accept the term Abolitionist with qualifications. They do not come out square and open-handed, and affirm themselves to be Abolitionists. As a general rule, we are attempting to explain away the charge that this is an Abolition war. I hold that it is an Abolition war, because slavery has proved itself stronger than the Constitution; it has proved itself stronger than the Union; and has forced upon us the necessity of putting down slavery in order to save the Union, and in order to save the Constitution. (Applause.)

I look at this as an Abolition war instead of being a Union war, because I see that the lesser is included in the greater, and that you cannot have the lesser until you have the greater. You cannot have the Union, the Constitution, and Republican institutions, until you have stricken down that damning curse, and put it beyond the pale of the Republic. For, while it is in this country, it will make your Union impossible; it will make your Constitution impossible. I therefore call this just what the Democrats have charged it with being, an Abolition war. Let us emblazon it on our banners, and declare before the world that this is an Abolition war, (applause,) that it will prosper precisely in proportion as it takes upon itself this character. (Renewed applause.)

My respected friend, Mr. Purvis, called attention to the existence of prejudice against color in this country. This gives me great cause for apprehension, if not for alarm. I am afraid of this powerful element of prejudice against color. While it exists, I want the voice of the American Anti-Slavery Society to be continually protesting, continually exposing it. While it can be said that in this most anti-slavery city in the Northern States of our Union, in the city of Philadelphia, the city of Brotherly Love, the city of churches, the city of piety, the most genteel and respectable colored lady or gentleman may be kicked out of your commonest street car, we are in danger of a compromise. While it can be said that black men, fighting bravely for this country, are asked to take seven dollars per month, while the Government lays down as a rule or criterion of pay a complexional one, we are in danger of a compromise. While to be radical is to be unpopular, we are in danger of a compromise. While we have a large minority called Democratic, in every State of the North, we have a powerful nucleus for a most infernal reaction in favor of slavery. I know it is said that we have recently achieved vast political victories. I am glad of it. I value these victories, however, more for what they have prevented than for what they have actually accomplished. I should have been doubly sad at seeing any one of these States wheel into line with the Peace Democracy. But, however it may be in the State of Pennsylvania, I know that you may look for abolition in the creed of any party in New York with a microscope, and you will not find a single line of anti-slavery there. The victories were Union victories, victories to save the Union in such ways as the country may devise to save it. But whatever may have been the meaning of these majorities in regard to the Union, we know one thing, that the minorities, at least, mean slavery. They mean submission. They mean the degradation of the colored man. They mean every thing but open rebellion against the Federal Government in the North. But the mob, the rioters in the city of New York, convert that city into a hell, and its lower orders into demons, and dash out the brains of little children against the curbstones; and they mean any thing and every thing that the Devil exacts at their hands. While we had in this State a majority of but 15,000 over this pro-slavery Democratic party, they have a mighty minority, a dangerous minority. Keep in mind when these minorities were gotten. Powerful as they are, they were gotten when slavery, with bloody hands, was stabbing at the very heart of the nation itself. With all that disadvantage, they have piled up these powerful minorities.

We have work to do, friends and fellow-citizens, to look after these minorities. The day that shall see JEFF. DAVIS fling down his Montgomery Constitution, and call home his Generals, will be the most trying day to the virtue of this people that this country has ever seen. When the slaveholders shall give up the contest, and ask for readmission into the Union, then, as Mr. WILSON has told us, we shall see the trying time in this country. Your Democracy will clamor for peace, and for restoring the old order of things, because that old order of things was the life of the Democratic party. "You do take away mine house, when you take away the prop that sustains my house," and the support of the Democratic party we all know to be slavery. The Democratic party is for war for slavery; it is for peace for slavery; it is for the *habeas corpus* for slavery; it is against the *habeas corpus* for slavery; it was for the Florida war for slavery; it was for the Mexican war for slavery; it is for jury trial for traitors, for slavery; it is against jury trial for men claimed as fugitive slaves, for slavery. It has but one principle, one master; and it is guided, governed, and directed by it. I say that, with this party among us, flaunting its banners in our faces, with the New

York *World* scattered broadcast over the North, with the New York *Express*, with the mother and father and devil of them all, the New York *Herald*, (applause,) with those papers flooding our land, and coupling the term Abolitionist with all manner of coarse epithets, in all our hotels, at all our crossings, our highways and byways and railways all over the country, there is work to be done—a good deal of work to be done.

I have said that our work will not be done until the colored man is admitted a full member in good and regular standing in the American body politic. Men have very nice ideas about the body politic where I have travelled; and they don't like the idea of having the negro in the body politic. He may remain in this country, for he will be useful as a laborer—valuable, perhaps, in time of trouble, as a helper; but to make him a full and complete citizen, a legal voter, that would be contaminating the body politic. I was a little curious, some years ago, to find out what sort of a thing this body politic was; and I was very anxious to know especially about what amount of baseness, brutality, coarseness, ignorance, and bestiality could find its way into the body politic; and I was not long in finding it out. I took my stand near the little hole through which the body politic put its votes. (Laughter.) And first among the mob I saw Ignorance, unable to read its vote, asking *me* to read it, by the way, (great laughter,) depositing its vote in the body politic. Next I saw a man stepping up to the body politic, casting in his vote, having a black eye, and another one ready to be blacked, having been engaged in a street fight. I saw, again, Pat, fresh from the Emerald Isle, with the delightful brogue peculiar to him, stepping up—not walking, but leaning upon the arms of two of his friends, unable to stand, passing into the body politic! I came to the conclusion that this body politic was, after all, not quite so pure a body as the representations of its friends would lead us to believe.

I know it will be said that I ask you to make the black man a voter in the South. Yet you are for having brutality and ignorance introduced into the ballot-box. It is said that the colored man is ignorant, and therefore he shall not vote. In saying this, you lay down a rule for the black man that you apply to no other class of your citizens. I will hear nothing of degradation or of ignorance against the black man. If he knows enough to be hanged, he knows enough to vote. If he knows an honest man from a thief, he knows much more than some of our white voters. If he knows as much when sober as an Irishman knows when drunk, he knows enough to vote. If he knows enough to take up arms in defence of this Government, and bare his breast to the storm of rebel artillery, he knows enough to vote. (Great applause.)

Away with this talk of the want of knowledge on the part of the negro! I am about as big a negro as you will find any where about town; and any man that does not believe I know enough to vote, let him try it. I think I can convince him that I do. Let him run for office in my district, and solicit my vote, and I will show him.

All I ask, however, in regard to the blacks, is that whatever rule you adopt, whether of intelligence or wealth, as the condition of voting, you shall apply it equally to the black man. Do that, and I am satisfied, and eternal justice is satisfied; liberty, fraternity, equality, are satisfied; and the country will move on harmoniously.

Mr. President, I have a patriotic argument in favor of insisting upon the immediate enfranchisement of the slaves of the South; and it is this. When this rebellion shall have been put down, when the arms shall have fallen from the guilty hands of traitors, you will need the friendship of the slaves of the South, of those millions there. Four or five million men are not of inconsiderable importance at any time; but they will be doubly important when you come to reörganize and reëstablish republican institutions in the South. Will you mock those bondmen by breaking their chains with one hand, and with the other giving their rebel masters the elective franchise, and robbing them of theirs? I tell you the negro is your friend. You will make him your friend by emancipating him. But you will make him not only your friend in sentiment and heart by enfranchising him, but you will make him your best defender, your best protector against the traitors and the descendants of those traitors, who will inherit the hate, the bitter revenge which will crystallize all over the South, and seek to circumvent the Government that they could not throw off. You will need the black man there, as a watchman and patrol; and you may need him as a soldier. You may need him to uphold in peace, as he is now upholding in war, the star-spangled banner. (Applause.) I wish our excellent friend, Senator WILSON, would bend his energies to this point as well as the other — to let the negro have a vote. It will be helping him from the jaws of the wolf. We are surrounded by those that, like the wolf, will use their jaws, if you give the elective franchise to the descendants of the traitors, and keep it from the black man. We ought to be the voters there. We ought to be members of Congress. (Applause.) You may as well make up your minds that you have got to see something dark down that way. There is no way to get rid of it. I am a candidate already! (Laughter and applause.)

For twenty-five years, Mr. President, you know that when I got as far South as Philadelphia, I felt that I was rubbing against my prison wall, and could not go any further. I dared not go over yonder into Delaware. Twenty years ago, when I attended the first decade meeting of this Society, as I came along the vales and hills of Gettysburg, my good friends, the anti-slavery people along there, warned me to remain in the house during the day-time, and travel in the night, lest I should be kidnapped, and carried over into Maryland. My good friend, Dr. FUSSELL, was one of the number who did not think it safe for me to attend an Anti-Slavery meeting along the borders of this State. I can go down there now. I have been down there to see the President; and as you were not there, perhaps you may like to know how the President of the United States received a black man at the White House. I will tell you how he received me — just as you have seen one gentleman receive another (great applause); with a hand and a voice well-balanced between a kind cordiality and a respectful reserve. I tell you I felt big there! (Laughter.) Let me tell you how I got to him; because everybody can't get to him. He has to be a little guarded in admitting spectators. The manner of getting to him gave me an idea that the cause was rolling on. The stairway was crowded with applicants. Some of them looked eager; and I have no doubt some of them had a purpose in being there, and wanted to see the President for the good of the country! They were white; and as I was the only dark spot among them, I expected to have to wait at least half a day; I had heard of men waiting a week; but in two minutes after I sent in my card, the messenger came out, and respectfully invited "Mr. DOUGLASS" in. I could hear, in the eager multitude outside, as they saw me pressing and elbowing my way through, the remark, "Yes, damn it, I knew they would let the nigger through," in a kind of despairing voice — a Peace Democrat, I suppose. (Laughter.) When I went in, the President was sitting in his usual position, I was told, with his feet in different parts of the room, taking it easy. (Laughter.) Don't put this down, Mr. Reporter, I pray you; for I am going down there again to-morrow! (Laughter.) As I came in and approached him, the President began to rise, (laughter,) and he continued rising until he stood over me (laughter); and, reaching out his hand, he said, "Mr. DOUGLASS, I know you; I have read about you, and Mr. SEWARD has told me about you"; putting me quite at ease at once.

Now, you will want to know how I was impressed by him. I will tell you that, too. He impressed me as being just what every one of you have been in the habit of calling him — an honest man. (Applause.) I never met with a man, who, on the first blush, impressed me more entirely with his sincerity, with his devotion to his country, and with his determination to save it at all hazards. (Applause.) He told me (I think he did me more honor than I deserve) that I had made a little speech, somewhere in New York, and it had got into the papers, and among the things I had said was this: That if I were called upon to state what I regarded as the most sad and most disheartening feature in our present political and military situation, it would not be the various disasters experienced by our armies and our navies, on flood and field, but it would be the tardy, hesitating, vacillating policy of the President of the United States; and the President said to me, "Mr. DOUGLASS, I have been charged with being tardy, and the like"; and he went on, and partly admitted that he might seem slow; but he said, "I am charged with vacillating; but, Mr. DOUGLASS, I do not think that charge can be sustained; I think it cannot be shown that when I have once taken a position, I have ever retreated from it." (Applause.) That I regarded as the most significant point in what he said during our interview. I told him that he had been somewhat slow in proclaiming equal protection to our colored soldiers and prisoners; and he said that the country needed talking up to that point. He hesitated in regard to it, when he felt that the country was not ready for it. He knew that the colored man throughout this country was a despised man, a hated man, and that if he at first came out with such a proclamation, all the hatred which is poured on the head of the negro race would be visited on his administration. He said that there was preparatory work needed, and that that preparatory work had now been done. And he said, "Remember this, Mr. DOUGLASS; remember that Milliken's Bend, Port Hudson and Fort Wagner are recent events; and that these were necessary to prepare the way for this very proclamation of mine." I thought it was reasonable, but came to the conclusion that while ABRAHAM LINCOLN will not go down to posterity as ABRAHAM the Great, or as ABRAHAM the Wise, or as

ABRAHAM the Eloquent, although he is all three, wise, great and eloquent, he will go down to posterity, if the country is saved, as Honest ABRAHAM (applause); and going down thus, his name may be written any where in this wide world of ours side by side with that of WASHINGTON, without disparaging the latter. (Renewed applause.)

But we are not to be saved by the captain, at this time, but by the crew. We are not to be saved by ABRAHAM LINCOLN, but by that power behind the throne, greater than the throne itself. You and I and all of us have this matter in hand. Men talk about saving the Union, and restoring the Union as it was. They delude themselves with the miserable idea that that old Union can be brought to life again. That old Union, whose canonized bones we so quietly inurned under the shattered walls of Sumter, can never come to life again. It is dead, and you cannot put life in it. The first ball shot at Sumter caused it to fall as dead as the body of Julius Cæsar, when stabbed by Brutus. We do not want it. We have outlived the old Union. We had outlived it long before the rebellion came to tell us — I mean the Union, under the old pro-slavery interpretation of it — and had become ashamed of it. The South hated it with our anti-slavery interpretation, and the North hated it with the Southern interpretation of its requirements. We had already come to think with horror of the idea of being called upon, here in our churches and literary societies, to take up arms, and go down South and pour the leaden death into the breasts of the slaves, in case they should rise for liberty; and the better part of the people did not mean to do it. They shuddered at the idea of so sacrilegious a crime. They had already become utterly disgusted with the idea of playing the part of bloodhounds for the slave-masters, watch-dogs for the plantations. They had come to detest the principle upon which the Slave States had a larger representation in Congress than the Free States. They had already come to think that the little finger of dear old JOHN BROWN was worth more to the world than all the slaveholders in Virginia put together. (Applause.) What business, then, have we to fight for the old Union? We are not fighting for it. We are fighting for something incomparably better than the old Union. We are fighting for unity; unity of idea, unity of sentiment, unity of object, unity of institutions, in which there shall be no North, no South, no East, no West, no black, no white, but a solidarity of the nation, making every slave free, and every free man a voter. (Great applause.)

TRIBUTE TO GEORGE THOMPSON.

The President.—In 1830, when the great struggle was going on in England for the abolition of slavery in the West Indies, a young man made his appearance in London, and presented himself at the office of the Anti-Slavery Society, proposing to become a lecturer in the field. He was accepted, and went forth and vindicated the right of the slave to his freedom, and held up to the abhorrence of the English people the sin and the shame of West India slavery. Having seen that struggle successfully through, and carried through partly by his own efforts, on invitation from me, I being on that side of the Atlantic at the time, he generously turned his back on his well-won popularity and brightening prospects, and came over to our country to plead the same cause, and for the same class of victims, essentially, to be redeemed from the horrors of slavery, and to help make our land free, great and glorious. He came over in 1834, and was mobbed and hunted like a partridge on the mountains wherever he travelled. His words were irresistible; his eloquence was potent; and the enemies of emancipation knew full well that if he were permitted to have the ear of the people, he would sweep the whole country with the power of Niagara. And therefore they sought his life, and it was with the greatest difficulty that he got out of the country, and that his life was thereby saved.

In 1850, the same noble advocate of freedom ventured once more to come over to America, and make us a visit. He was then a member of Parliament, representing the Tower Hamlets, and his reception was in many respects indicative of a very great and cheering change of public sentiment. Still he was dogged and hooted at, clamored down in public meetings, and every insult was heaped upon him by the enemies of emancipation.

The same individual contemplates coming to our country in the course of the present month, to begin the joyous new year with us, and to give us his congratulations in view of the progress of our glorious cause, and once more look into the faces of his old friends. (Applause.) I therefore offer the following resolution to the Society:

Resolved, That this meeting, learning that it is the purpose of our honored and well-tried trans-Atlantic friend and coadjutor, George Thompson, soon to revisit this country, extends to him in advance fraternal welcome and warm congratulation; and, voluntarily consecrating himself, as he has done, for nearly three years past, in the most generous, disinterested and self-sacrificing manner, to the service of our country and the support of the American Government, and to the work of thwarting the insidious machinations of rebel emissaries abroad, and stimulating the popular sentiment of England to proclaim its abhorrence of this accursed Slaveholders' Rebellion, and to compel the British Government to withhold all recognition of the independence of the Southern Confederacy, we feel that we may assure him, in behalf of all loyal men in the country, a grateful recognition of his patriotic services, and a flattering ovation wherever he may have an opportunity to address them.

The resolution was unanimously adopted.

TRIBUTE TO BENJAMIN LUNDY.

The President. During our meetings, our friends have been giving reminiscences; and if you will allow me, for a moment, to revert to the past, I will tell you how I became an Abolitionist, that honor may be given to whom honor is due, to one whose memory ought to be preserved to the latest generation as the distinguished pioneer in this great struggle.

In 1827, I went to Boston, and edited a paper called *The National Philanthropist*. It was devoted to the cause of Temperance. Up to that hour, I had known little or nothing of slavery, as to the number of slaves held, or as to where they were held. So completely had the whole question been put out of sight, that I was almost wholly ignorant in respect to it. Among my exchange papers I received a little dingy monthly periodical, called the *Genius of Universal Emancipation*, published in the city of Baltimore, by BENJAMIN LUNDY, a member of the Society of Friends. On reading it, my attention was instantly arrested, and my interest strongly awakened. I was beginning to be initiated in the broad and good work of reform. As I read it, my heart was touched, and my understanding enlightened. I wrote for my paper a friendly notice of the publication, and again and again referred to it. After a little while, who should knock at the door of our house but BENJAMIN LUNDY, from Baltimore, very desirous to see me, on an anti-slavery mission to Boston? Then I had an opportunity to become personally acquainted with him, and from his own lips to gain that information of which I was so destitute. He warmed my heart and fired my spirit; and I did at that time all I could to facilitate the object of his visit by getting up anti-slavery meetings for him, obtaining subscribers for his paper, etc., etc.

In 1828, I went to Bennington, Vt., and edited a paper called *The Journal of the Times*, which was in part a political and in part a reformatory paper. When the gentlemen came to me from Vermont to see if I would edit the paper, they told me it was to be in support of the election of JOHN QUINCY ADAMS as against ANDREW JACKSON; and as I was decidedly in favor of Mr. ADAMS, and had some distrust of military men, I could readily accede to their views. But I said, Gentlemen, if I go, I must have the liberty of advocating in the columns of the paper the Anti-Slavery cause, the Temperance cause, the Peace cause, and the cause of Moral Reform. It was a very singular kind of political paper; but they gave me *carte blanche*, and I agreed to undertake the enterprise. The anti-slavery feeling which I had imbibed in Boston was growing more and more in my soul, and I wrote more and more on that subject for my paper. The consequence was, that one day who should present himself again at my door but BENJAMIN LUNDY, of Baltimore? He had taken his staff in hand, and travelled all the way to the Green Mountains. He came to lay it on my conscience and my soul that I should join him in this work of seeking the abolition of slavery; and he so presented the case, with the growing disposition that I had to take hold of the cause, that I said to him, " I will join you as soon as my engagement ends here; and then we will see what can be done."

The proposition upon his part was, that we should convert the little monthly into a large and handsome weekly paper. I was to be the principal editor, while he was to be a travelling editor and lecturer, for the purpose of diffusing information and getting subscribers. But he did not assist me a great deal in that way, because, as soon as I got to Baltimore, I had my eyes opened in regard to the absurdity and delusion of gradual emancipation; and I said to my friend LUNDY, " If I join you now, I must hoist the banner of immediate, unconditional, everlasting emancipation." (Applause.) He said, " Very well; write as you choose; and as you feel that you must go for Immediate Emancipation, put your initials to your articles, and I will put my initials to mine; and then the readers will know how to divide the responsibility between us." To this I agreed. But I drove off subscribers four or five times as fast as he could get them! From the moment that the doctrine of Immediate Emancipation was enunciated in the columns of the *Genius*, as it had not been up to that hour, it was like a bombshell in the camp of the subscribers themselves; and from every direction letters poured in that they had not bargained for such a paper as that, or for such doctrines, and they desired to have no more copies sent to them. So that the experiment failed, and we had to separate. BENJAMIN LUNDY took his paper, and had it transformed again into a little monthly, which afterwards passed from his hands, and became *The Pennsylvania Freeman*.

Now, if I have in any way, however humble, done any thing toward calling attention to the question of slavery, or bringing about the glorious prospect of a complete jubilee in our country at no distant day, I feel that I owe every thing in this matter, instrumentally, and under GOD, to BENJAMIN LUNDY. For had it not been for him, I know not where I should have been at the present time. My eyes might have been sealed for my whole lifetime, and, possibly, though I trust in GOD I could not have been, I might have been led off, in some direction or other, so far as even to care nothing for slavery in our country. I feel it due to the memory of one who devoted so many years of his life so faithfully to the cause of the oppressed, that I should state this reminiscence.

Mr. GARRISON, after paying this tribute to Mr. LUNDY, closed his address as follows:—

It has been very pleasant to me to see how united we have been all the way through this meeting; not one, apparently, disposed to censure any thing said here in favor of universal liberty. It is very pleasant indeed to my spirit. Sometimes, I know, eggs and brickbats are to be preferred to popular good-will and approval. Sometimes popular good-will and approval are to be preferred to rotten eggs and brickbats. Other things being equal, popular good-will and approval are preferable to brickbats and rotten eggs. As no principle has been compromised, as we have been faithful to our duty, as we have endeavored to remember those in bonds as bound with them, it is cheering to see this large assembly, and the tens and hundreds of thousands elsewhere, all mingling together, forgetting the things that are behind, and pressing onward to the mark of our high calling—immediate and everlasting emancipation. (Applause.)

Two or three questions, and I conclude: Do you wish to see this rebellion put down? [VOICES — "Yes," "Yes."] What is it in this country that has rebelled? Is it freedom? ["No."] Then it is slavery that is in rebellion, is it not? ["Yes."] Are you for the abolition of slavery? ["Yes," "Yes."] So am I; it is a unanimous vote. Amen and amen; glory, hallelujah! (Applause.) In carrying this thing through, though at first it must be through the desolation of war by the depravity and fiendish obstinacy of the South, carrying it through will not be to curse the South, but to bless her with freedom and free institutions, free speech, a free press, free men, and free laborers, to open the windows of heaven, and to cause GOD to pour down his blessings, so that there shall not be room to contain them. O, the glorious prospect beyond this war! — the glorious hope of thus repaying the South for her oppression, not with vengeance, but with love and good-will! We are struggling to save the slaveholders as men. We are struggling to redeem the slaves as men. In their redemption, the land shall be redeemed, and GOD shall be our GOD, and peace shall be all through our borders, from the Atlantic to the Pacific, and there shall be none to molest or to make afraid. Our work is before us, not completed, as has well and often been said to-day. It is going on. We will not yield one jot or tittle; we will not grow weary until every slave is free.

> "Gray Plymouth Rock hath yet a tongue,
> And Concord is not dumb;
> And voices from our fathers' graves
> And from the future come;
> They call on us to stand our ground;
> They charge us still to be
> Not only free from chains ourselves,
> But foremost to make free."

ANNE DICKINSON followed with a glowing and eloquent appeal, of which, as we have no adequate report, we will not attempt to give a sketch. Suffice it to say, that she was received with great enthusiasm, and that her remarks gave great pleasure to the crowded assembly.

The Society then adjourned, *sine die*.

ANNALS OF WOMEN'S ANTI-SLAVERY SOCIETIES.

BY MARY GREW, OF PHILADELPHIA.*

The trumpet-call which, thirty years ago, summoned the American people to moral warfare against the system of American slavery, aroused in the souls of a few earnest women a consciousness of personal responsibility for the existence of that great national sin, and a consciousness of power to promote its overthrow. They clearly perceived, both intellectually and spiritually, that the truth of the inherent sinfulness of slavery, and the correlative right and duty between the slave and his master of immediate emancipation, were the only principles which could permanently vivify an enterprise for the destruction of a system intimately inwrought with the political, religious, and social life of the nation. Their first step was to organize themselves for effective effort for the promulgation of these truths.

Previous to the organization of the American Anti-Slavery Society, two Female Anti-Slavery Societies were formed in Massachusetts; the first, in Reading, in the month of March, 1833; the second, in Boston, in October of the same year. In December following, the Philadelphia Female Anti-Slavery Society was organized, and at about the same time, the Female Anti-Slavery Society of Amesbury, Mass. During the few years immediately following, numerous State, County, and City Anti-Slavery Societies were formed throughout the Free States, both East and West, and among them were many organizations of women. Of these were the Concord, Lynn, Providence, Brooklyn, New York, Pittsburg, and Massillon Female Anti-Slavery Societies. All these associations were auxiliary in fact, and many of them in name, to the American Anti-Slavery Society; based upon the same principles, working with the same measures, and inspired by the same hope. An examination of early anti-slavery records reveals the fact that many of these women were active and influential members of churches of various denominations, who brought into this new enterprise the energy, zeal, and executive ability acquired in their ecclesiastical and moral training; and that they began their work in confident faith that a general dissemination of the truth relative to the character of American slavery would speed-

---

* This paper was read to the Society, by Miss Grew, on the afternoon of the first day of the meeting.

ily array the power of these churches against a system essentially anti-Christian. It cannot be claimed for them that they counted the cost of the warfare upon which they were entering, nor the number of the years which lay stretched out in the dim future, between their first battle and their final victory. It was well for them, well for the cause to which they had vowed allegiance, that this knowledge lay beyond their reach. The soul that would not have fainted or faltered before the prefigured vision of that long period of toil and strife, was, yet, stronger for the buoyant hope of early victory, and addressed itself to the labors of each successive year all the more ardently for the bright possibility that its close might usher in the jubilee.

As they went on, they found their work widening, their responsibility deepening, at every step. It is now a page of history, it was then a startling revelation daily made, a painful experience daily borne, that the churches which had nurtured their sons and daughters on the *words* of Christian love and human brotherhood, had no desire to see them practically illustrated towards the slave or the negro. With more of keen disappointment and sorrow than of indignation did we look on the strange spectacle of the American Church standing by to keep the garments of an enraged populace, stoning the Stephens of that martyr age.

In October, 1835, the Boston Female Anti-Slavery Society learned what was the degree of free speech which Massachusetts would allow and protect. Their announcement of their Annual Meeting to be held at Congress Hall for the transaction of business, elicited threatening and scurrilous articles from the daily newspapers, indirectly invoking popular violence upon the anticipated meeting. Alarmed by these indications, the proprietor of the Hall refused to open it, and the meeting was necessarily postponed. That was a critical hour for the slave in the South, for freedom of speech in the North, and for the friends of both. In itself, it was a question of little importance whether a small and obscure Society should hold, publicly or privately, a meeting for the transaction of its business. Viewed with reference to its *immediate* consequences only, it seemed that obstinacy and folly would counsel the former, and wisdom the latter course. But the Boston Female Anti-Slavery Society, in deciding this question, looked beneath the surface of things, looked beyond the present hour. They knew that they stood that day, in Boston, the representatives, not only of two and a half millions of American slaves calling for help in the name of Justice, but, also, of the right of freedom of speech and of the press in the Free States of America. They could not estimate then, we cannot compute now, the immense, far-reaching consequences for good or evil, which hung on that decision. From the records of those soul-trying scenes, we learn that one question was asked and answered by their own souls, and their path of duty lay clearly revealed: "Upon whom dare those call to resist the popular voice, who have themselves been silenced by its tumult?"

Then followed the public advertisement of their meeting, and their assembling at No. 46 Washington street, on that memorable 21st of October, 1833, when that famous mob of "gentlemen of property and standing" assaulted them with violence, and the Mayor of Boston told them that he had no power to protect such a meeting.

These events stand out, with prominence, in a review of the life, now become history, of the Women's Anti-Slavery Societies of this country; for they were the commencement of a long course of struggles against tyranny, and resistance to popular clamor in the advocacy of the slave's right to personal and political freedom.

A few years later, Anti-Slavery Women instituted an Annual Convention, to be composed of delegates from their various Societies, the object of which was "to interest women in the subject of anti-slavery, and to establish a system of operations throughout every town and village which should exert a powerful influence in the abolition of American slavery."

The first of this series of Conventions was held in the city of New York, in May, 1837. The Resolutions adopted and the Addresses and Letters issued by that body indicate the wide scope which our enterprise had, at that period, attained; and evince a clear apprehension of its growing demands, and a strong and solemn purpose to meet them faithfully.

The second of these Conventions was held in Philadelphia, in May, 1838, during that well-remembered week when the Slave Power ruled this city, and its vassals sought to appease it by a burnt-offering of a Temple of Liberty. Women who sat in their imperilled houses that day, thinking on the National inheritance awaiting their children, read, by the light of those fires, new lessons of duty to their country and their race. That Convention, driven from one place of meeting to another, at last assembled in a school-room, which was opened to them by one who regarded the security of private property as of less importance than the defence of a great moral principle. The records of their closing session show that in the midst of their own fiery trials, and their sympathetic sufferings with our colored fellow-citizens who were victims of popular fury, they were jubilant over the triumph of Liberty in the British West Indies, the glad tidings of which were then resounding through our land; and were strong in faith and hope of the emancipation of the American slave. Another fact is clearly revealed by the records of these Conventions. It is that Abolitionists long clung, tenaciously, to the American Church, cherishing the belief that there was spiritual vitality enough in it to exorcise the spirit of slavery; and that it was with great reluctance that, after earnest and persistent efforts to arouse this vitality, they were convinced that the great body of the American Church was so thoroughly corrupted, by its alliances with slavery, that separation from it was a Christian duty.

The third Convention assembled in Philadelphia, in May, 1839, and occupied the building of the Pennsylvania Riding School, which, the Minutes tell us, was the only building of sufficient size which could be procured in the city for that purpose. The Mayor of the city, alarmed for the safety of the public peace, called upon LUCRETIA MOTT, and offered several suggestions for the conduct of the Convention, which he thought might aid in warding off threatened danger. It is interesting, now, to read that conversation, eminently characteristic of the two parties represented by the colloquists.

We find on the Minutes of this Convention a Resolution of adjournment to meet in the city of Boston in the year 1840. But the adjourned meeting was never held, and the third was the last of this series of Conventions.

The informing spirit of the Anti-Slavery enterprise had been leading its followers in a way which they knew not. Opening their eyes to one truth, and setting their hands with earnest purpose to one course of action, they soon perceived the scope of their vision broadening, and new fields of labor spreading out before them. Women whose souls burned with indignation against the monstrous injustice of slaveholding, or melted in pity for the slave, began to plead the cause of emancipation in public assemblies of men and women; and men, working heartily and zealously in the same cause, discovered

that, as concert of action between men and women was important to
success, so mutual counsel and discussion in their business meetings
were convenient and profitable. The American Anti-Slavery Society, at its Annual Meeting in 1840, decided for itself that such
mutual conference was right and expedient, and thenceforward women shared with men the management of its business, spoke from its
platform, and were commissioned as its lecturing agents. Anti-Slavery Conventions composed exclusively of women were no longer
needed, as they served no purpose which was not better served on a
broader basis of operation. Some of our Women's Anti-Slavery
Societies retained their distinct organization, and others were gradually merged in State or County Societies.

Two Institutions established by the Boston and Philadelphia Female Anti-Slavery Societies, and which became very important auxiliaries in our cause, have a prominent place in the scenes which we are
reviewing. These are the series of Annual Fairs commenced in Boston in the year 1835, and in Philadelphia in 1836. The former soon
passed from a Metropolitan into a National Institution; and the latter, in the progress of years, became in fact and in name the Pennsylvania Anti-Slavery Fair, though they continued under the control
and management of their originators. These have been of vast importance to our cause, in furnishing pecuniary support to the organ
of the National Society, and to other instrumentalities by which our
work has been done. And independently of such service, they have
been of immense value as mediums of moral influence. Their social
attractions brought many young persons within the hearing of anti-
slavery truth; the opportunity of *working* for the objects of their
sympathy crystallized sentiment into principle; the annual gatherings
of the old and young, the veterans and the neophytes of our ranks,
in scenes where the freedom of social intercourse mingled with the
spirit of an anti-slavery meeting, were Passover Festivals, whither
"our tribes went up" with gladness, and found refreshment and
strength. Occasionally they became mediums of strength to our
souls by a sterner ministration. There were times when the populace,
consenting to be the tool of the Slave Power, demanded the suppression of these Fairs, and the municipal authority sympathized with a
lawless mob, or shrank from the duty of opposing it. Four years
ago, some of you stood in this Hall in very different circumstances
from these which surround us to-day. Then, the banner which we

hung out from its walls disturbed the peace of Philadelphia, because it bade the nation " Proclaim liberty throughout all the land, to all the inhabitants thereof." Some of you well remember that remarkable conference which we held in the centre of this room, standing with the officers of the law, who were in most uncomfortable strait betwixt their sense of obligation to do what they were bidden, and their reluctance to perform the disgraceful errand on which they had been sent. On that occasion, our opponents succeeded in ejecting the Pennsylvania Anti-Slavery Fair from this Hall, and the doors of another were immediately opened to it, by one of our citizens, who, in the darkest and stormiest days of our conflict, *never* closed those doors against us.

Many of you remember, also, the yet more trying circumstances in which this Fair was held a year later, when the anticipation of the dissolution of the Union had alarmed the commercial classes in the North, and the suppression of an Anti-Slavery Bazaar was regarded by some of our citizens as an opportune peace-offering to the South, and we were once more called to stand for the defence of the people's right of peaceful assemblage. The vigilance of our Mayor and his officers frustrated the purpose of the mob; and we regarded the maintenance of our right thus to assemble the chief success of our Fair of 1860.

The Philadelphia Female Anti-Slavery Society has preserved its distinct organization, and now awaits, with its coadjutors of the past thirty years, the hour when the shout of final victory shall burst from all our host, proclaiming that the work of the American Abolitionists is accomplished. That hour draws nigh. At the close of thirty years of warfare, we stand to-day in the midst of national convulsion—of a great moral revolution. Old things have passed away, and we hear a voice out of heaven proclaiming, "Behold, I make all things new!" The long and weary hours of darkness passed, we look around us, and

> " Lo! our foemen of the night
> Are brothers at the dawn of day."

Our watchwords are caught by other lips, and echoed through the land. Our Banner of Emancipation clings to the flag-staff of the Stars and Stripes, and soon will wave as broadly over the nation. " Who knoweth not that the hand of the Lord hath wrought this?"

Verily, it is fitting that we, who, side by side, have toiled and fought for thirty years, should come hither to-day, to grasp one another's hands in fraternal congratulation, and to unite our unutterable thanksgivings that America's Day of Jubilee has dawned, and its sun is high in the heavens. With its glory streaming down upon us, and the song of our ransomed brethren in our ears, we bow in adoration before the Power and Wisdom and Love which is guiding this mighty revolution, and cry: "Thy will be done on earth as it is done in heaven."

APPENDIX.

LETTER FROM JOHN JAY, ESQ.

To Messrs. J. M. McKim, *and others, Committee of the American Anti-Slavery Society:*

GENTLEMEN, — It is with regret that I find myself unable to accept the invitation with which you have honored me to assist at the celebration of your Thirtieth Anniversary.

The term of a generation has elapsed since that eventful assemblage at Philadelphia in 1833, and we who survive are permitted to see the great objects which were then proposed in the course of rapid accomplishment.

Slavery has already ceased to have a constitutional or legal existence in the rebel States, and the faith of the National Government and the American people has been solemnly pledged to that act, by the Commander-in-Chief of our Army and Navy; and at his command, also, rightfully issued under the same war power and on grounds of military necessity, the colored people are being raised to the rank of soldiers and citizens. But we cannot overlook the fact that these objects of our life-long devotion are being effected by other arguments than the narrow constitutional means and moral suasion to which the founders of your Society so rigidly limited its efforts.

Man proposes, but God orders; and it was ordained that the Slave Power of America, hardening its heart like its prototype of Egypt, and raising its bloody hand against the American people, to the end that it might erect a slave empire on the ruins of our Republic, should, by its own act, forfeit the constitutional guarantees by which it was protected, and should itself invite its extinguishment by the tramp of armies and the crash of battle. While the slaveholders in their madness have thus inaugurated a war in which slavery is to perish, it is to be remembered that their allies at the North persistently allured them to their doom.

The first gun aimed against Sumter, and which sounded the knell of slavery, would never have been fired but for the assurance given by Democratic leaders at the North, who believed the masses to be as rotten as themselves, that they would assist the rebels in revolutionizing the government; and when the war had progressed for nearly two years, these rebel sympathizers, foiled in their effort to convince the nation that it had no right to defend its existence, attempted to stay the national arm by discouraging volunteering at the North, and so compelled the President to call upon the black man to assist in maintaining our constitutional integrity. How promptly that call has been responded to, how gallantly he has done his duty as a soldier at Port Hudson, Milliken's Bend, and Fort Wagner, and how popular the scheme of enlisting colored troops has become, from the simple fact, that every black man who joins the army enables a white man to stay at home, are matters familiar to us all; and we can hardly fail to admire the inscrutable ways of Providence, as we wonderingly behold the abolition of slavery and the elevation of the colored race, for which we had labored for a quarter of a century with such small success, now being rapidly and effectually accomplished through the agency of JEFFERSON DAVIS, Mr. VALLANDIGHAM, and Gov. SEYMOUR. He maketh, says Holy Writ, the wrath of man to praise Him, and the remainder of wrath shall He restrain.

A time so full of excitement as the present is not the most fitting for a calm review of the history of the Society, whose birth you are met to celebrate; and yet, as our work is so nearly finished, and your next decade will probably dawn upon the American continent unpolluted by the footstep of a slave, it may be well now to recal the political principles declared in the Constitution of your Society, as established at Philadelphia, and reäffirmed in the face of the malignant persecutions to which its early members were subjected. They are not to be lightly overlooked by the future historian of America; for when the story of their struggle is truly told, there will be no brighter page in American history than that which records their pure philanthropy, their intelligent patriotism, their wise statesmanship, their moral courage, and their heroic defence of Christian principle and constitutional right against the domineering power of an overwhelming and brutal majority.

If the founders of the American Anti-Slavery Society must yield to JEFFERSON DAVIS and his confreres, so far as the merit goes of organizing a thoroughly efficient project of immediate abolition, by so much as the bayonet and the bullet, iron-clads and monitors, Greek-fire and swamp angels are more convincing arguments than slow appeals to the conscience and the reason — especially when the one is blunted and the other perverted — they need yield to none in the claim which their children will make for them, that they were the exemplars of that spirit of devotion to Christian truth and American principle that to-day like a halo enwraps our country, and unites us in a common resolve to maintain, at whatever cost, against Southern slavery and European neutrality, the unity, the greatness, and the freedom of our Republic.

I am aware that this view differs somewhat from the portrait which has been usually painted of American Abolitionists; that they have been pictured as disunionists, amalgamationists and incendiaries, anxious to interfere with slavery in defiance of the Constitution, and to incite servile insurrection without regard to humanity. But who was the painter of these darkly shadowed and distorted features?

The Slave Power, disguised as a conservator of the Constitution, and attempting to escape the issue which we tendered by inventing fraudulent side issues. Now that the Slave Power is stripped of the mask under which it dared to impeach the patriotism of the Abolitionists, the American people will at their leisure review the charges which many of them have long believed.

One quality is already accorded to them, even by their intelligent opponents, and that is, moral courage, indomitable pluck. A handful of men, without power, wealth, or official influence, they arrayed themselves against American slavery, reigning supreme in Church and State, as did the English Quakers against the British slave trade; and although they had none other than moral weapons and an armory of facts, the Slave Power recognized them at once as an adversary to be feared and to be crushed; for it dreaded, as was frankly admitted, their influence not simply with the people of the North, but upon the consciences of the slaveholders themselves.

The members of your Society were compelled to meet the furious onset of the Slave Power almost from the moment of their organization. Villified by a slaveholding President, whose message they answered with a protest of great dignity and force; denounced in both Houses of Congress by slaveholders and their tools; slandered by a demoralized press; derided from the bench; sneered at by the bar, and damned from the pulpit; hooted at in political and religious conventions; tabood in would-be-aristocratic circles; threatened with legislative pains and penalties for exercising their constitutional prerogatives; howled at by ruffian mobs, their houses sacked, their churches invaded, their presses destroyed, their liberties violated, they maintained their integrity with undaunted front, yielding no iota of principle, but grandly fulfilling the injunction, "Stand like a beaten anvil!" Every new outrage, as they multiplied throughout the North, such as the dragging of a clergyman from his pulpit in New Hampshire, and his sentence, by a convenient magistrate, as a common brawler, to fifteen days' hard labor, for having preached an anti-slavery sermon; or the leading of Mr. Garrison, that early and faithful pioneer of freedom, about the streets of Boston with a rope around his body, amid the plaudits of "gentlemen of property and standing"; or the murder of the brave Lovejoy, forerunner of the countless thousands since murdered by the same accursed power; so far from intimidating the Abolitionists, only inspired them with a sterner determination to rescue the country from the ruffianism of slavery, and they stood, and on the page of history will for ever stand, the successful champions of those constitutional rights, freedom of conscience and of speech, freedom of the press and of debate, and the right of petition.

In vindicating the founders of the Society from the charges preferred against them by the slaveholders, and on the strength of which they were so bitterly persecuted—charges which were swallowed with disgraceful credulity by willing dupes, and which even now are sometimes repeated by men who lay claim to an ordinary degree of intelligence—it is necessary to refer to some historical facts, in order that the opinions of individuals or of societies at a later date may not be confounded with the principles, pledges and conduct of the national organization formed at Philadelphia.

The principal charges on which its founders were arraigned were these:

1. That they disregarded and repudiated the Constitution of the United States.
2. That they were in favor of a dissolution of the Union.
3. That they advocated the right of Congress to abolish slavery in the States.
4. That they favored marriages between blacks and whites.
5. That they approved of and incited insurrection among the slaves.

When the Anti-Slavery Convention met at Philadelphia, Judge JAY, who was prevented from attending as a delegate, urged upon them, by letter, the necessity of an explicit declaration of their political principles, to meet the baseless charges already made against them.

The first number of *The Emancipator* had shortly before announced that "constitutional restrictions, independently of other considerations, forbid all other than moral interference with slavery in the Southern States;" and the Convention incorporated three distinct propositions in the Constitution of the American Anti-Slavery Society:

1. That each State in which slavery exists has, by the Constitution of the United States, the exclusive right to legislate in regard to abolition in that State.
2. That they would endeavor, in a constitutional way, to influence Congress to put an end to the domestic slave trade, and to abolish slavery in the District of Columbia, and likewise to prevent the extension of slavery to any State that might thereafter be admitted to the Union.
3. That the Society would never in any way countenance the oppressed in vindicating their rights by resorting to physical force.

Under this Constitution and these distinct pledges, the Society rapidly increased in numbers, strength and influence. Its lecturers, agents, newspapers and publications aroused the country, and auxiliary societies sprang up far and near, numbering in 1836, 527; in 1837, 1,006; in 1838, 1,256; and in 1839, 1,650 auxiliaries had adopted the principles of its Constitution.

It was to crush anti-slavery effort under these clearly-defined limitations that mobs were inaugurated, in 1834, to sack churches and houses in New York, and to insult Mr. GARRISON in Boston, and "conservative meetings" were held in various Northern cities, "to consign to execration" the Abolitionists as "abandoned knaves and hypocrites."

In 1835, the Board of your Society issued an address to the public, for the advisement of those who had been led to believe that they

" were pursuing measures at variance not only with the constitutional rights of the South, but with the precepts of humanity and religion."

The address was signed by ARTHUR TAPPAN, President, and also by JOHN RANKIN, WILLIAM JAY, ELIZUR WRIGHT, A. L. COX, LEWIS TAPPAN, SAM. E. CORNISH, S. S. JOSSELYN, and THEODORE S. WRIGHT. As it excited marked attention both in America and in Europe, and is the fullest official exposition of the views of the Society, you will perhaps allow me to quote briefly its several heads. They were as follows:

1. That Congress has no more right to abolish slavery in the Southern States than in the French West India Islands.

2. That the exercise of any other than moral influence to induce abolition by the State Legislatures would be unconstitutional.

3. That Congress had the right to abolish slavery in the District of Columbia, and that it was their duty to efface so foul a stain from the national escutcheon.

4. That American citizens have the right to express and publish their opinions of the Constitution, laws and institutions of any and every State and nation under heaven, and "we never intend to surrender the liberty of speech, of the press, or of conscience—blessings we have inherited from our fathers, and which we mean, so far as we are able, to transmit unimpaired to our children."

5. That they had uniformly deprecated all forcible attempts on the part of the slaves to recover their freedom.

6. That they would deplore any servile insurrection, on account of the calamities that would attend it, and the occasion it might give for increased severity.

7. That the charge that they had sent publications to the South, designed to incite the slaves to insurrection, was utterly and unequivocally false.

8. That the charge that they had sent any publications to the slaves was false.

9. That they had employed no agents in the Slave States to distribute their publications.

10. They reiterated their conviction that slavery was sinful, and injurious to the country, and that immediate abolition would be both safe and wise, and that they had no intention of refraining from the expression of such views in future.

11. They reiterated their views in reference to the elevation of the colored people.

12. "We are accused of acts that tend to a dissolution of the Union, and even of wishing to destroy it. We have never calculated 'the value of the Union,' because we believe it to be INESTIMABLE, and that the abolition of slavery will remove the chief danger of its dissolution."

In conclusion, they said: "Such, fellow-citizens, are our principles. Are they unworthy of Republicans and of Christians?" And, after referring to the unconstitutional usurpation of the government to protect slavery, and to prevent free discussion and the freedom of the mails, they closed with the prophetic warning: "Surely, we need not remind you that if you submit to such an encroachment on your liberties, the days of our Republic are numbered; and that although Abolitionists may be the first, they will not be the last victims offered at the shrine of arbitrary power."

As the country, under the stirring appeals and startling facts put forth by the American Society, its auxiliaries and its members, awoke to a new appreciation of the evils and dangers of slavery to the Republic as well as to the slave, some earnest Abolitionists, stung by a sense of its excessive wrong, and unwilling to await the slow remedy of moral suasion, or limited Congressional interference, sought to find some shorter method of accomplishing its destruction. Here and there, one inclined to the belief that Congress could constitutionally abolish it; others, that its very existence was unconstitutional, and should be so declared by the Supreme Court; and a few, at a later period, that it could be effected only by a dissolution of the Union.

But all of these suggestions were absolutely irreconcilable with the Constitution adopted in Philadelphia. In 1838, the late ALVAN STEWART, Esq., of Utica, attempted to change that Constitution by an elaborate argument in favor of the right of Congress to abolish slavery in the States, and the proposed amendment was urged with great vigor and eloquence; but it was as vigorously resisted, as unsound in principle and inconsistent with good faith, and the attempt signally failed.

In the same year, the Massachusetts Society reconsidered some resolution that had been hastily adopted, and resolved, "That Congress has no power to abolish slavery in the several States of this Union."

The same year, Mr. ELLIS GRAY LORING wrote to Judge JAY, from Boston: "I know of but one or two persons here who believe in the power of Congress over slavery in the States."

With the division that occurred a year or two later in the American Society, the removal of the old Board to Boston, and the formation in New York of the American and Foreign Anti-Slavery Society, the national unity of the organization was broken, and widely differing views began to be expressed by anti-slavery men, who did not hold to the principles declared at Philadelphia, upon the religious and political bearings of the question.

Prominent individuals divided upon the status of slavery, and the best mode of overthrowing it; and neither the Liberty party, headed by those veteran Abolitionists, GERRIT SMITH and WILLIAM GOODELL, nor WENDELL PHILLIPS, the golden-mouthed exponent of the views entertained at Boston, fairly represented the constitutional principles defined by the American Society, and adopted by nearly two thousand auxiliary associations.

But—and this is an historic fact of interest and importance—as the increasing insolence and usurpation of the Slave Power induced the conviction that if the Abolitionists had commenced the struggle to obtain freedom for the slave, the American people must continue it to preserve their own; and with their characteristic common sense, the people devoted themselves to the task of overthrowing its power and checking its extension, and organized for the purpose, under the wise lead of Abolitionists, in 1855, the Republican party. They incorporated into that platform the identical constitutional principles on which, thirty years ago, the American Anti-Slavery Society took its stand.

On these principles, for the holding of which we and our fathers were denounced as incendiaries and fanatics, FREMONT was nominated and LINCOLN was elected; and the sufficiency of those principles—the restriction of slavery extension, the abolition of slavery in the District, and of the inter-State slave trade, and the emancipation of the National Government from the control of the Slave Power—to cripple and eventually to destroy slavery, was significantly recognized by the slaveholders themselves when they resolved, some twenty-five or thirty years ago, that the instant those principles were triumphant in the National Government, they would anticipate the overthrow of slavery by overthrowing the Republic.

Prejudices deeply seated may obscure, perhaps, for another generation, the credit due to the gentlemen whose careful action in convention you are met to celebrate; but the candid historian will admit that they exhibited not a blind devotion to the cause of the slave. but a conscientious regard to the integrity of the Constitution, and the welfare and happiness of the country. He will record that it was the Abolitionists who, avoiding all infringement on the constitutional rights of the slaveholders, would allow no infringement on their own, and that to them belongs the honor of vindicating the right of petition, and maintaining against brute violence and legislative menace freedom of speech and of the press. While he will be compelled to acknowledge that in many things they were defeated, that they opposed unsuccessfully the Seminole war and the annexation of Texas under the late rebel JOHN TYLER, that they failed in arresting that most wicked war waged by the Slave Power against Mexico under JAMES K. POLK, and that accursed act, the Fugitive Slave Bill, under the renegade Abolitionist, MILLARD FILLMORE, and the removal, under FRANKLIN PIERCE, of the ancient landmark fixed by the Missouri Compromise, he may say with truth, that they checkmated the Slave Power under JAMES BUCHANAN in its efforts to force slavery into Kansas, and that they for ever terminated its usurped supremacy upon the continent, when, defeating the traitors BELL and BRECKINRIDGE, they elected as President ABRAHAM LINCOLN.

Whatever errors of opinion or of action there may have been on the part of individuals or societies at a recent date, the political principles declared at Philadelphia have stood the test of time and trial, and have received the emphatic endorsement of the American people; and the Anti-Slavery movement in the United States, with few exceptions that more plainly show the rule, has been marked by statesmanlike characteristics, now crowned with success, and by a love of country that no delay, injustice or disappointment could impair or disturb.

Their progress was not always observed by the unobservant, and we heard occasionally that Abolition was dead; but when the hour came that the Slave Power, drunken with blood and insolent with oppression, deemed itself strong enough to destroy the Republic, anticipating an easy victory by the aid of its fellow-traitors in the North, the hour had come also, although they knew it not, when the loyal American people were educated to that point of patriotism, pluck and constitutional strength, that they were able to meet the blow, treacherously as it was given, and to return it with a vigor that is sending slavery and the rebellion to a common grave.

It is an interesting fact, that while the rebel slaveholders, who still regard as their friends the Peace Democrats and conditional Unionists at the North, who veil their treason under very thin disguise, both slaveholders and slaves, long before the Proclamation of Emancipation, foresaw the inevitable issue of the contest; and BEAUREGARD came much nearer the truth than he has sometimes done, when he forbade his rebel troops to call by any other name than Abolitionist, every soldier who followed the old flag of his country, keeping step to the music of the Union, and ready to die in its defence.

As we recall reverently the dead upon your roll of those who met at Philadelphia, to issue what has since proven to be a second Declaration of Independence, let us remember also, tenderly, our brave heroes, who, slain by slavery, sleep beneath the battle-fields of the Republic, and their comrades, our sons and brothers, who now maintain against that inhuman power the integrity, the supremacy, and the honor of our country.

Always, gentlemen, most faithfully yours,

JOHN JAY.

LETTER FROM ARCHIBALD A. McINTYRE.

PHILADELPHIA, Dec. 1, 1863.

J. M. McKIM, ESQ.:

DEAR SIR,— A kind invitation was received to attend a meeting of your Society, to be held on the 3d and 4th inst.

While I have to decline it because of pressing engagements, I cannot but express my full conviction in the complete success of a cause, which, like yours, is right in itself, and which is sought to be promoted by instrumentalities only which are sanctioned by law, morality and religion. Efforts made to reform, based on " the conviction and repentance " of the wrong-doer, must in the end succeed, particularly when that wrong-doer is a community.

Very respectfully, yours,

ARCHIBALD A. McINTYRE.

LETTER FROM REV. CHARLES G. AMES.

ALBANY, N. Y., Dec. 1, 1863.

DEAR MR. GARRISON:

I greatly wish I could accept your kind invitation to be one of the favored many who will meet in Holy Convocation at Philadelphia this week: much more might I wish myself worthy to be counted as one of those who, by bearing the burden and heat of the day, have been the instruments of Higher Wisdom in bringing the Good Time so near. But as one born out of due time—as one born too late to be a worker in the earlier and more trying days when "not crime itself was so fatal to a man as to be known to hold abolition sentiments"—I do most heartily rejoice that other men have labored with such rich results. As I give thanks to God for all good, so do I thank him for the American Abolitionists, and for their noble work, which has made a true Republic—a Christian Commonwealth—possible in America. Of all the warriors which this continent has produced, from sturdy MILES STANDISH down to UNCONDITIONAL-SURRENDER GRANT, I should most delight to crown with garlands of honor the brave men and women who have fought through the Thirty Years' War with Slavery.

Though I have never thought it wise or necessary to burn down our political house in order to clear it of vermin—though I have always believed that "Union" would sooner or later be understood to mean "Liberty"—yet I have also rejoiced to recognize that deep conservatism which has ever been at the bottom of all anti-slavery radicalism, and have been captivated by that sublime faith in God and Truth, and the Brotherhood of all Human Interests, which has not ceased, through all these dreary years, to cry aloud in the ears of this guilty nation, "Let justice be done, and the heavens *won't* fall!"

I join with you in thanking God for the victories of the Past, and also in taking courage for the battles of the Future. For *there is much heavy work waiting to be done.* In the first place, we must clinch the nail already driven, by maintaining the legal validity and securing the practical efficiency of the Great Proclamation. The highest military authority, pressed by an unparalleled national crisis, has done what JOHN QUINCY ADAMS said any General might do — has declared, concerning more than three million slaves held by the public enemy, that they "are, and henceforward shall be, free." Powerful combinations will be formed to secure the return of the rebel States with no guaranty for the enforcement of this national decree of freedom: the plain English of which is, that, for the sake of reinvesting traitors with their forfeited rights of citizenship, we will permit the reënslavement of these loyal millions, in violation of the plighted faith of our Government. For the sake of a false, treacherous and dishonorable peace, we will make ourselves active accomplices in the blackest crime in history! It would scarcely be more monstrous, if we were to send proposals to the rebels, "If you will resume your old, hypocritical pretence of allegiance, and live at peace with us, we will consent to the butchery of all the soldiers now in arms against you, of all Southern Unionists whose presence offends you, and of all Northern men whose opinions are hostile to slavery!" It is for anti-slavery men to teach this nation that all acceptable peace-offerings must be laid on the altar of Liberty, and not on the altar of Despotism. And it is for anti-slavery men to see to it that "the promise of freedom, being made," *shall* be "kept."

What more effective way of clinching this nail, so well driven into the coffin of our national Tormentor, than by striking straight, bold, hard blows in favor of "liberty throughout *all* the land unto *all* the inhabitants thereof"? If there are honest differences as to methods; if we do not all see clearly the wisdom or constitutionality of Congressional legislation against slavery in the non-seceding States, except on the basis of coöperation with those States; the least we can do is to insist that Congress must exercise its conceded power to invite and secure that coöperation. When it is wholly apparent that "Freedom for All" is the settled policy and purpose of that loyal mass which constitutes the nation, and which alone has the right to govern, Slavery in every Border State, as in Missouri, will be seen on its knees, in an agony of vain supplication for a little more time to make its will, chatter its prayers, gather up its robes, and get ready to die as becomes its Christian professions. For we must, henceforth, reckon among "the powers that be," which "are ordained of God," and which "bear not the sword in vain," a compact, earnest, almost savage party of Emancipationists (not "Abolitionists"—oh, no *indeed!*) in every Border State; for even Kentucky must soon come pouting into line, jostled and crowded forward by her more sensible neighbors. When slavery, hotly pressed by foes who are dead in earnest, can only act on the defensive, and is confronted on its own ground by a free press and free assemblies of the people, the fight may be sharp, but it must be short. It will be glad to die all the sooner for being assured that the loyal sense and sympathy of the whole nation take sides with its assailants; and we must take care that such assurance is amply justified.

May I say one thing more, which lies much on my heart? You, of all men, know best how to excuse the many things which try to get themselves spoken, when these sacred subjects are once broached.

We must stand by the Freedmen like brothers, through their trying period of transition — through the weary wilderness of years which will still stretch between their Egypt and their Canaan, even after they have clambered out of the bed of this Red Sea. We must nurse their infant liberty till it can go alone and defend itself. The negro, like another man, must indeed work out his own salvation, and fight his own battle; but we are bound to see fair play. The malignant, murderous prejudice and piratical rapacity of the white man must not be allowed to override the weakness, inexperience, ignorance and simplicity of a people just born into the world; nor to force unrighteous inferences from their faults and follies; nor to cheat them of the means of honest living and growing. *Equality of rights before the law* must not only be recognized in *form*, but must be secured in *fact*, as a thing of the spirit and the life, or Emancipation is only a victorious failure.

You asked me to "send a word of cheer"; and, lo! I fall to talking of more burdens yet to be borne, and more duties yet to be done. Happily, the lovers of God and man have learned that duty is joy, and that hard work is heavenly pleasure. What greater privilege than to meet the rising occasion, and pour on the strained and sensitive ear-drum of this awakened nation the clear, wise, warm message of Humanity and Justice? Never was the lesson more needed; never could it be more welcome; never could it sound so much like the trump of God.

Welcome, day of judgment! Depart, ye cursed, who have betrayed and crucified the Christ in the person of his poor and helpless brothers! Come forward, ye blessed, who have been true to the rights of the least and the lowest — to the rights of those who could not recompense your fidelity! Inherit the kingdom! It is yours henceforward; and ye shall sit on the right hand of Power.

Yours, in the patience of hope and the labor of love,

CHARLES G. AMES.

LETTER FROM JESSE STEDMAN.

SPRINGFIELD, (Vt.) Nov. 25, 1863.

MY DEAR SIR:

Your invitation to attend the Convention of the American Anti-Slavery Society at the city of Philadelphia, on the 3d and 4th of December, came duly to hand, and I do assure you no man, more than myself, will feel a deeper interest in its action, or would more enjoy a brief interview with the early pioneers of this Heaven-appointed cause, in a city whose founder never stained his hands with human blood, nor his soul with a touch of that abomination of abominations, human bondage; and no man more than myself regards the importance of *decided, united* and untiring action in the cause of emancipation at this momentous crisis, when all, or nearly all, are disposed, either from policy or principle, to lend a helping hand.

I would accept aid coming from *any* quarter and from almost *any* motive, to exterminate and utterly *annihilate* the *cause* of all our national calamities. The most absurd and dangerous policy is to turn the Abolition cause over to the Government, as some seem disposed to do, when the second "ruler in the kingdom" tells the world " slavery is their business, not mine," and very complacently talks about "*returning prodigals*"! Returning prodigals, forsooth!!

Thieves, murderers, pirates ranked under the mild cognomen of prodigals! A prodigal, in the common acceptation of the term, is an angel of light in the comparison, as he may not be guilty of a single act which the law regards criminal. I have less confidence than most men in the President, the Cabinet, or members of Congress, with a few honorable exceptions in regard to the latter, as to any action of either based upon the principle of immediate, universal emancipation as the duty of the Government and right of the slave; and hence I regard the action of the American Anti-Slavery Society in this momentous crisis of immeasurable importance. The wants of the thousands already free, and the millions yet in bondage, if ever free, in the necessaries of life and education to render them fit subjects for civilized life, present an outlay and amount of labor to be done the most appalling. But, Mr. President, I am aware I hardly need urge the Convention to action when there are so many who have been longer in the harness, and have labored so much more effectively than myself. In this connection, I cannot but advert to the changed condition of public opinion since the burning of Pennsylvania Hall, an age ago, in the city where you assemble, dedicated to free discussion. *Then* my blood rose to fever heat, and has remained there most of the time since. May your labor be crowned with success, and that speedily; and God grant that *moral necessity* may complete what military necessity commenced, and the joyous shouts of thirty-three million, free as the air of heaven, shake the continent from centre to circumference, and the benediction of the world and the blessing of God rest upon all who have lent a helping hand to deliver the oppressed from the power of the oppressor!

JESSE STEDMAN.

LETTER FROM GEORGE WILLIAM CURTIS.

NORTH SHORE, (Staten Island, N. Y.) Nov., 1863.

DEAR SIR:

I have the invitation to your meetings on the 3d and 4th of December, but my engagements will take me far away at that time. I do not wonder that you congratulate yourselves, for History will record that the Abolitionists were the vanguard of American liberty, not only in asserting the natural right of every man to personal freedom, but in maintaining through the fiery tempest of hostile public opinion the right of free speech, which is the corner-stone of a Republic of all the people like ours.

I rejoice with you that we have lived to the day in which the people of this country plainly see that Liberty, and Liberty alone, is Union.

Faithfully, yours,
GEORGE WILLIAM CURTIS.

LETTER FROM REV. JEHIEL CLAFLIN.

EAST WESTMORELAND, (N. H.) Nov. 28, 1863.

DEAR GARRISON:

Your circular and letter of the 23d inst., inviting me to be present at the decade celebration in the city of Philadelphia, on the 3d and 4th of December proximo, was received; and as I shall be denied the pleasure of being present in person to participate in the proceedings of that memorable and joyous occasion, allow me, dear sir, through you, to congratulate the veteran pioneers and faithful coadjutors in meeting each other again, after a long and arduous warfare, in the "city of brotherly love," where, thirty years ago, they met to inaugurate the grandest and most sublime movement since the Christian era. Being based, not on expediency but on principle, and depending, not on numbers but on the truth and the justice of their cause, they could not but have the sanction and approval of a just God and all-wise Ruler of the Universe; and relying on his all-potent arm for aid, their ultimate success could be but a question of time. And although many of the loved and dearly-remembered ones, co-laborers in this humanitary and Heaven-approved enterprise, have fallen in the midst of the "irrepressible conflict," yet it has pleased the all-wise and merciful Father graciously to spare the precious life of him, who, under God, was the first to call to repentance this guilty and oppressive nation—" to undo the heavy burdens, to break every yoke, and let the oppressed go free "; and though one after another of the faithful ones has fallen, battling nobly in the true heroic and martyr spirit for the deliverance of the oppressed, " remembering those in bonds as bound with them," yet others, catching the spirit of the noble dead, have risen up as new recruits to fill the ranks, and help carry forward to final completion the great work so nobly begun. The occasion will be a rare one for those who have consecrated the strength of their years and manhood in the cause of the oppressed. Those who will be gathered there to greet each other again and renew old acquaintance, will gather new strength and new inspiration to press on to final victory this mighty death-grapple with the legions and powers of darkness. The true friends of immediate emancipation and universal freedom have abundant cause of rejoicing and hope, in view of what has already been accomplished in the result of their faithful and indefatigable labors; "but the end is not yet." Slavery is a monster tenacious of life; but the harpoons of truth have been thrown by skillful hands, and the hideous monster is now writhing in his death-throes. Hitherto our cause has been unpopular, but now its advocates and friends may be counted by many thousands; since, to be such, no longer endangers one's reputation or popularity; yet, coming in at the eleventh hour, " they shall receive their penny." Recounting on this occasion, as you certainly will, the marvellous changes in the public mind and heart in this nation in regard to this great question of the age, you may very pertinently ask,

"What hath God wrought?" Thanking God for his favor and help in the past, let us gird up afresh with unfaltering fidelity and hope for the last decisive and final victory over the serried hosts of darkness, conscious that our duty is not done and our work not complete until the last fetter is broken from the limbs of the last slave in the land. Let every true Abolitionist be encouraged, now that the North has been aroused, and has leaped to "arms," and marshalled its hosts to vindicate our cause and the rights of humanity in "black and white." Let every heart and hand be quickened to new zeal and activity in the meritorious work of redeeming humanity from the iron grasp of tyrants and oppressors.

Let us all be hopeful that God, after having sufficiently chastened us, as a nation, for our pride, avarice, ambition, ingratitude and oppression, will yet bring us out of this fiery ordeal a united, prosperous and happy people, to be in the future not a warning but an example to all the nations of the earth.

Feeling it an honor, of which I am not worthy, to have my humble name linked with the noble and honored champions of impartial and universal freedom, and praying that God's blessing may attend your gathering, I am, with much esteem, your fellow-laborer,

JEHIEL CLAFLIN.

LETTER FROM SARAH M. GRIMKE.

WEST NEWTON, Nov. 30, 1863.

DEAR BROTHER GARRISON:

How my heart yearns to be with you on this soul-stirring and glorious occasion — the third decade of your untiring and unflinching efforts in the cause of Human Rights! What a jubilee to my spirit would it be to mingle with you in this celebration!

When our revolutionary fathers drew the sword to establish the great principles they promulgated, of the right of every human being to life, liberty, and the pursuit of happiness, they achieved, in their heroic and successful struggle for independence, the greatest triumph the world had then witnessed for liberty and self-government. But, alas! they too soon proved that the blessings they had won were only to be enjoyed by the white man — they sat down under their vines and fig trees, and sang hosannas to the Highest for their deliverance. In the songs of their jubilee, they heard not "the trampled negro's smothered cries."

To you and your coadjutors it was reserved to hear the groans of the oppressed — to cry aloud and spare not — to lift up your voices in the palmiest days of a haughty and prosperous nation, and proclaim on the house-tops that all their righteousness was but filthy rags — yea, they were a stench in the nostrils of Jehovah. To you, and to those who have stood by you in the day of conflict, it has been reserved to fight the battle of the weak against the strong; of the down-trodden against the mighty; of the prisoner, scourged and tortured, against his tyrant; of the bereaved and bleeding mother against the relentless wretch who robs her of her child; of all those helpless babes, robbed of their birthright, and doomed to hopeless bondage, against the fiend who perpetrated this highest crime against God and Humanity. The blessing of these destitute ones will be your exceeding great reward.

Now you stand on the height you have reached with so much toil, and suffering, and patience, and fortitude. In surveying the past, you hear the blessed language, "Well done, good and faithful servants! enter ye into the joy of your Lord." In surveying the present, the word greets your ear, "Speak to my people that they *go forward*." In surveying the future, you behold the glory of the Lord covering the earth, and you, too, may sing Hosanna to the Highest. Truly, if our forefathers did the work of noble men, nobly you have done the work of God in a godlike spirit.

This blessed war is working out the salvation of the Anglo-Saxon as well as of the African race. The eyes of the nation are being anointed with the eye-salve of the King of heaven, and thousand voices swell the anthem of praise and thanksgiving for what has been done; and lips, touched with living coals from God's altar, breathe the prayer, "Let not thine hand spare, nor thine eye pity, till judgment be brought forth unto victory."

This war, the holiest ever waged, is emphatically God's war; and whether the nation will or not, He will carry it on to its grand consummation, until every American enjoys the rights claimed for him in our Declaration of Independence.

Will not some hero arise, ere this conflict closes, on whom will rest the mantle of Toussaint L'Ouverture? Earnestly do I pray that, from among the ranks of our colored brethren, a savior may arise, who will make this war resplendent with his deeds of valor, courage, wisdom and fortitude; and who will be deservedly hailed as the final Deliverer of his people.

Yours, faithfully,
SARAH M. GRIMKE.

LETTER FROM REV. DAVID THURSTON.

LITCHFIELD CORNER, Me., Nov. 20, 1863.

DEAR SIR:

I thank you for the invitation to the thirtieth anniversary of our Society at Philadelphia. I call it ours, because I aided in its organization, and have never formally withdrawn from it. Though for reasons which seemed to me satisfactory, I have taken no part in its meetings of late, I have never departed from its principles, as stated in our DECLARATION — the immediate and entire abolition of slavery in the United States, "by all those instrumentalities sanctioned by law, humanity and religion; and thus to deliver our land from its deadliest curse, and to wipe out the foulest stain which rests upon our national escutcheon." Not a month before we met at Philadelphia to form an Anti-Slavery Society, I had preached three sermons on the subject of slavery, and, among other things, said that "it ought immediately to cease, because its continuance is preparing the way for civil war." Here I freely and thankfully acknowledge my indebtedness to you for enlightening me on the horrid cruelty and abominable wickedness of holding and using men as articles of property. No human enactments (falsely called laws) can change a being, created with the faculties necessary to make him a moral agent accountable to his Creator, into an article of property, a marketable commodity. Never have I failed to bear testimony against slaveholding as a practice fraught with wrongs and woes unutterable. I do not call it an *institution* or a *system*, for it is neither. I constantly maintain the inherent, imprescriptable right of the slaves to freedom.

Because, as a nation, we have withheld from them that sacred right, at the same time proclaiming our belief that all men are endowed by their Creator with the inalienable rights to life, liberty, and the pursuit of happiness, in the righteous Providence of God, the leaders in the rebellion have risen up to punish us and themselves for our atrocious wickedness. "Howbeit, they do not mean so, neither do their hearts think so." We are experiencing the scourges of the just indignation of God against us. Shall not we continue to feel them, till we remove the great, not the only, cause of them, by giving freedom to all the enslaved? As the nation refused to do what Abolitionists have been laboring to have them do, these thirty years, Jehovah has taken the work into His hands, and He will do it effectually. What wonderful changes in regard to slavery are taking place! Ecclesiastical organizations, which, heretofore, have utterly refused or ignored any action in relation to slavery, are now passing resolutions condemning the practice. Even the American Board of Commissioners for Foreign Missions, at their late meeting, passed, unanimously, a "resolution of thanks to God that the entire abolition of slavery on the North American Continent is an inevitable, and not far distant, result of the war."

In regard to what has already been done for the overthrow of slavery, and what we joyfully anticipate is to be done, we may exclaim, "Behold what a great matter a little fire has kindled!" Surely, the agency of God is to be devoutly recognized and gratefully acknowledged in these changes. "He is pouring contempt upon princes, and setting the poor on high from affliction, and making him families like a flock. The righteous see it and rejoice, and all iniquity shall stop her mouth. He disappointeth the devices of the crafty, so that their hands cannot perform their enterprise."

Probably not many of those whose names are attached to our Declaration still survive. I may be one of the oldest, having past my *eighty-fourth year nine months*, and still able to plead the cause of the oppressed. Gladly would I be with you on the 3d and 4th of December, to recount some of the conflicts, trials, discouragements and hopes, through which our cause has passed. Surely, we may "thank God and take courage," for the right will ultimately prevail. Domestic affliction must prevent my personal attendance. Give my kind regards to those pioneers in the good Abolition cause, who may be present at the contemplated meeting. I rejoice with them in the brightening prospect of having our country freed from that most inhuman and flagitiously wicked practice, which has exerted such a fearfully demoralizing influence through the whole land.

On behalf of the oppressed, I am truly with you,

DAVID THURSTON.

WM. LLOYD GARRISON.

LETTER FROM GEORGE E. BAKER.

WASHINGTON, Dec. 2, 1863.

GENTLEMEN:

Your invitation to attend the celebration of the Third Decade of the American Anti-Slavery Society was received by me with grateful feelings. Circumstances prevent my accepting it. Cheering as the prospect now is of the abolition of American slavery, there never was a time more favorable for a bold discussion of its nature and evils, nor a time when such discussion was more necessary. The people need a fuller appreciation of the intrinsic wickedness of slavery. JOHN WESLEY indulged in no figure of speech when he said, "American slavery is the *sum* of all villanies." He spoke truly and literally. If we could add up, as we add up a column of figures, Murder, Theft, Adultery, Fraud, etc., the total would be—Slavery. The slaveholder is guilty, not of one of the great sins only, but of all combined. Yet how many regard slavery chiefly as an economic evil, a question of expediency!

The rapid extinction of slavery now going on, at such fearful cost of blood and treasure, was foreseen by some of our great statesmen. They seem to have been of two classes. Mr. EVERETT, in his Gettysburg Oration, intimates that he saw it, and strove, "perhaps too long," to avert the catastrophe by compromise. He represents one, and much the larger, class.

Mr. SEWARD, on the other hand, saw the result forty years ago, and sought to save the country from convulsion and war by constantly raising his voice of warning, and by counselling the putting away of slavery through peaceful measures. To this end, with a small minority of his fellow-citizens, he labored. To this end, also, CHANNING, GARRISON, GERRIT SMITH, SUMNER and others wrote and spoke. "Man proposes, but God disposes." An almighty Power has taken the work from finite hands, and now we wait for the salvation of God.
Your friend and servant,

GEO. E. BAKER.

LETTER FROM JOSHUA COFFIN.

NEWBURY, (Mass.) Nov. 30, 1863.

DEAR GARRISON:

* * * What changes have taken place since December, 1833, and who then supposed that slavery would receive its death-blow by the hands of slavery itself? The first gun fired at Sumter was the death-knell of slavery. It will die hard, but die it must, although it may take a long time yet before the dying carcase is entirely dead, or buried beyond the hope of resurrection. As it is every day revealing its detestable character, it is every day changing the opinions of thousands, who have hitherto, like the priest and Levite, passed by on the other side, and been determined not to trouble themselves with such little things as the "nigger" question.

I wish I could be with you in Philadelphia this week; but as I cannot be with you in the flesh, I shall be with you in the spirit. I wish you a successful meeting, and hope that ere another decade shall have passed, the triumph of anti-slavery principles will be complete, and that the whole continent will join in the jubilee song, having been "regenerated and disenthralled by the irresistible genius of universal emancipation," directed as it undoubtedly has been by God's goodness, "whose ways are not as our ways, nor His thoughts as our thoughts." The counsels of Ahithophel have been turned to foolishness, and, like him, the leaders of the rebellion are hanging themselves. Please give my respects to all who may inquire about me, whom I formerly knew in Philadelphia, especially those who signed the Declaration in 1833. I wish I could see them all, and hear the addresses, and shake hands with those whom you may see and hear. But enough. Success to you, and may you and I live to see the consummation of our wishes!

Yours, truly, JOSHUA COFFIN.

LETTER FROM JOHN M. LANGSTON.

OBERLIN, Dec. 3, 1863.

WILLIAM LLOYD GARRISON, ESQ.:

DEAR SIR,—Accept my thanks for your earnest and manly efforts in behalf of the American slave. You and your noble coadjutors have brought our whole land under lasting gratitude to you. It would afford me vast pleasure to be in Philadelphia to-day to aid in commemorating the Thirtieth Anniversary of the American Anti-Slavery Society. Ill health prevents my being with you to-morrow. Up to last evening, I had hoped to be with you. I can now only thank you for your kind invitation to be present, and thank you for what, under God, you have been able to do for the American people and the American slave. For in laboring to secure the emancipation of the slave, you achieved the enfranchisement of all the people. And let all the people be grateful!

Yours, for God and Humanity, JOHN M. LANGSTON.

[From the New York Tribune of December 3, 1863.]

THE ANTI-SLAVERY ANNIVERSARY AT PHILADELPHIA.

Thirty years ago to-day, a few men met in Philadelphia to form the American Anti-Slavery Society. The Convention was not only small in numbers, but, with rare exceptions, its members were unknown beyond their own neighborhoods. The most conspicuous were the Rev. BERIAH GREEN, then recently Professor of Sacred Literature in Western Reserve College; LEWIS TAPPAN, an enterprising merchant of this city; JOHN G. WHITTIER, the Quaker poet; WM. LLOYD GARRISON, then as now the editor of the Boston *Liberator*; Dr. A. L. COX, a skillful physician of this city; SAMUEL J. MAY and AMOS A. PHELPS, clergymen of Massachusetts; WILLIAM GOODELL, then editor of the *Genius of Temperance*; ELIZUR WRIGHT, JR., since known as the translator of LA FONTAINE; the Rev. S. S. JOCELYN, of this city, and Dr. E. A. ATLEE and J. MILLER MCKIM, of Philadelphia. The Convention numbered sixty-two persons, from ten States. Prof. GREEN officiated as President, and Messrs. TAPPAN and WHITTIER as Secretaries. A Declaration of Principles and Purposes, from the emphatic and eloquent pen of Mr. GARRISON, was adopted, and "The American Anti-Slavery Society," based on the doctrine of immediate emancipation without expatriation, organized. The officers of the Society were then chosen. Its President was ARTHUR TAPPAN, the senior partner of one of our oldest mercantile firms, and widely known for his munificent contributions to the religious and benevolent institutions of the country. Among its other officers were SAMUEL FESSENDEN, the head of the Maine bar, and the father of the present able Senator in Congress from that State, the Rev. Dr. LORD, President of Dartmouth College, Professors FITCH and IVES, of Yale College, BENJAMIN LUNDY, one of the earliest anti-slavery pioneers, JOSHUA LEAVITT, the editor successively of the New York *Evangelist*, *The Emancipator*, and *The Independent*, Professor SHEPARD, of Bangor Theological Seminary, THEODORE D. WELD, and ELLIS GRAY LORING, DAVID LEE CHILD, and SAMUEL E. SEWALL, members of the Boston bar. Looking confidently into the future, the Declaration of the Convention, signed by all its members, proclaimed: "Our trust for victory is solely in God. We may be personally defeated, but our principles never. Truth, Justice, Reason, Humanity, must and will gloriously triumph." In a sketch of the proceedings of the Convention, a leading delegate, through an anti-slavery periodical, said: "The members of the Convention and their associates will never cease from their labors till their cause is triumphant. The God of Truth and Justice is with them, and will finally prevail."

No reflecting man can doubt that the historian of the conflict between Freedom and Slavery which has convulsed this nation for the last thirty years will assign a very important part in the great movement to the Society whose organization we have briefly sketched. From the start, it entered upon its seemingly almost hopeless work with an energy and a will that nothing could discourage or dismay. In the language of Mr. GARRISON, "it *would* be heard."

Its first battle was for freedom of speech and the press. And, in the face of riots and lynchings, and murders even, and while its meetings were broken up by mobs, and its presses thrown into rivers, and its orators and editors shut up in prisons or shot down at their posts, it fought out this fight during five or six years with a persistency and a courage which have few parallels in the annals of progress and reform. The heroism of this small body of proscribed men and women wrung plaudits from their opponents. The late WILLIAM LEGGETT wrote of them, twenty-eight years ago : " It would seem as if God had winnowed the population of the country to select a choice few, whom nothing can drive from the exercise of their right to discuss the question of slavery." Commenting upon the anti-abolition riots that disgraced this city in 1834, during which the house of LEWIS TAPPAN was sacked and his furniture reduced to ashes, Mr. CHARLES KING, then editor of the New York *American*, said, " Fire cannot burn their convictions out of these men." Nor did it! Unseduced by blandishments, and undeterred by violence, the Abolitionists kept straight on, urging their obnoxious doctrines upon public attention, not always in the mildest terms nor with the sweetest temper, but with stern facts and sturdy arguments, until they compelled the nation to stand still and listen.

Mingling with this contest for free speech and free printing, though initiated at a little later period in the conflict, was the memorable struggle for the right of petition. In 1835 and 1836, the Anti-Slavery societies began to petition Congress for the abolition of slavery in the District of Columbia, and the inhibition of the inter-State slave trade, and kindred measures. Though few at the outset, the number of petitioners swelled during the next two or three years till it reached in one Congress three-fourths of a million. It would belie obvious facts to call all these petitioners " Abolitionists." In the defence of the right of petition, as also that of the freedom of speech and the press, it became evident to considerate men that not alone was the right to discuss and petition in regard to slavery involved, but that vital constitutional principles were at stake, and that these must be defended against their assailants, irrespective of the merits of the particular subject over which the battle was waged, or the popularity or prestige of the persons whose privileges were put in peril.

It was upon these broad grounds that the venerable JOHN QUINCY ADAMS early became the champion of freedom of debate and the right of petition in the House of Representatives, where, for twelve years, he grappled with the Slave Power, making, not America only, but the civilized world, resound with the clash of the conflict. Doubtless posterity will regard this as the most honorable and brilliant chapter in the long and eventful life of this extraordinary man. The service he rendered to the cause of Freedom during these years was of incalculable value. The exalted positions he had held, his multifarious learning, his world-wide renown, lent lustre to the cause, while his exhaustless resources, his skill in debate, his dauntless courage and indomitable will, were a tower of strength to its friends, and a never-failing source of mortification and discomfiture to its foes.

The freedom of speech and debate, and the right of petition, had hardly been secured, before the subject of the annexation of Texas, and the consequent enlargement of the area of slavery, arrested the public attention. While thousands of our best and wisest men of all creeds and parties early took alarm at this attempt to commit the country to a policy of aggression upon the rights of foreign States, it is due to truth to say that the Abolitionists and their immediate coadjutors were the only classes who resisted annexation upon purely anti-slavery grounds. This contest, opening in 1837, continued, with occasional lulls, until the Presidential campaign of 1844, when it largely mingled in the discussions of the two parties that divided the country, the conspirators against national honor achieving a triumph in the election of JAMES K. POLK over HENRY CLAY.

It was now eleven years since the American Anti-Slavery Society was formed. During this period, kindred societies had been organized in every considerable town and village in the Free States, whose members numbered scores of thousands. These associations had employed hundreds of agents, who had traversed the country delivering addresses in all the principal centres of population. They had established newspapers in all the Northern States, and had circulated pamphlets and tracts by the million. Not only had they petitioned Congress, but they had besieged the Legislatures of the Free States, demanding that they themselves memorialize Congress in behalf of Emancipation, and protest against the abridgment of the right of debate and petition, and the annexation of Texas to the Union. Vermont and Massachusetts responded favorably to their demands in 1837, and other States subsequently copied their example, till at one period the Legislature of every State, not hopelessly bound in the fetters of a pro-slavery democracy, spoke words more or less emphatic for the slave and his champions. The Abolitionists had also made their power felt at the ballot-box, either by voting for the most acceptable candidates of the Whig and Democratic parties, or by bringing out candidates of their own. Their principles had likewise made a strong lodgment in the leading religious denominations of the country. Indeed, at the period of the inauguration of Mr. POLK, and the consequent consummation of the Texas villany, neither House of Congress, no State Legislature, no ecclesiastical body, no educational convention, no benevolent society, no political assemblage, could meet without finding itself launched upon a wide sea of discussion concerning slavery. The most superficial observer could not fail to see, nor the most indifferent spectator to feel, that the principles of the Abolitionists, after passing through the ordeal of long years of reproach and persecution, had taken fast hold upon the intellect and conscience of great masses of the American people.

The annexation of Texas was followed by the Mexican war, which brought in its train large accessions of territory. The whole nation was now compelled to stand face to face with the long dreaded and much avoided subject of slavery. Congress and the country were convulsed. The greatest minds of the times were forced to grapple with the agitating theme. The discussion summoned to the forum the loftiest statesmanship; it sent to the closet the ripest scholarship; it levied contributions upon the eloquence, the learning, the genius of the Senate, the Synod and the School, until all ranks and conditions of men were involved in the agitation.

After the advent of the Wilmot Proviso in 1847–8, the slavery agitation passed beyond the pale of the Abolitionists. Yet, from that important epoch onward till secession reared its treasonable crest, not a fundamental argument was employed against slavery, nor a vital principle enunciated, nor a sound view of the Constitution exhibited, nor an important fact presented, nor a prime objection answered, nor a glowing appeal in behalf of liberty uttered, which had not been previously employed, enunciated, exhibited, presented, answered and uttered by the Abolitionists. So true is this, that to minds familiar with the anti-slavery literature of the era, the speeches and prelections of those statesmen and orators who, for the last twelve or fifteen years, have fulmined in the Senate and on the rostrum, while spurning the imputation of being "Abolitionists," have seemed to be the cast-off robes, furbished up for the occasion, of the very class whom they affected to repudiate, if not despise.

During the Wilmot Proviso struggle, and its closely following contest over the compromise measures of 1850, the radical anti-slavery politicians of the country organized the Free-Soil party, the voting Abolitionists generally rallying to its support. Four years later, the Slave Power dictated the repeal of the Missouri Compromise, which speedily bore its natural fruit in the raids and rascalities, the frauds and felonies perpetrated in Kansas. These crimes stimulated to action the spirit of Northern freemen. They combined to resist these outrages upon Liberty and Law, and gave body and form to their determination by organizing the Republican party. At the election of 1856, the Slave Oligarchy triumphed, and triumphed, thank God, for the last time in a Presidential contest. Not heeding the ominous gathering in the Northern skies, the conspirators celebrated their triumph by endeavoring to sacrifice Human Freedom on the altar of the Dred Scott infamy, and to crucify Representative government on the Lecompton swindle. The sequel is known. The anti-slavery sentiment of the country was equal to the exigency. It consolidated its ranks. DOUGLAS revolted, split the Democracy in twain, and ABRAHAM LINCOLN took the Presidential chair.

Throughout the series of great events we have noticed, the course of the Abolitionists was marvellously direct and straight-forward.

They aimed their blows right at the core of slavery, denouncing it as a sin whose only appropriate remedy was immediate and unconditional repentance. Amid convulsions that made the continent tremble, this small band of reformers pursued their line of policy with a directness that finds its fitting illustration in the parallel of latitude, which crosses wide oceans, climbs high mountains, penetrates deep valleys, and traverses broad plains, without variableness or shadow of turning. Yet, notwithstanding this, it requires no spirit of divination to perceive that the organization of the Anti-Slavery Society in 1833, and the election of a Republican President in 1860, bear to each other the relation of remote cause and ultimate effect.

We utter no eulogium upon the Abolitionists. Posterity will do them justice, awarding praise and blame with impartial hand. Like other reformers, some of them have sometimes been impatient if not intolerant of those who were less quick to see, less keen to feel, less prompt to act than themselves. Their great work hastens to completion. We venture the prediction, that if any of those who aided in forming the Society of 1833 shall live till a third of a century shall have passed since that event, they will greet a day whose rising sun will not shed his beams upon a single negro slave in all our broad land.

[A.—p. 6.]

Since this speech was made, JOHN GREENLEAF WHITTIER has sent to the Editor of the Boston *Transcript* the following letter, by which it appears that Mr. GARRISON would have been liberated from prison by HENRY CLAY, had he not been anticipated by ARTHUR TAPPAN. The fact is of some historical interest.

The editor of the Louisville (Ky.) *Journal*, in an article on the release of the editor of *The Liberator* from prison in Baltimore, in 1830, makes the following statement:—

"Mr. CLAY related to us the facts in July, 1830. A few months before, Mr. GARRISON, editor of an emancipation paper in Baltimore, was prosecuted, imprisoned, and fined for a libel on Woolfolk. Not being able to pay the fine, his imprisonment was prolonged on that account. Mr. WHITTIER, an entire stranger to Mr. CLAY, wrote to him as a philanthropist, begging him to pay the fine, and thus procure Mr. GARRISON's release. Mr. CLAY wrote to his old friend, HEZEKIAH NILES, of *Niles's Register*, asking whether Mr. GARRISON was a worthy man, and saying that, if he was so, he would pay one half the fine, provided Mr. NILES or others would pay the other half. Mr. NILES wrote back, stating that, on the whole, he thought Mr. GARRISON worthy. Mr. CLAY at once remitted the money for half of the fine, the other half was paid, and GARRISON was discharged.

"It is not pleasant to have to add, that, some time afterwards, both WHITTIER and GARRISON wrote bitter things against Mr. CLAY."

The facts in the case are simply these: During the imprisonment of my friend GARRISON, I ventured to address a line to HENRY CLAY, asking him to use his influence with his political and personal friends in Baltimore to procure his release. I neither asked nor expected him to pay himself the fine and costs. I had no definite idea upon what terms, if at all, his release could be effected, or whether, in the words of Dumbedikes to Jeanie Deans, "Siller would do it." My appeal, wisely or otherwise, was made to a distinguished political man in behalf of one of his most ardent supporters, who must have been already known to him as the first editor in New England to nominate him for the Presidency, in an able and vigorous article published in the Bennington (Vt.) *Journal of the Times*, of March 27, 1829, and which was widely copied and commended. It is proper to say that my letter was written without the knowledge of my friend GARRISON.

In a letter which I received some time after from the Kentucky statesman, he informed me that he had written to a friend in Baltimore, in conformity with my wishes; but that he had just learned from his correspondent that he had been anticipated, and that the liberation had been effected without the aid he would otherwise have given. The fine and costs were in fact paid by ARTHUR TAPPAN, Esq., of New York.

The promptness of HENRY CLAY's response to my appeal was honorable in itself, and characteristic of one who was always true to his political and personal friends. The implied charge of ingratitude suggested by my old friend PRENTICE is perhaps hardly worth noticing. What HENRY CLAY proposed to do for GARRISON was no more than he would have done, and should have done, for any one who had established a similar claim upon his favor. As to myself, I could scarcely be said to be an "*entire* stranger" to him; for young and obscure as I was, I had in the Boston *Manufacturer* advocated his claims with such zeal and earnestness, that I was selected as the successor of the editor of the journal himself, and in the Hartford (Ct.) "*N. E. Review*" assisted, as he will doubtless remember, in writing "The Life of Henry Clay," and declined, on account of illness, an invitation from the National Republican Committee to fill a vacancy in the delegation of Connecticut to the Convention which nominated him in 1831. I mention this merely to show that my letter, under the circumstances, was not altogether boyish presumption.

That, in the progress of the great struggle between Freedom and Slavery, both GARRISON and myself have felt compelled to speak freely of the position and avowed sentiments of HENRY CLAY, is certainly true. But for myself, I can say that this was always done more in sorrow than in anger, and accompanied with a profound regret that one in many respects so noble, and endowed with such wonderful gifts, should allow his great influence to be felt in support of a system which his reason and conscience condemned.

JOHN G. WHITTIER.

AMESBURY, 11th 3d mo., 1864.

[B.—p. 40.]

ORIGINAL SIGNERS OF THE DECLARATION OF SENTIMENTS.

(Those marked with an asterisk have deceased.)

Maine.

DAVID THURSTON, JOSEPH SOUTHWICK,
NATHAN WINSLOW,* JAMES F. OTIS,
ISAAC WINSLOW.

New Hampshire.
DAVID CAMBELL.*

Vermont.
ORSON S. MURRAY.

Massachusetts.

DAVID S. SOUTHMAYD,* JAMES G. BARBADOES,*
EFFINGHAM L. CAPRON,* DAVID T. KIMBALL, JR.,
JOSHUA COFFIN, DANIEL E. JEWETT,
AMOS A. PHELPS,* JOHN REID CAMBELL,*
JOHN G. WHITTIER, NATHANIEL SOUTHARD,*
HORACE P. WAKEFIELD, ARNOLD BUFFUM,*
WILLIAM LLOYD GARRISON.

Rhode Island.
JOHN PRENTICE, GEORGE W. BENSON, RAY POTTER.*

Connecticut.

SAMUEL JOSEPH MAY, EDWIN A. STILLMAN,
ALPHEUS KINGSLEY, SIMEON S. JOCELYN,
ROBERT BERNARD HALL.

New York.

BERIAH GREEN, WILLIAM GOODELL,
LEWIS TAPPAN, ELIZUR WRIGHT, JR.,
JOHN RANKIN, CHARLES W. DENISON,
WILLIAM GREEN, JR., GEORGE BOURNE,*
ABRAHAM L. COX, JOHN FROST.*

New Jersey.
JONA. PARKHURST,* CHALKLEY GILLINGHAM, JAMES WHITE.*

Pennsylvania.

EVAN LEWIS,* AARON VICKERS,
EDWIN A. ATLEE,* JAMES LOUGHHEAD,
ROBERT PURVIS, JOHN R. SLEEPER,
JAMES McCRUMMELL, THOMAS WHITSON,
THOMAS SHIPLEY, EDWIN P. ATLEE,*
BARTHOLOMEW FUSSELL, JOHN SHARP, JR.,
ENOCH MACK, DAVID JONES,
JOHN McCOLLOUGH, LUCAS GILLINGHAM,
JAMES M. McKIM, JAMES MOTT,
SUMNER STEBBINS.

Ohio.
JOHN M. STERLING, MILTON SUTLIFF, LEVI SUTLIFF.

A NORTHERN SONG.

BY JOHN G. WHITTIER.

Now joy and thanks for evermore!
   The dreary night has well-nigh passed;
The slumbers of the North are o'er,
   The giant stands erect at last!

More than we hoped in that dark time,
   When faint with watching, few and worn,
We saw no welcome day-star climb
   The cold gray pathway of the morn.

O, weary hours! O, night of years!
   What storms our darkling pathway swept,
Where, beating back our thronging fears,
   By faith alone our march we kept!

How jeered the scoffing crowd behind,
   How mocked before the tyrant train,
As, one by one, the true and kind
   Fell fainting in our path of pain!

They died — their brave hearts breaking slow —
   But, self-forgetful to the last,
In words of cheer and bugle-glow,
   Their breath upon the darkness passed!

A mighty host on either hand
   Stood waiting for the dawn of day,
To crush like reeds our feeble band! —
   The morn has come — and where are they?

Troop after troop its line forsakes,
   With peace-white banners waving free,
And from our own the glad shout breaks,
   Of "Freedom and Fraternity!"

Like mist before the growing light,
   The hostile cohorts melt away:
Hurrah! our foemen of the night
   Are brothers at the dawn of day!

As unto these repentant ones
   We open wide our toil-worn ranks,
Along our line a murmur runs
   Of song, and praise, and grateful thanks.

CATALOGUE
OF
ANTI-SLAVERY PUBLICATIONS IN AMERICA.

[The following list does not pretend to completeness. On the contrary, a full list of works printed, or reprinted, in the United States on the subject of slavery, with a view to its abolition, would probably swell to nearly double the length of this. It goes forth, however, as the commencement of a better one. Titles of anti-slavery works, not included in this list, with names of authors, (where known,) and dates and places of publication, may be communicated to SAMUEL MAY, Jr., 221 Washington street, Boston.]

1750---1830.

Considerations on the Keeping of Negroes, &c. By JOHN WOOLMAN. 1754 to 1762.

ANTHONY BENEZET wrote and published on Slavery, between 1750 and 1774. A small tract of extracts: Philadelphia, 1858.

Notes on the State of Virginia. With an Appendix. By THOMAS JEFFERSON. 1787. [The 8th edition appeared in 1801.]

Various publications by Dr. BENJAMIN FRANKLIN and Dr. BENJAMIN RUSH appeared soon after 1787.

Constitution of a Society for Abolishing the Slave Trade. With several Acts of the Legislatures of Massachusetts, Connecticut, and Rhode Island, for that purpose. pp. 19. Providence. Printed by JOHN CARTER. 1789.

The Injustice and Impolicy of the Slave Trade, and of the Slavery of the Africans, illustrated in a Sermon before the Connecticut Society for the Promotion of Freedom and for the Relief of Persons unlawfully holden in Bondage; at their Annual Meeting in New Haven, September 15, 1791. By JONATHAN EDWARDS, D. D. [the younger.]

A Portraiture of Domestic Slavery in the United States. By JESSE TORREY, Jun. Philadelphia, 1817.

Memoirs of NAIMBANNA, an African Prince. Philadelphia. 1799.

Horrors of Slavery: in Two Parts. By JOHN KENRICK. Cambridge. 1817. "A copy of this work was placed by the author on the desk of every member of Congress when it was published."

Free Remarks, &c., respecting the Exclusion of Slavery from the Territories and New States. By a Philadelphian. 1819.

Speech of Mr. PLUMER, of New Hampshire, (in Congress,) on the Missouri Question, Feb. 21, 1820.

Reflections occasioned by the late Disturbances in Charleston. By ACHATES. Charleston, S. C., 1822. "Ascribed to the pen of Gen. THOMAS PINKNEY."— *Lundy's Genius of Universal Emancipation*, vol. 1, p. 147.

Oration on the Abolition of the Slave Trade. By JEREMIAH GLOUCESTER. Philadelphia. 1823.

Remarks Addressed to the Citizens of Illinois on the Proposed Introduction of Slavery. [About 1824.]

Information concerning the Present State of the Slave Trade. 1824.
A Treatise on Slavery, showing the Evil of Slaveholding, &c. &c. By JAMES DUNCAN. 1824. Republished, 1840.
Information for the Free People of Colour who are inclined to Emigrate to Hayti. Philadelphia. 1825.
Remarks on Slavery in the United States. From the *Christian Examiner*. By S. E. SEWALL. 1827.
A Sketch of the Laws relating to Slavery. By GEORGE M. STROUD. 1827. [2d edition, abridged. Philadelphia, 1856. 12 mo., pp. 125.]
Memorial of Inhabitants of the District of Columbia, praying for the Gradual Abolition of Slavery there. 1828.
WALKER'S Appeal ; in Four Articles, together with a Preamble to the Colored Citizens of the World, but in particular and very expressly to those of the United States of America. Written in Boston, in the State of Massachusetts, Sept. 28, 1829. By DAVID WALKER.
Speech of Hon. CHARLES MINER, of Pennsylvania, in U. S. House of Representatives. 1829. [Reprinted at Bethania, Pa., 1832.]
Remarks on the Character of ELIAS HICKS and his Exertions in the Abolition of Slavery. 1830.

1831.

Discourse on Slavery in the United States. By SAMUEL J. MAY.
Address, delivered to the Free People of Colour in Philadelphia, New York, and other cities, during the month of June, 1831. By WM. LLOYD GARRISON.
The Practicability of the Abolition of Slavery. A Lecture at Stockbridge. By H. D. SEDGWICK, Esq.
Address to Christians of all Denominations on the Inconsistency of Admitting Slaveholders to Communion and Church Membership. By EVAN LEWIS. Philadelphia. pp. 19.
Fragment of a Letter on the Slavery of the Negroes, written in 1776 ; by THOMAS DAY, Esq., Author of "Sandford and Merton."
Authentic and Impartial Narrative of the Tragical Scene in Southampton County Va., Aug. 22d, 1830. [The Southampton Insurrection.] By SAMUEL WARNER.

1832.

Thoughts on African Colonization. By WM. LLOYD GARRISON.
Four Sermons, at Western Reserve College. By BERIAH GREEN. [November and December.]
Speech of JOHN THOMPSON BROWN, in the House of Delegates of Virginia, on the Abolition of Slavery, Jan. 18, 1832. Richmond.
Speech of WILLIAM H. BRODNAX, in the House of Delegates of Virginia, on the Policy of the State with respect to its Colored Population, Jan. 19, 1832. Richmond.
Review of the Debate in the Virginia Legislature of 1831 and 1832. By THOMAS R. DEW, Professor in William and Mary College. Richmond.
A Plea for the Slave. To all Professing Christians in America.
Epistle from the Yearly Meeting of Friends in Philadelphia to the People of Colour.
Letters on the Colonization Society, and Its Probable Results. By M. CAREY.

1833.

The Right of Colored People to Education Vindicated. Letters to ANDREW T. JUDSON, Esq., and others, in Canterbury, (Conn.) relative to Miss CRANDALL and Her School for Colored Females. By SAMUEL J. MAY.

Detail of Plan for Improvement of Negroes on Plantations. By THOMAS S. CLAY.
Letters on Slavery. By Rev. J. D. PAXTON.
Constitution of the American Anti-Slavery Society; with the Declaration of Sentiments, and Address to the Public, issued by the Executive Committee.
An Appeal in Favor of that Class of Americans called Africans. By Mrs. CHILD.
Exposition of Anti-Slavery Principles and Plans. By Rev. S. J. MAY.
The Sin of Slavery and its Remedy. By ELIZUR WRIGHT, Jr., Professor in Western Reserve College.
Speeches at the Anti-Colonization Meeting in London, July 18, 1833, by CROPPER, GARRISON, O'CONNELL, and others.
Address in Boston, New York, and Philadelphia, before the Free People of Color, in April, 1833. By WM. LLOYD GARRISON.
The West India Question. By CHARLES STUART.
Facts proving the good conduct and prosperity of Emancipated Negroes.
The Despotism of Freedom; — or American Slavery the worst in the world. Address by DAVID L. CHILD.
Strictures on African Slavery. By SAMUEL CROTHERS.
Justice and Expediency; or Slavery considered with a view to its rightful remedy. By J. G. WHITTIER.
Reply to the Richmond (Va.) *Jeffersonian and Times.* By J. G. WHITTIER.
Memorial of Free People of Color of Philadelphia to the Senate and Representatives of Pennsylvania.
Address to the Coloured People of Philadelphia. By EVAN LEWIS.
Sketch of the Character and Defence of the Principles of WILLIAM LLOYD GARRISON. An Address before the Maine Anti-Slavery Society. By JAMES F. OTIS.
Address to the Citizens of Philadelphia, on Slavery. By EDWIN P. ATLEE.
Fruits of Colonizationism. The Canterbury [Conn.] Persecution.

1834.

Letter to the Editors of the *Christian Examiner.* By Rev. SAMUEL J. MAY.
The Maryland Scheme of Expatriation Examined. By a Friend of Liberty.
Report of the Arguments of Counsel in the case of PRUDENCE CRANDALL.
Man-stealing and Slavery denounced by the Presbyterian and Methodist Churches. By Rev. GEORGE BOURNE.
Address of the Starkborough and Lincoln Anti-Slavery Societies.
Brief Sketch of the trial of WM. LLOYD GARRISON for an alleged libel on FRANCIS TODD.
Letter to the Churches. By JAMES G. BIRNEY.
Sermon by Rev. JAMES T. DICKINSON, at Norwich, Conn., July 4th.
Oration on the 1st August, at South Reading, Mass. By DAVID L. CHILD.
Appeal to the New England and New Hampshire Methodist Conferences. By SHIPLEY W. WILLSON and others.
Eulogium upon Wilberforce. By DAVID PAUL BROWN.
Letter on Colonization. By Hon. JAMES G. BIRNEY.
Pictures of Slavery. By Rev. GEORGE BOURNE.
Debate at Lane Seminary; Speech of J. A. THOME, and Letter of Dr. S. H. COX.
Address before the Salem Anti-Slavery Society. By CYRUS P. GROSVENOR.
Constitution of the Newburyport Anti-Slavery Society.
The Gospel of the Typical Servitude. By SAMUEL CROTHERS, Greenfield, Ohio.
The Oasis. By Mrs. L. M. CHILD.
Lectures on Slavery and its Remedy. By AMOS A. PHELPS.

Remarks on Slavery and Emancipation. Boston.
GEORGE FOX and his First Disciples; or the Society of Friends as it was and as it is. By WILLIAM HOWITT. [From *Tait's Magazine*.]
Review of J. W. NEVIN'S Summary, &c. By Rev. JAMES H. DICKEY, of Salem, Ross County, Ohio.
JAMES G. BIRNEY'S First and Second Letters to the Ministry and Elders of the Presbyterian Church.
Statement of the Reasons which induced the Students of Lane Seminary to Dissolve their Connexion, &c.

1835.

Address at Middlebury, by request of Vermont Anti-Slavery Society. By OLIVER JOHNSON.
Inquiry into the Character and Tendency of the American Colonization and the American Anti-Slavery Societies. By Judge WM. JAY.
Testimony of God against Slavery, &c. &c. By Rev. LAROY SUNDERLAND.
Letter to a Member of Congress, from an English Clergyman.
Slavery. By WILLIAM E. CHANNING. 18 mo., pp. 167.
Report on the Condition of Colored People in the State of Ohio.
Fast Day Sermon on Slavery in Dover, N. H. By Rev. DAVID ROOT.
The Enemies of the Constitution Discovered. By DEFENSOR.
Mob, under Pretence of Law; Trial of Rev. George Storrs at Northfield, N. H.
Liberty Triumphant; a Sermon at Haverhill, by Rev. DAVID ROOT.
Address before the Foundry Missionary Society, Washington, Jan. 15, 1835. By Rev. G. G. COOKMAN, of the Methodist Episcopal Church.
The Book and Slavery Irreconcileable. By Rev. GEORGE BOURNE.
Address to the Members of the Religious Society of Friends, on the Duty of Declining the Use of the Products of Slave Labour. By CHARLES MARRIOTT.

1836.

Proceedings of the Rhode Island Anti-Slavery Convention, February, 1836. With a " Declaration," &c., by WILLIAM GOODELL.
Things for Northern Men to Do. By BERIAH GREEN.
Remarks by SAMUEL HOAR, of Massachusetts, in the House of Representatives, January, 1836. [Slavery and the Right of Petition.]
Account of Interviews between Committee of the Massachusetts Anti-Slavery Society and the Committee of the Legislature.
A Full Statement of the Reasons which were in part offered to the Committee of the Legislature of Massachusetts, &c. &c. &c.
Slavery and the Domestic Slave Trade. By Prof. E. A. ANDREWS.
Songs of the Free, and Hymns of Christian Freedom. Compiled by M. W. CHAPMAN.
Review of Remarks on Dr. CHANNING'S "Slavery"; by a Citizen of Massachusetts.
Freedom's Defence; or a Candid Examination of Hon. JOHN C. CALHOUN'S Report on the Freedom of the Press. By CINCINNATUS.
Synod of Kentucky's Plan of Emancipation.
Collection of [Five] Valuable Documents. [BIRNEY'S Third Letter, &c. &c.]
Review, by a Pittsburgher, of a Pamphlet on Slavery, from the *Biblical Repertory*
Plea before C. J. SHAW, in the case of Commonwealth *vs.* Thomas Aves. By ELLIS GRAY LORING.
Discussion on American Slavery between GEORGE THOMPSON, Esq., and Rev. ROBERT J. BRECKINRIDGE, in Glasgow; with an Appendix, by CHARLES C. BURLEIGH. Boston : Isaac Knapp.

Trial of REUBEN CRANDALL, M. D., for circulating Anti-Slavery Publications.
The War in Texas, &c., the Result of a long premeditated crusade against the Government by Slaveholders, &c.
Anti-Slavery Catechism. } By Mrs. L. MARIA CHILD.
Authentic Anecdotes of American Slavery. } (Some of these, perhaps, of an earlier date.)
Evils of Slavery and Cure of Slavery. }
The Fountain. }
Right and Wrong in Boston. Parts 1, 2, 3. By M. W. CHAPMAN.
Memoir of WILLIAM WILBERFORCE. By THOMAS PRICE. 2d American edition.
Epistle to the Clergy of the Southern States. By SARAH M. GRIMKE.
Appeal to the Christian Women of the South. By ANGELINA E. GRIMKE.
A Fast-Day Sermon. By Rev. E. J. FULLER.
Address on the Fourth of July, at Boston and Salem. By CHARLES FITCH.
Letter to Hon. HARRISON GRAY OTIS, PELEG SPRAGUE, and RICHARD FLETCHER. [By Dr. G. BRADFORD.]
Archy Moore. [By RICHARD HILDRETH.]
Narrative of AMOS DRESSER, &c. &c.
Voices of Freedom. By JOHN G. WHITTIER. [This little volume went through many editions.]

1837.

JOHN QUINCY ADAMS's 4th of July Oration at Newburyport.
Liberty. A Collection of Sentiments. Compiled by JULIUS R. AMES.
Sentiments Expressed by Southerners.   "   "   "
Historical Evidence concerning the Effects of Immediate Emancipation.
Letter of GERRIT SMITH to Rev. JAMES SMYLIE, of Mississippi.
The War in Texas; — to reëstablish, extend and perpetuate Slavery.
Discourse on American Slavery, at Mendon, Mass., July 4, 1837. By ADIN BALLOU.
JOHN QUINCY ADAMS's Letters to his Constituents, and Speech in Congress, &c.
Appeal to the Women of the nominally Free States, by Anti-Slavery Convention of American Women.
Letter to the Hon. HENRY CLAY, on the Annexation of Texas to the United States. By WILLIAM E. CHANNING.
Letter of WILLIAM E. CHANNING to JAMES G. BIRNEY. [Written in 1836.]
Slavery Illustrated in its Effects upon Woman, &c. By Miss GRIMKE.
These Bad Times the product of Bad Morals. Sermon by Rev. S. J. MAY.
Remarks of HENRY B. STANTON in the Representatives' Hall, Feb. 22 and 23, 1837.
Does the Bible Sanction Slavery?
The "Negro Pew," &c.
Slaveholding Weighed in the Balance of Truth. By CHARLES FITCH.
Views on Colonization. By Rev. JAMES NOURSE.
An Essay on Slavery and Abolitionism. By CATHARINE E. BEECHER.
Speech of Hon. WILLIAM SLADE, of Vermont, on the Abolition of Slavery and the Slave Trade in the District of Columbia. House of Representatives, Dec. 20.
Proceedings of Convention of Ministers on the subject of Slavery, in Worcester County, Dec. 5 and 6, 1837; and, by adjournment, January, 1838. Speech at said Convention, by Rev. GEORGE ALLEN.
Treatise on the Intellectual Character and Civil and Political Condition of the Colored People of the United States. By Rev. HOSEA EASTON, a Colored Man.
Constitutional Argument. By ALVAN STEWART.
FATHER WARD's Letter to Prof. STUART, on Prof. STUART's Letter to Dr. FISK. [JONATHAN WARD, Brentwood, N. H.]

1838.

Immediate Emancipation ; and Remarks on Compensation. By CHARLES STUART.
Trial of Rev. John B. Mahan, in Kentucky.
Letters on American Slavery, addressed to Mr. THOMAS RANKIN. By JOHN RANKIN, [of Virginia, afterwards of Ohio,] Pastor of Presbyterian Church in Ripley, Ohio.
Letters to CATHARINE E. BEECHER. By ANGELINA E. GRIMKE.
Letters from the West Indies. By Prof. HOVEY.
Address at the Broadway Tabernacle, New York, August 1, 1838. By WM. LLOYD GARRISON.
The Generous Planter and His Carpenter Ben. (4th edition, 1838.)
Report of a Delegate to the Women's Anti-Slavery Convention at Philadelphia. [With a notice of the burning of Pennsylvania Hall.]
Emancipation in the West Indies, &c. By JAMES A. THOME and J. HORACE KIMBALL.
Narrative of JAMES WILLIAMS, an American Slave. [Drawn up by J. G. WHITTIER.]
Report on the Powers and Duties of Congress upon Slavery and the Slave Trade.
Correspondence between Hon. F. H. ELMORE and JAMES G. BIRNEY.
Appeal to the Methodist Episcopal Church. By Rev. ORANGE SCOTT.
Proceedings of a Meeting to form the Broadway Tabernacle Anti-Slavery Society.
Address to the Abolitionists of Massachusetts on the subject of Political Action. [Drafted by ELLIS GRAY LORING.]
Rights of Colored Men to Suffrage, Citizenship, &c. &c. By WM. YATES.
Alton Trials. [Destruction of Rev. E. P. LOVEJOY'S Press; and his Murder.]
Power of Congress over the District of Columbia. By WYTHE.
The Martyr of Freedom. A Discourse at East Machias, Me. By Rev. T. T. STONE.
Appeal of Forty Thousand Citizens, threatened with Disfranchisement. [Philadelphia.]
Present State and Condition of the Free People of Color of Philadelphia.
A Sermon on Holding Communion with Extortioners. By JOHN M. PUTNAM, Pastor of Church in Dunbarton, N. H.
Why Work for the Slave ? By NATHANIEL SOUTHARD.
Address before the Concord (N. H.) Female Anti-Slavery Society. By NATHANIEL P. ROGERS.
Brief Remarks on CATHARINE E. BEECHER'S Essay on Slavery. By the Author of "Archy Moore."
Speech of JOHN QUINCY ADAMS, on the Texas Question.
Letter from JAMES BOYLE to WILLIAM L. GARRISON, &c.
A Letter to the Abolitionists. By WILLIAM E. CHANNING, D. D.

1839.

The Chattel Principle the Abhorrence of Jesus Christ and His Apostles ; or, The New Testament against Slavery. By BERIAH GREEN, President of Oneida Institute.
Letter to W. E. CHANNING, D. D., on the Abuse of the Flag of the United States in the Island of Cuba, in Promoting the Slave Trade. By R. R. MADDEN.
The Testimony of God against Slavery; with Notes. By Rev. LaROY SUNDERLAND.
Anti-Slavery Manual. By Rev. LaROY SUNDERLAND.
Report of the Holden (Mass.) Slave Case.
Speech of Hon. THOMAS MORRIS, of Ohio, in Reply to the Speech of the Hon. HENRY CLAY [on Anti-Slavery Petitions]. Senate, Feb. 9, 1839.
Trial of the Amistad African Captives, at Hartford.

The Martyr Age of the United States. By HARRIET MARTINEAU.
Remarks on the Slavery Question. Letter to JONATHAN PHILLIPS, Esq. By WM. E. CHANNING.
American Slavery as It Is: Testimony of a Thousand Witnesses. By THEODORE D. WELD.
Right and Wrong in Massachusetts. By MARIA WESTON CHAPMAN.
Condition of Free People of Color in the United States.
Condition of the People of Color in Ohio, with Interesting Anecdotes.
Work for Abolitionists.
Letter on the Political Obligations of Abolitionists, by JAMES G. BIRNEY; With a Reply, by WM. LLOYD GARRISON.
Address before the Old Colony A. S. Society, at South Scituate, July 4. By WM. LLOYD GARRISON.
Thoughts on the Duty of the Episcopal Church in Relation to Slavery. By JOHN JAY.
The Kidnapped Clergyman; or, Experience the best Teacher.
An Inquiry into the Condition and Prospects of the African Race in the United States; and the Means of Bettering its Fortunes.
The North Star. Edited by JOHN G. WHITTIER.
Slaveholding a *Malum in Se*, or Invariably Sinful. By E. R. TYLER. 2d Edition.
Introductory Lecture before the Adelphic Union. By EDMUND QUINCY.
Anti-Slavery Lecturer. [Utica, N. Y.]

1840.

Africans Taken in the Amistad. President Van Buren's Message, and Documents.
Discourse on Life and Character of Rev. CHARLES FOLLEN, L.L. D.; before the Massachusetts Anti-Slavery Society. By SAMUEL J. MAY.
Emancipation. By WILLIAM E. CHANNING. pp. 111.
Despotism in America. By RICHARD HILDRETH. 2d edition.
Slavery *vs.* the Bible. Correspondence of the General Conference of Maine and the Presbytery of Tombecbee, Mississippi. With Appendix, by CYRUS P. GROSVENOR.
Familiar Letters to HENRY CLAY, describing a Winter in the West Indies. By J. J. GURNEY.
Address from Convention of American Women to the Society of Friends, on the subject of Slavery.
Proceedings of the Society of Friends in the case of WILLIAM BASSETT.
Pinda; a True Tale. By MARIA WESTON CHAPMAN.
Exposition of Proceedings in Relation to JOHN P. DARG, the Elopement of his Alleged Slave, &c.
Two Sermons on the Kind Treatment, and on the Emancipation of Slaves. Preached at Mobile. By Rev. GEORGE F. SIMMONS.
Extracts from the American Slave Code.

1841.

Iniquity and a Meeting. A Discourse at Whitesboro', N. Y., Jan. 31, 1841. By BERIAH GREEN.
Three Months in Great Britain. By JAMES MOTT.
Right and Wrong amongst the Abolitionists of the United States. By JOHN A. COLLINS.
ROGER S. BALDWIN's Argument before the U. S. Supreme Court in the case of the African Cinquez or Jinque.
Argument of JOHN QUINCY ADAMS in the same case.

Correspondence between OLIVER JOHNSON and GEORGE F. WHITE, a Minister of the Society of Friends.
Origin and True Causes of the Texas Insurrection, commenced in 1835. By COLUMBUS.
The West Indies. By Mrs. NANCY PRINCE.

1842.

Ten Years of Experience. By MARIA WESTON CHAPMAN.
Address at Lenox on Emancipation, Aug. 1st. By WM. E. CHANNING.
The American Churches the Bulwarks of American Slavery. By an American. [JAMES G. BIRNEY. First published in England. 3d American Edition, 1842.]
Correspondence of West Brookfield Anti-Slavery Society and Rev. MOSES CHASE.
The Duty of the Free States. Parts 1 and 2. Suggested by the Case of the "Creole." By WM. E. CHANNING.
Discourse on the State of the Country. By Rev. CALEB STETSON.
Discourse on the Covenant with Judas. By Rev. JOHN PIERPONT.
The Creole Case; with the Comments of the New York *American*.
Address of JOHN QUINCY ADAMS to his Constituents at Braintree.
Narrative of LUNSFORD LANE, formerly of Raleigh, N. C.

1843.

DANIEL O'CONNELL's Letter to the Cincinnati Repeal Association.
A Sermon on Slavery. 1841; repeated and published, 1843. By THEO. PARKER.
The Brotherhood of Thieves; or, A True Picture of the American Church and Clergy. By STEPHEN S. FOSTER.
Church Affairs in West Brookfield. (With result of Council in Deacon J. HENSHAW's case.)
ISAAC T. HOPPER's Narrative of Proceedings in New York Monthly Meeting against himself and others. 18 mo., pp. 126.
Christmas, and Poems on Slavery, for Christmas, 1843. [By THOMAS HILL, now President of Harvard College.]
Poems on Slavery. By H. W. LONGFELLOW.
The Virginia Philosopher; or, Few Lucky Slave-Catchers: a Poem. [By Dr. DANIEL MANN.]
Address of the New England Anti-Slavery Convention to the Slaves of the United States; with an Address to President TYLER.
Sermon on Slavery. By JAMES FREEMAN CLARKE.
Sonnets and other Poems. By WM. LLOYD GARRISON.
The Voice of Duty. A 4th of July Discourse at Westminster, Mass. By ADIN BALLOU.

1844.

View of the Action of the Federal Government in behalf of Slavery. By WILLIAM JAY.
Address at Concord, on Emancipation, Aug. 1st. By R. W. EMERSON.
Exposition of Difficulties in West Brookfield. [By JOHN M. FISK.]
Methodist Episcopal Church and Slavery. By LUTHER LEE.
The Principle of Reform. A Discourse, by Rev. CALEB STETSON.
Thoughts on the Proposed Annexation of Texas to the United States. By VETO.
Views of American Constitutional Law in its bearing upon American Slavery. By WILLIAM GOODELL.
Sketches of the Life and Writings of JAMES G. BIRNEY. By BERIAH GREEN.

1845.

Address at Syracuse, on Emancipation, Aug. 1st. By SAMUEL J. MAY.
The Constitution a Pro-Slavery Compact ; or, Selections from the Madison Papers, &c. [By WENDELL PHILLIPS.]
Can Abolitionists Vote or Take Office under the U. S. Constitution ? [By WENDELL PHILLIPS.]
How to Settle the Texas Question.
Narrative of the Life of FREDERICK DOUGLASS, an American Slave. Written by Himself.
Comeouterism. Duty of Secession from a Corrupt Church. By WILLIAM GOODELL.
Proceedings of a Convention of Delegates on the Annexation of Texas.
A Protest against American Slavery, by One Hundred and Seventy-Three Unitarian Ministers.
The Unconstitutionality of Slavery. By LYSANDER SPOONER.
Address on the Annexation of Texas, and the Aspect of Slavery in the United States. By STEPHEN C. PHILLIPS.
Tracts of New England Anti-Slavery Tract Association. [J. W. ALDEN, Agent.]
Review of Correspondence on Slavery between Rev. Drs. FULLER, of Beaufort, S. C., and WAYLAND, of Providence, R. I. By CYRUS P. GROSVENOR.
The Unconstitutionality of Slavery. By G. W. F. MELLEN.

1846.

Correspondence between Rev. SAMUEL H. COX, D. D., and FREDERICK DOUGLASS, a Fugitive Slave.
Correspondence between the Church in Uxbridge and Dr. A. C. TAFT.
Papers on the Slave Power. By JOHN G. PALFREY.
An Inquiry into the Scriptural Views of Slavery. By ALBERT BARNES.
The Slave ; or, Memoirs of ARCHY MOORE. [By RICHARD HILDRETH.] 6th Edition, 1846.
The Branded Hand. Trial and Imprisonment of JONATHAN WALKER, at Pensacola, Florida.
Slavery, and the Slaveholder's Religion, &c. By SAMUEL BROOKE.
Address of Committee of Faneuil Hall Meeting, held Sept. 24, 1846, on the recent case of kidnapping [at South Boston.]

1847.

Slaveholding Examined in the Light of the Holy Bible. By WM. H. BRISBANE.
Resistance to Slavery every Man's Duty. By Rev. GEORGE ALLEN.
Letter from Bridgwater, England, to Bridgewater, New England, and Reply.
Eulogy on the Life and Character of THOMAS CLARKSON. By CHARLES L. REASON.
Address of the Macedon Convention, by WM. GOODELL and GERRIT SMITH.
Lectures before Salem Female Anti-Slavery Society. By WM. W. BROWN.
Position and Duties of the North with regard to Slavery. By ANDREW P. PEABODY.
Review of LYSANDER SPOONER'S Essay on the Unconstitutionality of Slavery. By WENDELL PHILLIPS.
Narrative of WILLIAM W. BROWN, a Fugitive Slave. Written by Himself. [Repeated Editions.]
The Church as It is ; or, The Forlorn Hope of Slavery. By PARKER PILLSBURY.
Facts for the People; Showing the Relations of the U. S. Government to Slavery, &c. By LORING MOODY.
Life of BENJAMIN LUNDY.
Memoir of the Martyr TORREY. [CHARLES T.]

1848.

Letter to the People of the United States touching the Matter of Slavery. By THEODORE PARKER.
Letters to Prof. STOWE and Dr. BACON, &c. &c. By AMOS A. PHELPS.
The Constitutionality of Slavery. [By WM. I. BOWDITCH.]
Conscience the Best Policy. The Least of Two Evils. Two Sermons, by Rev. JOHN WEISS, at New Bedford.
Letter from FREDERICK DOUGLASS to his old Master, THOMAS AULD.
The Anti-Slavery Harp. A Collection of Songs. By WILLIAM W. BROWN.
The Application of Religion to Politics. By JAMES RICHARDSON.
The Black Code of the District of Columbia, in force Sept. 1, 1848. By W. G SNETHEN.
The Young Abolitionists. By J. ELIZABETH JONES.

1849.

Argument of CHARLES SUMNER, Esq., against Separate Colored Schools.
Speech in Congress of HORACE MANN, on Slavery, and the Slave Trade in the District of Columbia.
A Review of the Causes and Consequences of the Mexican War. By WILLIAM JAY.
Slavery and the Constitution. By WM. I. BOWDITCH.
Statistical Inquiry into the Condition of the Free People of Color of the City and Districts of Philadelphia.
Report of the Committee on Slavery to the Convention of Congregational Ministers of Massachusetts. Presented May 30.

1850.

Pictures of the Peculiar Institution, in Louisiana and Mississippi. By an Eye Witness.
The Anti-Slavery Reform. Its Principles and Method. By WM. I. BOWDITCH.
The Experience of THOMAS JONES, a Slave for 43 years.
Review of WEBSTER'S (7th of March) Speech on Slavery. By WENDELL PHILLIPS.
Speech of THEODORE PARKER (in review of WEBSTER'S Speech.)
Reply to WEBSTER. By Hon. WM. JAY.
Discourse on Recapture of Fugitive Slaves. By WM. C. WHITCOMB, of Stoneham.
The Fugitive Slave Law. A Discourse at West Bridgewater. By J. G. FORMAN.
Proceedings of the U. S. Senate on the Fugitive Slave Bill, &c. &c. &c., with the Speeches of Messrs. DAVIS, WINTHROP, and others.
The Function and Place of Conscience. A Sermon for the Times. By THEODORE PARKER.
The Fugitive Slave Bill, its History, &c. With an account of the Seizure of JAMES HAMLET.
The War with Mexico Reviewed. By ABIEL ABBOTT LIVERMORE.
Narrative of SOJOURNER TRUTH, a Northern Slave, emancipated in 1828.
Narrative of the Life and Travels of Mrs. NANCY PRINCE.
Facts for Baptist Churches. Collected, &c., by A. T. FOSS and E. MATHEWS. pp. 408.
Remarks by Rev. G. W. PERKINS on Prof. STUART'S "Conscience and the Constitution."
New Dangers to Freedom and New Duties for its Defenders. A Letter by HORACE MANN.

1851.

Slavery in the United States: its Evils, Remedies, &c. By Rev. EPHRAIM PEABODY.
Address before Salem Female Anti-Slavery Society. By THOMAS T. STONE.
Duty of Disobedience to Wicked Laws. A Sermon on Fugitive Slave Law. By CHARLES BEECHER.
Limits of Civil Obedience. A Discourse at Dorchester. By NATHANIEL HALL.
The Grand Issue. By SAMUEL WILLARD.
Letter to Hon. SAMUEL A. ELIOT, on his Apology for Voting for the Fugitive Slave Bill. By HANCOCK.
The Moving Power. A Discourse on the Fugitive Slave Law. By W. H. FURNESS.
The Gospel applied to the Fugitive Slave Law. A Sermon at Hingham. By OLIVER STEARNS.
Discourse on the Boston Fugitive Slave Case. By W. H. FURNESS.
Conscience and the State. A Discourse in Providence. By Rev. F. H. HEDGE.
The Fugitive Slave Law. Speech in Congress of HORACE MANN.
The Fugitive Slave Law. Speech at Lancaster, by HORACE MANN.
The Chief Sins of the People. A Sermon on Fast Day. By Rev. THEO. PARKER.
The Three Chief Safeguards of Society. A Sermon. By THEODORE PARKER.
Public Spirit and Mobs. Two Sermons at Springfield. By GEORGE F. SIMMONS.
The Supremacy of God's Word Asserted, in opposition to the Fugitive Slave Bill. By Rev. NATHANIEL WEST.
United States vs. Charles G. Davis.
Speech of SAMUEL J. MAY to the Convention of Onondaga County, on the rescue of JERRY.
Letters and Speeches of HORACE MANN.
The Higher Law tried by Reason and Authority.
Our Nation's Sins and Christian Duty. By DANIEL FOSTER.
Politics and the Pulpit. Shall we Compromise? From the *Independent*.

1852.

Examination of the Charges of Mr. JOHN SCOBLE and Mr. LEWIS TAPPAN, against the American Anti-Slavery Society. By EDMUND QUINCY.
Services of Colored Americans in the Wars of 1776 and 1812. 8vo., pp. 40. [Subsequently enlarged to a Volume.] By WM. C. NELL.
Letter to LOUIS KOSSUTH, in behalf of the American Anti-Slavery Society. 8vo., pp. 112. [By WM. LLOYD GARRISON.]
History of the Trial of CASTNER HANWAY and others.
Argument on the Fugitive Slave Law, at Syracuse. By GERRIT SMITH.
The Boston Kidnapping. A Discourse. By THEODORE PARKER.
Discourse on the Death of DANIEL WEBSTER. By THEODORE PARKER.
Freedom National; Slavery Sectional. Speech of Hon. CHARLES SUMNER in the Senate of the United States.
Thrice Through the Furnace. [By Mrs. SOPHIA L. LITTLE.]
The White Slave; or, Memoirs of a Fugitive. [By RICHARD HILDRETH.] (An enlargement of "Archy Moore.")
Uncle Tom's Cabin; or, Life Among the Lowly. By HARRIET BEECHER STOWE. 2 vols.
Selections from the Writings and Speeches of WM. LLOYD GARRISON. pp. 416.
History of Slavery and Anti-Slavery. By WILLIAM GOODELL. pp. 604.
Five Years' Progress of the Slave Power.
Six Years in a Georgia Prison. By LEWIS W. PAINE.

1853.

Withdrawal from American Tract Society, on the Ground of Alliance with the Slave Power Proved, &c. &c. By Judge WM. JAY.
Our Rights as Men. An Address before Legislative Committee. By WM. J. WATKINS.
Words for Working Men. [Including JOHN WESLEY's "Thoughts on Slavery."]
A Key to Uncle Tom's Cabin, &c. By HARRIET BEECHER STOWE. Royal 8vo., pp. 262.
Platform of the American Anti-Slavery Society, and its Auxiliaries.
Fellowship with Slavery. [Rhode Island Evangelical Consociation.] Rev. S. WOLCOTT.
Facts and Opinions touching the American Colonization Society. By G. B. STEBBINS. [With a Preface, by Hon. WM. JAY.]
Miscellaneous Writings on Slavery. By WM. JAY. Boston, 12 mo., pp. 670.
Speeches in Congress. By JOSHUA R. GIDDINGS. Boston, 12 mo., pp. 511.
ISAAC T. HOPPER; A True Life. By L. MARIA CHILD.
Personal Memoir of Captain DANIEL DRAYTON.
American Slave Code. By WM. GOODELL.
White Slavery in the Barbary States. By Hon. CHARLES SUMNER.

1854.

Biography of MAHOMMAH G. BAQUAQUA, a Native of Africa. Detroit. 8 vo., pp. 66. By SAMUEL MOORE, Esq.
The North and the South. Reprinted from the New York *Tribune*.
Educational Laws of Virginia. Personal Narrative of Mrs. MARGARET DOUGLASS.
No Compromise with Slavery. An Address in New York by WM. LLOYD GARRISON.
The Rendition of ANTHONY BURNS. By WM. I. BOWDITCH.
Reform and Repeal. Legal Anarchy. Two Sermons by Rev. JOHN WEISS.
Christian Duty. Three Discourses with reference to the Enforcement of the Fugitive Slave Law in Boston and New York. By W. H. FURNESS.
The New Crime against Humanity. A Sermon, by THEODORE PARKER. (June 4.)
The New Commandment. A Discourse at Salem, by O. B. FROTHINGHAM. (June 4.)
Massachusetts in Mourning. A Sermon in Worcester, by T. W. HIGGINSON. (June 4.)
The Bad Friday. A Sermon in West Roxbury, by E. B. WILLSON. (June 4.)
The Rendition of ANTHONY BURNS, its Causes and Consequences. A Discourse in Boston, by J. F. CLARKE. (June 4.)
The Crisis of Freedom. A Sermon at Lynn, by SAMUEL JOHNSON. (June 11.)
The Laws of God and the Statutes of Man. A Sermon by THEODORE PARKER. (June 18.)
Sermon of the Dangers which Threaten the Rights of Man in America. By THEODORE PARKER. (July 2.)
West India Emancipation. A Speech at Abington, Aug. 1. By WM. LLOYD GARRISON.
Address at Quincy. By CHARLES FRANCIS ADAMS.
Our Country's Sin. A Sermon to the Nestorian Mission in Persia. By Rev. JUSTIN PERKINS, D. D.
Autographs for Freedom.
Despotism in America. [Enlarged edition.] By R. HILDRETH.
Narrative of LEWIS and MILTON CLARKE ; once Slaves in Kentucky.

1855.

The Boston Mob of "Gentlemen"—of 1835. Proceedings of the Twentieth Anniversary of said Mob.

A Series of Twenty Tracts of the AMERICAN ANTI-SLAVERY SOCIETY. [These Tracts were by W. I. BOWDITCH, Esq., Hon. J. G. PALFREY, Mrs. M. W. CHAPMAN, Mrs. HARRIET B. STOWE, Mrs. FOLLEN, T. W. HIGGINSON, S. S. FOSTER, O. B. FROTH-INGHAM, R. HILDRETH, SAMUEL MAY, Jr., C. C. BURLEIGH, Miss S. C. CABOT, Rev. CHARLES BEECHER, C. K. WHIPPLE, Miss JANE WHITING.
Narrative of Facts in the Case of PASSMORE WILLIAMSON.
Sketches of Slave Life, &c. By PETER RANDOLPH, an Emancipated Slave. [With Preface, by SAMUEL MAY, Jr.]
Letters on Slavery to Pro-Slavery Men. By O. S. FREEMAN. [Dr. ROGERS.]
The Trial of Theodore Parker, for the "Misdemeanor" of a Speech in Faneuil Hall against Kidnapping, before the Circuit Court of the United States, April 3, 1855. With the Defence, by THEODORE PARKER.
Argument of WENDELL PHILLIPS, Esq., before Committee on Federal Relations, in support of the Petitions for the Removal of Edward Greeley Loring from office of Judge of Probate.
Principles of the Revolution. By JOSHUA P. BLANCHARD.
Report of Radical Political Abolitionists' Convention, at Syracuse.
Proceedings of the First State Convention of the Colored Citizens of the State of California. Sacramento.
My Bondage and My Freedom. By FREDERICK DOUGLASS.
Speeches by GERRIT SMITH.
Memoir of HENRY BIBB, a Fugitive Slave.
The Hour and the Man. By HARRIET MARTINEAU.
Writings and Speeches on Slavery. By ALVAN STEWART.
Twelve Years a Slave. Narrative of SOLOMON NORTHUP. [A Northern man Kidnapped.]
Additional Speeches, Addresses, &c. By THEODORE PARKER.
An Inside View of Slavery; or, A Tour Among the Planters. By C. G. PARSONS, M. D.
The North-Side View of Slavery; the Canadian Refugees' own Narratives. By BENJAMIN DREW.
Caste; A Story of Republican Equality. By SIDNEY A. STORY, Jr.
Biography of an American Bondman. By his Daughter.

1856.

Wolfsden. By Dr. DANIEL MANN.
The Crimes against Kansas. Speech of Hon. CHARLES SUMNER, in the United States Senate, May 19 and 20.
Six Months in Kansas. By a Lady of Boston.
Dred: A Tale of the Great Dismal Swamp. By HARRIET BEECHER STOWE.
The Kidnapped and the Ransomed: being the Personal Recollections of PETER STILL and his wife VINA, after forty years of Slavery. With a Biographical Sketch of SETH CONCKLIN. By W. H. FURNESS, D. D.
Anthony Burns; A History. By CHARLES EMERY STEVENS.
Condition of the Free and Slave States. By HENRY CHASE and CHARLES W. SANBORN.
Address on the Power of the Slave States, and the Duties of the Free States. By JOSIAH QUINCY.
Address before the Citizens of Cambridge. By JOEL PARKER. [Relating to Slavery in the Territories, its Extension, &c.]
History of the Struggle for Slavery Extension or Restriction in the United States. By HORACE GREELEY.

Speech of Rev. O. B. FROTHINGHAM, before American Anti-Slavery Society.
The Sumner Outrage. Meeting at Cambridge, with the Speeches.
Case of PASSMORE WILLIAMSON. Proceedings of Court, &c.
A Journey in the Seaboard Slave States, &c. &c. By FREDERICK LAW OLMSTEAD. pp. 723.
Whig Policy Analyzed and Illustrated. By JOSIAH QUINCY.
The Responsibility of the North in relation to Slavery : Cambridge.
Triumph of Equal School Rights in Boston. Proceedings of a Meeting, &c., December 17, 1855.
A Review of the Official Apologies of the American Tract Society.
Kansas, her Struggle and her Defence. By Rev. J. E. RAY.
The Anti-Slavery Movement. A Lecture by FREDERICK DOUGLASS.
Revolution or Reform. By EDMUND H. SEARS.

1857.

Letter to the Committee of the American Tract Society. By WM. JAY.
The New Revolution. A Speech by THOMAS W. HIGGINSON.
The Genius and Posture of America. A 4th of July Oration at Boston. By WM. R. ALGER.
Significance of the Struggle between Liberty and Slavery. A Discourse at Portland. By Rev. FREDERICK FROTHINGHAM.
Manifest Destiny of the American Union. Reprinted from the *Westminster Review.* [By HARRIET MARTINEAU.]
Autobiography of a Female Slave. [By Miss MATTIE GRIFFITH.]
The Impending Crisis of the South, &c. By HINTON ROWAN HELPER. pp. 420.
The Legion of Liberty and Force of Truth. [Compiled by J. R. AMES.] A new Edition. pp. 336.
Journey Through Texas. By FRED. LAW OLMSTEAD.
Is Slavery a Blessing? Reply to Prof. BLEDSOE's Essay, &c. By a Citizen of the South.
Church and Slavery. By Rev. ALBERT BARNES.
Slavery. By Rev. ALBERT BARNES.
God against Slavery. By Rev. G. B. CHEEVER, D. D.
Herod, John, and Jesus ; or, the Christian Cure for Slavery. By A. D. MAYO.
To the Friends of the A. B. C. F. M. By C. K. W.

1858.

The Southern Platform ; or, Manual of Southern Sentiment on Slavery. By DANIEL R. GOODLOE.
Proceedings of the Free Convention at Rutland, Vt. [Slavery in part.]
The Suppressed Tract ! and The Rejected Tract ! [American Tract Society.]
The Family Relation as Affected by Slavery. [By C. K. WHIPPLE.]
Address of the American Tract Society, Boston.
The Bible against Oppression. [No. 1 of the (Boston) American Tract Society.]
The Escape ; or, A Leap for Freedom. A Drama. By WM. WELLS BROWN.
The Exiles of Florida ; or, The Crimes of our Government against the Maroons, etc. By J. R. GIDDINGS. 12 mo., pp. 338.
Father Henson's Story of his own Life. With an Introduction, by Mrs. H. B. STOWE.
Proceedings of the Anti-Slavery Convention at West Randolph, Vt. Aug., 1858.
Speech of Rev. HENRY BLEBY, Missionary from Barbadoes, on the Results of Emancipation in the British West India Colonies.

The Sin of Slavery, the Guilt of the Church, and Duty of the Ministry. By Rev. GEORGE B. CHEEVER, D. D.
The Fire and Hammer of God's Word against the Sin of Slavery. By Rev. GEORGE B. CHEEVER, D. D.

1859.

Statistics of Free and Slave Labor in the United States of America. By JAS. HAUGHTON.
The Right of Property in Man [considered.] A Discourse. By W. H. FURNESS.
The Blessings of Abolition. A Discourse. By W. H. FURNESS.
To the Friends of Equal Rights in Rhode Island. [On the Schools.] By GEORGE T. DOWNING and others.
The Methodist Church and Slavery. By CHARLES K. WHIPPLE.
No Slave-hunting in the old Bay State. Speech of CHARLES C. BURLEIGH. (January.)
No Slave-hunting in the old Bay State. Speech of WENDELL PHILLIPS, before Legislative Committee on Federal Relations. (February.)
The American Tract Society, Boston. [By C. K. WHIPPLE.]
Slavery and the American Board of Commissioners for Foreign Missions. [By C. K. WHIPPLE.]
Great Auction Sale of Slaves at Savannah, Georgia, March, 1859. [Slaves of Pierce M. Butler, of Philadelphia.] 24 mo., pp. 28.
"No Fetters in the Bay State." Speech of WM. LLOYD GARRISON before Legislative Committee on Federal Relations. (February.)
Present Condition of the Free Colored People of the United States. By Rev. JAMES F. CLARKE. [From *Christian Examiner* for March, 1859.]
The Slave Auction. By Dr. JOHN THEOPHILUS KRAMER, late of New Orleans, La.
Fraternity Lecture, by WENDELL PHILLIPS, Esq.; also, his Letter to Judge Shaw and President Walker. (October.)
Sermon on the Tragedy at Harper's Ferry. By Rev. GEORGE B. CHEEVER, D. D. (November.)
Causes and Consequences of the Affair at Harper's Ferry. A Sermon by JAMES F. CLARKE. (November.)
Harper's Ferry and its Lesson. A Sermon for the Times. By Rev. E. M. WHEELOCK. (November.)
Two Sermons on Slavery and its Hero Victim. By Rev. NATHANIEL HALL. (December.)
Tribute to the Memory of Charles F. Hovey, Esq. [Died April 28, 1859.]
The Fellowship of Slaveholders Incompatible with a Christian Profession.
The Lesson of the Hour. Lecture at Brooklyn, November 1, 1859. By WENDELL PHILLIPS.
The Natick Resolution; or, Resistance to Slaveholders, &c. &c. By HENRY C. WRIGHT.
Memoir of the Life of J. W. Loguen.
The Roving Editor; or, Talks with Slaves. By JAMES REDPATH.

1860.

A Series of Twenty-Five Tracts (new) of the AMERICAN ANTI-SLAVERY SOCIETY. [These Tracts were by Mrs. L. MARIA CHILD, WM. LLOYD GARRISON, JOSHUA COFFIN, WENDELL PHILLIPS, SAMUEL MAY, Jr., and others.)
Review of Gov. Banks's Veto on Enrolment of Colored Militia. By F. W. BIRD.
No Rights, No Duties. Letter of HENRY C. WRIGHT to Hon. HENRY WILSON.
Harper's Ferry Invasion. Senate Document.

The Guilt of Slavery and the Crime of Slaveholding demonstrated from the Hebrew and Greek Scriptures. By Rev. GEORGE B. CHEEVER, D. D. pp. 472.
Demonstrations in favour of Dr. Cheever, in Scotland. Speeches of Drs. CANDLISH, GUTHRIE, ALEXANDER, and others.
The American Board and American Slavery. Speech of THEODORE TILTON, at Brooklyn. (January.)
Harrington; a Story of True Love. [By WM. D. O'CONNOR.]
The John Brown Invasion. An Authentic History of the Harper's Ferry Tragedy.
John Brown's Expedition Reviewed, in a Letter from THEODORE PARKER, at Rome, to FRANCIS JACKSON, in Boston.
The Anti-Slavery History of the John Brown Year. [Being Annual Report of the American Anti-Slavery Society, for the year ending May 1, 1860.]
The Public Life of Captain John Brown. By JAMES REDPATH.
Echoes of Harper's Ferry. By JAMES REDPATH.
The Barbarism of Slavery. Speech of Hon. CHARLES SUMNER, in the United States Senate, June 4, 1860.

1861.

Emancipation; Its Justice, Expediency, and Necessity. An Address at Boston, by Hon. GEORGE S. BOUTWELL.
Relation of the American Board of Commissioners for Foreign Missions to Slavery. By CHARLES K. WHIPPLE.
The Uprising of a Great People. By COUNT GASPARIN. [Translated by MARY L. BOOTH.]
The War for the Union. A Lecture in New York, by WENDELL PHILLIPS. December, 1861.
The War of Secession. By JOSHUA P. BLANCHARD.
A Voice from Harper's Ferry. By OSBORNE P. ANDERSON. [One of John Brown's men.]
Linda. Incidents in the Life of a Slave Girl. Written by herself. [Mrs. HARRIET JACOBS.] Edited by Mrs. L. MARIA CHILD.
Sermons and Speeches of GERRIT SMITH, New York. pp. 198.
The Life and Letters of Captain John Brown, &c., with Notices of some of his Confederates. Edited by RICHARD D. WEBB. London. Not re-published, but extensively circulated, in this country.

1862.

Emancipation in the West Indies. By F. B. SANBORN.
The Birth and Death of Nations. By JAMES MCKAYE.
The Rejected Stone; or, Insurrection vs. Resurrection in America. By a Native of Virginia. [Rev. M. D. CONWAY.] 12 mo., pp. 131.
The Golden Hour. By MONCURE D. CONWAY. pp. 160.
The Ordeal of Free Labor in the British West Indies. By WM. G. SEWELL. pp 325.
Discourse before American Baptist Home Missionary Society, at Providence, May 29, 1862. "God Timing all National Changes," &c. By Rev. Dr. WILLIAM R. WILLIAMS.
Record of an Obscure Man.
Tragedy of Errors. — By Mrs. MARY LOWELL PUTNAM.
Tragedy of Success.
The Story of the Guard: A Chronicle of the War. By JESSIE BENTON FREMONT.
The Abolitionists, and their Relation to the War. A Lecture in New York, by WM. LLOYD GARRISON, January, 1862.

Speech of GERRIT SMITH on the Country. At New York, December 21, 1862.
The True Story of the Barons of the South. By E. W. REYNOLDS. With an Introduction, by Rev. S. J. MAY.
Historical Notes on the Employment of Negroes in the American Army of the Revolution. By GEORGE H. MOORE, Librarian of New York Historical Society.
Among the Pines; or, South in Secession Time. By EDMUND KIRKE.

1863.

Speeches, Lectures, and Letters. By WENDELL PHILLIPS. pp. 562.
The Black Man, his Antecedents, his Genius, and his Achievements. By WM. WELLS BROWN. 12 mo., pp. 288.
Cochin. The Results of Slavery. } Translated by MARY L. BOOTH.
 " The Results of Emancipation. }
Discourse of WENDELL PHILLIPS, Esq., on a Metropolitan Police.
The Negro. A Speech in New York, by THEODORE TILTON. (May.)
The New Gospel of Peace. In two Parts.
An Historical Research respecting the Opinions of the Founders of the Republic, on Negroes as Slaves, as Citizens, and as Soldiers. Read before the Massachusetts Historical Society. By GEORGE LIVERMORE.
Songs of the Freedmen of Port Royal. By Miss LUCY McKIM.
My Southern Friends. By EDMUND KIRKE.
Preliminary Report Touching the Condition and Management of Emancipated Refugees; made to the Secretary of War by the American Freedmen's Inquiry Commission, June 30, 1863. [ROBERT DALE OWEN, JAMES McKAYE, SAMUEL G. HOWE, Commissioners.]

The Anti-Slavery Poetry of JOHN G. WHITTIER, JOHN PIERPONT, JAMES RUSSELL LOWELL, GEORGE S. BURLEIGH, JULIA WARD HOWE, and others, never wanting in rebuke of the wrong, or in animating support of the right, rendered unspeakable service to the cause at every stage of its progress.

SOCIETIES, CONVENTIONS, &c.

Constitution of the New England Anti-Slavery Society; with an Address to the Public. 1832.
Annual Reports of Massachusetts Anti-Slavery Society. [Formed 1831; originally called New England Anti-Slavery Society. Reports continued to 1853; then merged in American Society's Reports.]
Proceedings of the Anti-Slavery Convention at Philadelphia, Dec. 4, 5, and 6, 1833.
Annual Reports of American Anti-Slavery Society. [Formed December, 1833.]
Report and Proceedings of Providence Anti-Slavery Society. With an Exposition of the Principles and Purposes of the Abolitionists. By S. J. MAY. 1833.
Proceedings of New England Anti-Slavery Convention. 1834, 1835, 1836, 1837.
Annual Reports of Rhode Island Anti-Slavery Society.
 "   "   New Hampshire "   " 1835, &c.
 "   "   Pennsylvania   "   "
 "   "   Boston Female "   " [Commencing 1834.]
Address of New York Young Men's Anti-Slavery Society. 1834.
Proceedings of New Hampshire Anti-Slavery Convention, at Concord, Nov., 1834.
   "   " Ohio   "   " at Putnam, April, 1835.
First Annual Report of Union College Anti-Slavery Society. 1836.

Proceedings of the New York Anti-Slavery Convention at Utica; and New York Anti-Slavery Society, held at Peterboro'. Oct., 1835.
First Annual Report of Union College Anti-Slavery Society. With an Address. By GEORGE L. LEROW. 1836.
Address of the New York City Anti-Slavery Society. 1833.
First Annual Report of Ladies' New York City Anti-Slavery Society. 1836.
Proceedings of First Annual Meeting of New York State Anti-Slavery Society, at Utica. 1836.
Proceedings of Pennsylvania Convention, at Harrisburg. 1837.
Annual Reports of Philadelphia Female Anti-Slavery Society. [First published Report in 1837; continued to present time.]
Annual Reports of American and Foreign Anti-Slavery Society. [Formed 1840.]
Proceedings of American Anti-Slavery Society at its Second Decade. 1853.
" of Pennsylvania Yearly Meeting of Progressive Friends. [Commencing 1853; continued to present time.]
First Annual Report of New York Anti-Slavery Society. 1854.
Reports of the National Anti-Slavery Bazaar, held in Boston. 1855. 1858.
Proceedings of the State Disunion Convention at Worcester, Mass. 1857.
Legislative Documents of various States.
Congressional Documents.
Issues of the Loyal Publication Societies of New York, Philadelphia, and Boston.

ANTI-SLAVERY JOURNALS AND PERIODICALS.

THE GENIUS OF UNIVERSAL EMANCIPATION. Benjamin Lundy, Editor. Commenced in or near 1821, at Baltimore.

THE LIBERATOR. William Lloyd Garrison, Editor. Commenced January 1, 1831, at Boston, and still continued.

THE EMANCIPATOR. Commenced 1834, at New York; continued about ten years.

HERALD OF FREEDOM. Edited in succession by Joseph Horace Kimball, (3 years;) Nathaniel Peabody Rogers, (6 years;) and Parker Pillsbury, (2 years.) Commenced at Concord, New Hampshire, in 1835; continued till June, 1846.

THE NATIONAL ENQUIRER. Benjamin Lundy, Editor. Commenced at Philadelphia, 1836; continued two years.

THE PENNSYLVANIA FREEMAN.* John G. Whittier, first Editor. Commenced at Philadelphia, 1838; continued to 1854.

THE MASSACHUSETTS ABOLITIONIST. Amos A. Phelps, Editor. Commenced at Boston, 1838. United with EMANCIPATOR soon after.

THE CRADLE OF LIBERTY. William Lloyd Garrison, Editor. 1839.

THE NATIONAL PHILANTHROPIST. Cincinnati.

*All know what service Mr. Whittier has rendered to the Anti-Slavery cause by his poetry. It is not so generally known how much labor he has performed as an Anti-Slavery editor. He first edited, in 1836, the Essex *Gazette*, (Haverhill,) then the organ of the Essex County Anti-Slavery Society; next, the *Pennsylvania Freeman*, (Philadelphia,) organ of the Pennsylvania Anti-Slavery Society, in 1838 and 1839; the *Anti-Slavery Reporter*, (New York,) in 1841; the *Emancipator*, (New York,) for a short period in 1844; the *Middlesex Standard*, (Lowell,) 1845; was assistant editor of the *Essex Transcript*, 1846; and corresponding editor of the *National Era*, (Washington,) from 1847 to 1853.

THE NATIONAL ANTI-SLAVERY STANDARD. Successively edited by Nathaniel P. Rogers; David L. and Lydia Maria Child; Maria W. Chapman and others; Sydney H. Gay; Edmund Quincy; Oliver Johnson. Commenced June, 1840; continued to present time.

THE HERALD OF FREEDOM. Edited by N. P. Rogers. Commenced at Concord, New Hampshire, March, 1845; but soon afterwards removed to Lynn, Mass., and united with the PIONEER.

THE ANTI-SLAVERY BUGLE; commenced at Salem, Ohio, 1845. Continued until 1861.

THE NORTH STAR. Frederick Douglass, Editor, Commenced at Rochester, N. Y., December, 1847; afterwards called "Frederick Douglass's Paper"; discontinued 1863.

THE NATIONAL ERA. Gamaliel Bailey, Editor. Commenced at Washington, 1847; continued about twelve years.

THE RADICAL ABOLITIONIST. William Goodell, Editor. Commenced about 1855; discontinued 1859.

THE ANGLO-AFRICAN. New York.

THE PRINCIPIA. William Goodell, Editor. Commenced at New York, 1859; still continued.

VOICE OF FREEDOM. C. L. Knapp, Editor, Montpelier, Vt. 1839.

ALTON OBSERVER. Elijah P. Lovejoy, Editor. Alton, Ill. 1837.

CHARTER OAK. William H. Burleigh, Editor. Hartford, Conn.

HUMAN RIGHTS. LaRoy Sunderland, Editor.

FREE PRESS. Utica, N. Y. 1845.

INDIANA FREEMAN.

LIBERTY GAZETTE. Burlington, Vt.

ALBANY PATRIOT. William L. Chaplin, Editor. 1846.

GRANITE FREEMAN. 1846.

NOTE. Numerous journals, both at an early and a more recent date, were *in part* open to the advocacy of the Anti-Slavery cause, but also included a predominant range of other subjects, political, sectarian, and moral. Many of them rendered effective service to the Anti-Slavery reform.

ANTI-SLAVERY REPORTER. Commenced June, 1833.

ANTI-SLAVERY RECORD. 1835.

QUARTERLY ANTI-SLAVERY MAGAZINE. Elizur Wright, Jr., Editor. 1835-37.

ANTI-SLAVERY EXAMINER. 1838, &c.

THE SLAVE'S FRIEND. For Children.

THE MONTHLY OFFERING. John A. Collins, Editor. 1841, &c.

THE ANTI-SLAVERY ALMANAC was first published in 1836, by the American Anti-Slavery Society. Continued several years.

THE LIBERTY BELL. Edited and published annually in Boston, by Maria Weston Chapman. 1843 to 1858, (one or two years being omitted.).

ERRATUM. In Mrs. Mott's speech, for Ralph *Sangerford*, read Sandiford.